# The Power of Our Supreme Court

# The Power of Our Supreme Court

## of Our

## Supreme

## Court

### How Supreme Court
### Cases Shape Democracy

## MATT BEAT

CORAL GABLES

The Power of Our Supreme Court: How Supreme Court Cases Shape Democracy

Library of Congress Cataloging-in-Publication number: 2022943085
ISBN: (pb) 978-1-68481-068-0 (hc) 978-1-68481-275-2 (e) 978-1-68481-067-3
BISAC category code: LAW018000, LAW / Constitutional

Printed in the United States of America

# Contents

# Why I Wrote
# This Stuff

We find things that don't mean anything to us boring. If we can't connect with something, or see how it's relevant to our daily lives, how can we possibly be interested in it? As an educator, I have spent much of my time trying to convince people that boring stuff that *seems* irrelevant to them is *entirely relevant*.

Some things have been easier to make relevant than others. It's always easy for me to make anything to do with money relevant. Almost everyone constantly thinks about money, and most worry about it. Therefore, when I teach about the Great Depression, I can often draw them in with a story of a real sixty-year-old man who had spent his entire life working and saving money, only to lose all of it when his bank failed. He described how, later, after years of not being able to find work, he could only find shelter in a shantytown and had to wait in line for bread to not starve to death. We can connect to that stuff.

Other things are not so easy to make relevant. The Compromise of 1790, the first of three incredibly important compromises made between Northern and Southern politicians to keep the United States together, isn't interesting to learn about. Sure, it's a pivotal event in the country's early history, but it's kind of a boring story. It only means something to most of us when connected with the cultural divides of today.

Enter the Supreme Court of the United States. It's currently made up of nine people who arguably have more power than any politician or plutocrat in the United States. They are at the top of the American federal government's judicial branch, which *interprets* laws. Interprets? Well, humans can interpret things however they want, can't they? This, alone, is a tremendous power, and just five interpretations from the Court can be carved in stone as a precedent that can be used for decades, if not centuries. The Court has complete discretion over which cases it decides to hear. Of the 7,000 to 10,000 requests for cases it gets each year, it often only takes between eighty and eighty-five. It has the power to overthrow decisions of all courts underneath it.

The Supreme Court's power has grown tremendously since the early 1800s. Beginning with the case *Marbury v. Madison*, which institutionalized the idea of judicial review, the Court slowly became a powerful force to hold the other two branches of government, legislative and executive, accountable. Judicial review is the process by which the judicial branch can determine whether the executive and legislative branches' actions are constitutional. This means if the president issues an Executive Order the Court thinks is unconstitutional, they can strike it down. If Congress passes a law the Court thinks *is* constitutional, it can uphold it. Beginning in the 1950s, the Court became more overtly political. In the 1960s, it ramped up to a point where people began electing the president based on who they might appoint to join it.

In recent years, perhaps no other Supreme Court case has been more scrutinized than *Roe v. Wade*, which legalized abortion, or specifically said that a woman had the right to an abortion until a certain point in her pregnancy. The *Roe* decision sparked a contentious debate that continues to this day. Before *Roe*, abortion was not a major political, partisan issue.[1] Now, many Americans vote for politicians based on whether they are "pro-life," meaning they are against the *Roe* decision, or "pro-choice," meaning they are for the *Roe* decision. According to Gallup, one in four Americans won't vote for a politician unless they share their views about the *Roe* decision.[2] There is some evidence that Donald Trump got elected as president in 2016 because he switched from "pro-choice" to "pro-life" a few years before he ran.[3] Once he was in office, he appointed three justices who almost certainly are "pro-life." As a matter of fact, while I was writing this book, *Roe v. Wade* was overturned. Many voters were motivated to head to the polls for the 2022 midterm elections due to the overturning of *Roe*.[4]

But abortion is just one issue that the Supreme Court has decided on. Throughout American history, the Court has also shaped what we collectively define as "free speech," voting rights, equality under the law, privacy, freedom of and from religion, the rights of the accused, the types of punishments the accused get, and the role of the president, among other things. Not only that, but its impact has also grown almost out of necessity as in recent decades the legislative branch has become more and more polarized and unproductive. We live in an era when Congress compromises and forms coalitions less and less. Therefore, the Court has often stepped in to effectively legislate from the bench. One notable example of them doing this is *Obergefell v. Hodges*, which legalized same-sex marriage. There is no doubt that some of the most influential changes to American public policy have only occurred due to the Supreme Court.

Up to this point, I'm likely not telling you anything you already didn't know. 92 percent of Americans surveyed by CSPAN in 2018 agreed that the Supreme Court impacted

1   www.washingtonpost.com/news/made-by-history/wp/2018/01/22/how-abortion-became-the-single-most-important-litmus-test-in-american-politics
2   news.gallup.com/poll/313316/one-four-americans-consider-abortion-key-voting-issue.aspx
3   www.theatlantic.com/health/archive/2016/11/why-women-and-christians-backed-trump/507176
4   www.kff.org/other/poll-finding/2022-midterm-election-kff-ap-votecast-analysis/

their everyday lives. Yet, 52 percent of those same Americans surveyed couldn't name one Supreme Court justice.[5] While we understand the Court's importance, we are fairly ignorant of who they are and what they do. It's not our fault.

As I hinted at earlier, the Supreme Court is boring. It's made up of old people who often seem out of touch with most Americans. These old people are highly intelligent, using words like "henceforth" and "stipulation." They speak "legalese," or the language of the law, commonly spoken in courts and written into contracts.

Second, American public schools have failed to adequately teach students about the Supreme Court. Only nine states and the District of Columbia require one full school year of US government class to graduate high school. Thirty states require a half year of the class, and eleven states require no government class at all to graduate.[6] In Kansas, where I am from, students get half a year of government class. It wasn't enough for me. The vast majority of what I know about how the American government works I learned in college. In fact, I wasn't completely comfortable with my knowledge of it *until I had been teaching it for a couple of years*. Not only that, American teachers often have limited resources to teach their students. Increasingly, elected officials and parents micromanage what they can teach about the Supreme Court.

Speaking of which, I have taught American government to middle schoolers and juniors and seniors in high school. In Kansas, the standards do not require us to focus on the Supreme Court. This is perhaps understandable for middle schoolers, but unacceptable for high schoolers. Since I value the Supreme Court (in case you haven't realized that already), I dedicated more time to it than most American government teachers in my home state. One of the most engaging lessons I facilitated every semester involved my students pretending they were Supreme Court justices interpreting the Bill of Rights and Fourteenth Amendment to make a decision. Not only did the lesson cause my students to critically think, but it also led to some fantastic philosophical discussions. For example, when we looked at the landmark case *Texas v. Johnson*, in which the Court decided that flag burning was symbolic speech protected by the First Amendment, my classes were often split like the Court was. As students, I mean…justices, made their arguments, they quickly realized that "freedom of speech" was a nuanced and complex ideal that wasn't absolute. Overall, when my students had to interpret the US Constitution for themselves, they often had different interpretations. Despite all that, they also mostly ended up agreeing with how the Court decided, which I found revealing.

5   static.c-span.org/assets/documents/scotusSurvey/CSPAN%20PSB%202018%20Supreme%20
    Court%20Survey%20Agenda%20of%20Key%20Findings%20FINAL%208%2027.pdf
6   www.aft.org/ae/summer2018/shapiro_brown

But I am just one teacher. Each school year, I passionately taught about the Supreme Court to around 150 students, often about four weeks out of each semester or around twenty hours. Not only that, but I'm not in the classroom anymore.

Fortunately, I am still a teacher online. What I mean by that is that I'm a YouTuber who makes videos about the Supreme Court. The series is called Supreme Court Briefs, and the videos are short and accessible, filled with all kinds of animations, music, bad dad jokes, and other gimmicky bits to make the Court more engaging. Each episode focuses on a different Supreme Court case that I think is relevant to our lives. Nearly all of those cases are also featured in this book, as it turns out! I've learned that thousands of American government teachers have played my Supreme Court Briefs series to their students in the classroom. And that's not just high school teachers but also college professors. While this is amazing and makes me happy, over the past few years I've also learned that other people watch the series *for fun*. You read that right. Instead of watching Netflix or paint dry, they watch educational videos I made about important Supreme Court cases. Before you get too excited, Supreme Court Briefs is the least popular series on my channel. My Supreme Court videos perform worse than my other content. Many of the regular viewers of the series are not American. According to the analytics that YouTube provides, at least 35 percent of my Supreme Court Briefs viewers do not currently live in the United States.

Sure, I'm writing this book for anyone who wants to learn about the Supreme Court of the United States. However, I'm mostly writing this book for *apathetic Americans*. I've had American viewers reach out to me and tell me that my Supreme Court Briefs series filled the void of their ignorance of the Court. Often, they write that they never learned about the Court before watching my videos because they didn't get the opportunity to learn about it in school. More importantly, though, is when they tell me that my videos were the first thing they consumed that got them interested and even excited about the Supreme Court. That has become my main motivation. I don't want to offend anyone already heavily interested in the Supreme Court, but with my videos and this book, I'm not focused on you. Bring me the indifferent Americans. I will not sleep until you care.

# What the Heck Is the Supreme Court?

The Supreme Court of the United States, often referred to simply as SCOTUS, is the highest court of the judicial branch of the United States. It's the highest court in the country. *It has the final say on what the United States Constitution actually means.* Once the Court makes a decision, that's it, buddy. The only way the decision can be reversed is if the Supreme Court reverses it, which rarely happens.

However, when the Framers wrote the Constitution in 1789, they didn't mention much about the Supreme Court or the judicial branch.

It's all mostly spelled out in **Article 3:**

**Section 1:** The judicial power of the United States, shall be vested in one Supreme Court, and in such inferior courts as the Congress may from time to time ordain and establish. The judges, both of the supreme and inferior courts, shall hold their offices during good behavior, and shall, at stated times, receive for their services, a compensation, which shall not be diminished during their continuance in office.

**Section 2:** The judicial power shall extend to all cases, in law and equity, arising under this Constitution, the laws of the United States, and treaties made, or which shall be made, under their authority;—to all cases affecting ambassadors, other public ministers and consuls;—to all cases of admiralty and maritime jurisdiction;—to controversies to which the United States shall be a party;—to controversies between two or more states;—between a state and citizens of another state;—between citizens of different states;—between citizens of the same state claiming lands under grants of different states, and between a state, or the citizens thereof, and foreign states, citizens or subjects.

In all cases affecting ambassadors, other public ministers and consuls, and those in which a state shall be party, the Supreme Court shall have original jurisdiction. In all the other cases before mentioned, the Supreme Court shall have appellate jurisdiction, both as to law and fact, with such exceptions, and under such regulations as the Congress shall make.

The trial of all crimes, except in cases of impeachment, shall be by jury; and such trial shall be held in the state where the said crimes shall have been committed; but when not committed within any state, the trial shall be at such place or places as the Congress may by law have directed.

**Section 3:** Treason against the United States, shall consist only in levying war against them, or in adhering to their enemies, giving them aid and comfort. No person shall be convicted of treason unless on the testimony of two witnesses to the same overt act, or on confession in open court.

The Congress shall have power to declare the punishment of treason, but no attainder of treason shall work corruption of blood, or forfeiture except during the life of the person attainted.

That's it. Just 369 words. The only court specifically mentioned? The Supreme freaking Court (see the first sentence of Section 1).

**Article 2, Section 2,** also mentions how folks could join the Supreme Court:

(The President)…shall nominate, and by and with the Advice and Consent of the Senate, shall appoint…Judges of the supreme Court.

Yep, there is nothing in the Constitution about qualifications for Supreme Court justices. Heck, technically you could be in the Supreme Court and never passed the bar or went to law school. There's not even an age or citizenship requirement. If the president wanted to nominate their six-year-old Venezuelan nephew and the Senate approved it, that could happen. Is it likely that something like that could happen? No, but theoretically it could. Also, the Constitution does not mention term limits. Therefore, each justice has a lifetime tenure, meaning they can be on the court until they die, retire, quit, or are forcibly removed from office. Let me get this out of the way—no justice has ever been removed from office, and only one, Samuel Chase, has been impeached.

One thing was for sure—each justice would get a single vote in deciding the cases argued before it. They would presumably be less influenced by politics since they would never have to worry about being elected. They would hear the facts of each case and interpret the Constitution, hopefully objectively.

When the United States Congress first met in 1789, they realized they probably ought to elaborate more on what the Court looked like and did. However, it's important to remember that many of the first members of Congress were terrified of a strong judiciary. They thought courts having too much power would lead to tyranny. This is why half of the Bill of Rights protects citizens from judicial overreach. Yet, after months of debate, Congress passed the Judiciary Act of 1789.

First, the new law said there would be six justices of the Supreme Court. The justice who would preside over the Supreme Court is known as the chief justice. The chief justice is essentially the highest-ranking person in the entire judicial branch. They not only preside over oral arguments but also have tremendous influence in setting the Court's agenda. Each time a president is elected, the chief justice administers the oath of office, and if a president is impeached, they preside over the Senate during those proceedings. The other five members of the Supreme Court are called associate justices.

The Judiciary Act also said the Supreme Court would get together to hear cases twice a year, with the first session beginning on the first Monday of February and the second session beginning on the first Monday of August. The law divided the country into thirteen federal districts, each having one District Court and one judge. If someone didn't like a District Court judge's decision, they could appeal to a circuit court, presided by a local district judge and two Supreme Court justices. The law created the office of the Attorney General, who would head the Department of Justice, overseen by the president. The law gave the Supreme Court the power to settle disputes between states and to review certain judgments made by the highest court in any state.

Today, the Court mostly takes on cases that come by appeal, meaning a lower court has already made a decision on the case, but one party was upset with the decision. When the Court decides to hear such a case, it's called "appellate jurisdiction." There's also "original jurisdiction," meaning no other court had heard the case. Two common examples of original jurisdiction are when a case involves representatives from foreign governments and when a case involves a dispute between two different states' governments. A third way cases reach the Court is through a "writ of certiorari." This is an order from the Supreme Court to a lower court demanding they send records on a case to review. Just like with an appeal, this often occurs when one of the parties involved petitions the Supreme Court for certiorari.

Often the Court determines whether a law or action violates a civil right or civil liberty. A "civil right" is an individual right threatened by majorities to favor some over others. To protect civil rights, the Court must make sure majorities in the country are not discriminating against minorities. A "civil liberty," on the other hand, is an individual freedom threatened by people in power, usually those in government. To protect civil liberties, the Court must make sure those in power aren't abusing their power.

In some cases, the Supreme Court might make a decision based on the information provided to them without hearing arguments, if they all already agree. When this happens, it's called a "per curiam opinion," and none of the justices sign it.

However, that's the exception to the norm. Usually the Court hears arguments from both sides. After a case is accepted for full review and before oral arguments are made, lawyers on each side have to submit a "brief" or written statement that includes their legal arguments and other important stuff that supports their side. Other parties not directly involved in the case but still strongly interested in the outcome may also submit briefs, known as "amicus curiae."

After the briefs are filed, the justices hear oral arguments. A minimum of six justices must be present to hear a case. A lawyer representing each side gets up to thirty minutes to present their party's case. Justices can (and often do) interrupt them to challenge them or ask for further clarification. Oral arguments are not recorded on video, but since 1955 the audio has been recorded and available to the public. While justices may ban video cameras during oral arguments for many reasons, the main reason is that they worry that cameras will encourage showboating. Regardless, oral arguments are less secretive than they used to be. All oral arguments are open to the public, but seating is often limited and on a first-come basis.

Once in session, the Court usually hears two one-hour arguments a day on Mondays, Tuesdays, and Wednesdays, two weeks on and off. During an argument week, the justices meet in a private conference, closed to their staff, to discuss each case and take a preliminary vote. If the chief justice is in the majority for a decision, they decide who will write the opinion. If the chief justice is in the minority in a decision, the justice with the most seniority assigns who will write it.

Often, the Court doesn't announce its decision until several weeks or months after hearing oral arguments. No one outside the Court knows exactly when they will announce a decision, and there's not even a set time in which they have to reach a decision. However, all cases argued before the Court are usually decided before they take a summer break, often by the end of June.

The Court issues four different types of opinions. First, there are "unanimous opinions." That's when all the justices decide to vote the same way. If the decision is not unanimous, there will be a "majority opinion" and "dissenting opinion," which lay out why the justices decided the way they did. Finally, there are "concurring opinions" written by justices who agree with one side or the other but have different reasons for doing so and want everybody to know about it.

The Court interprets cases in two ways—broadly or narrowly. When they interpret a case broadly, they view it through a broader context. In other words, they consider a wide array of other cases and circumstances to provide a decision that can be more universally applied. When they interpret a case narrowly, they view a case with just the specific facts at hand. In narrow interpretations, they provide a decision unique to the specific case. Often, narrow interpretations open the door for many more cases to look at the same broader issue, while broad interpretations close that same door.

As I stated in the first chapter, the Court makes between eighty and eighty-five decisions each year. Most of these decisions go under the radar. However, occasionally they announce a controversial or extremely impactful decision that can cause a bit of a frenzy. More common are protests. While it's quite common for protests to occur in front of the United States Supreme Court building on the day of oral arguments for a case that will potentially have a big impact, it's common to see protestors show up after a decision that has a big impact is announced.

The Supreme Court Building may be iconic today as a place where the American public gathers, but it has only been around since 1935. In fact, the Supreme Court today looks much different than it did in 1789, when Congress passed and President George Washington signed the Judiciary Act. First, several more laws have been passed since then that have changed the role and makeup of the Court. More importantly, however, the Court has given itself more power over the years. In fact, it's never been more powerful than it is today. In the next chapter, we will examine how these nine people became nine of the most powerful people in history.

# Who Makes Up the Supreme Court?

We learned in the last chapter that the US Constitution lists no qualifications for Supreme Court judges. Technically, if the president nominates someone and a majority of the US Senate approves of them, they are in, regardless of whether they are "qualified" or not.

All in all, the Supreme Court has had some qualified people serve in it throughout its history. I always argue it's the most dignified and intelligent branch of the federal government. I mean no disrespect to the executive and legislative branches, but it's much easier to serve in those than the judicial branch. For example, at the time of the writing of this book, 12,421 people have served as either US Representatives, US Senators, or both in American history. Just *116* have ever served in the highest court in the land. In total, there have been 17 chief justices and 104 associate justices.

Fortunately, pretty much all of the 116 people who have served on the Court have been qualified. All 116 had experience as a lawyer. All 116 had either graduated from law school, taken law classes, been admitted to the bar, or practiced law for a living. The last justice appointed who didn't attend law school was James Byrnes, who served on the Court for only fifteen months between 1941 and 1942, the shortest tenure of any justice. Byrnes didn't graduate high school, but taught himself law and passed the bar at twenty-three years old. 41 of the 116 justices had no judicial experience before joining the Court. In other words, 41 of them had never been judges *until* they reached the Supreme Court. Eight justices served in private practice before they joined the Court. Three had been law school deans.

Perhaps surprisingly, several justices had been involved in either the executive branch or legislative branch for joining the Supreme Court. First, one was a US president! That'd be William Howard Taft, who was much happier as a Supreme Court justice than he ever was as commander in chief. Eleven served as governors. Twelve served as Attorney General, Deputy Attorney General, Assistant Attorney General, or Solicitor General. Seven served as US Department Secretaries. Dozens served in other, lower executive branch positions. Fifteen justices also had served or served afterward in the US Senate. Seventeen had served in the House of Representatives. In recent decades, perhaps to make the judicial branch more insulated from political pressures, presidents have nominated fewer folks to the Court who had previously been legislators.

Okay, so they've all been quite qualified, but have they all behaved? The Constitution states that justices "shall hold their offices during good behavior." So what if they *do* misbehave? Just like if the president misbehaves, if a justice misbehaves the US House of Representatives can impeach them. Impeachment does not mean they get charged with a crime. It simply means they are charged with misconduct. If the House votes to impeach, then it sends its articles of impeachment to the US Senate. The Senate then acts as the judiciary, considering evidence, hearing witnesses, and finally voting to acquit or convict the impeached justice.

Only one Supreme Court justice has ever been impeached—Samuel Chase. As a justice, the Federalist Chase had been an outspoken critic of the Democratic-Republican majority in Congress. Led by US Representative John Randolph and President Thomas Jefferson, the House voted to impeach Chase on March 12, 1804, accusing him of being biased with how he heard two politically sensitive cases. You read that correctly. *They impeached him for being biased.* The final article of impeachment accused Chase of promoting his political beliefs on the bench, and therefore "tending to prostitute the high judicial character with which he was invested, to the low purpose of an electioneering partizan." When Chase appeared before the Senate to defend himself, he said he was being impeached for his political beliefs instead of any real crime. Incredibly, Chase's defense team convinced several Democratic-Republican Senators to sympathize with them. On March 1, 1805, the Senate voted to acquit Chase on all counts. Chase resumed his duties on the Court and remained there for the rest of his life. No Supreme Court justice has ever been forcibly removed. Chase's impeachment was the closest we got to that.

More justices retire from office than die while in office. Each year, there's approximately a 2.6 percent chance a justice will die while in office, and a 2.8 percent chance a justice will retire.[7] The average age of a justice at the time of their appointment is fifty-three. The average age at the time of their retirement is sixty-nine. Most justices historically have been born in March. Historically, John has been the most common first name of justices. Harvard is the most common alma mater of all justices, and Episcopalian is the most common religion. Most have come from the state of New York. George Washington nominated more justices than all other presidents.

Of the 116 justices historically, all but *four* had predominately European ancestry. Sonia Sotomayor, who currently sits on the bench, is the first and only Hispanic Supreme

7   www.ncbi.nlm.nih.gov/pmc/articles/PMC3000028

Court justice. Six justices have been born outside of the United States. Only six women have ever served on the Supreme Court. Four *currently sit on the court.* William Douglas served on the Supreme Court longer than any other justice in American history. He served 13,358 days, or almost thirty-seven years. The longest-serving chief justice was John Marshall, who served in that position for more than thirty-four years. That said, the average length of service for all justices before the ones currently on the bench is about seventeen years. In recent decades, the average length of service has dramatically increased.

The current chief justice is John Roberts. He currently gets paid $280,500 a year. The other justices are Clarence Thomas, Samuel Alito, Sonia Sotomayor, Elena Kagan, Neil Gorsuch, Brett Kavanaugh, Amy Coney Barrett, and Ketanji Brown Jackson. They all currently get paid $268,300 a year.

In conclusion, Supreme Court justices are human beings. They have the same flaws as all human beings. They have conflicting biases and values, and often passionately disagree with each other about core issues. However, for the most part, these justices have learned to work with each other well. Despite ideological differences, there is a unique bond in the Court, and while we don't know much about what goes on inside The Marble Palace (a.k.a. the US Supreme Court Building), we do know that the members of the Court often become quite close. Look no further than the special connection between justices Ruth Bader Ginsburg and Antonin Scalia, who often voted differently while on the bench together, but often would attend the opera together. "How blessed I was," Ginsburg once wrote of Scalia, "to have a working colleague and dear friend of such captivating brilliance, high spirits and quick wit." In my opinion, brilliance, high spirits, and quick wit summarize the qualities of many Supreme Court justices in American history. My country has been lucky to have some good ones on the bench, and I don't see this trend reversing soon. I am often the first one in a conversation to defend them, even if I might disagree with them.

# A Brief History of the Supreme Court of the United States

In 1790, the Supreme Court met for the first time. The first chief justice, John Jay, led a meeting with fellow justices John Rutledge, William Cushing, James Wilson, John Blair, and James Iredell at the Merchants Exchange Building in New York City, which at the time was the country's capital city, on February 2, 1790. Yep, there were only six members of the Court. The Judiciary Act of 1789 only called for six justices on the bench. The meeting was mostly about boring, procedural stuff.

In the early years of the Court, justices had to travel for several months of the year and do circuit duty or participate in various circuit court decisions. Circuit courts used to be federal courts in various federal judicial districts. Today they make up the United States District Court system.

Most of the early decisions of the 1790s had little impact on the entire country. The first official Supreme Court case was *Van Staphorst v. Maryland* (1791). The Van Staphorst brothers had loaned money to Maryland's government during the American War of Independence, and Maryland had refused to pay it back under the terms the brothers demanded. It was so historically insignificant that the suit was settled before oral arguments. The first Supreme Court decision in American history was *West v. Barnes* (1791). William West, a farmer, judge, and general in the American War of Independence, got in trouble with another judge, David Barnes, for making loan payments in Rhode Island with paper currency instead of gold or silver. The Court ultimately sided with Barnes on procedural grounds—West missed a deadline to file paperwork. From 1791 to 1801, the Court met in Philadelphia's City Hall building.

Probably the most notable Supreme Court case of the 1790s was *Chisholm v. Georgia* (1793). Alexander Chisholm, a merchant, tried to sue Georgia's government over money due to him for goods that Robert Farquhar had supplied Georgia during the—you guessed it—American War of Independence. Georgia said that, as a sovereign state, it couldn't be sued. The Court ruled that they could be sued, and this ended up causing so much of a stir that Congress and state governments added the Eleventh Amendment to the US Constitution, which officially said states didn't get sovereign immunity from lawsuits made by citizens of other states in federal courts, among other things.

After John Jay stepped down as chief justice, John Rutledge took his place for a short while and then Oliver Ellsworth took his place for a few years. After the Federalist Party lost its majority in Congress due to the elections of 1800, they reduced the number of justices from six to five to prevent Thomas Jefferson, the new incoming president, from making an appointment.

However, it wasn't until John Marshall became the country's fourth chief justice in 1801 that things started to get juicy in the Court. Marshall remains the longest-serving and most influential chief justice in American history. His dominant personality, often through charm, quick wit, and humor, allowed him to regularly convince his fellow justices to agree with him. Marshall wrote almost half of all the decisions throughout his incredible tenure of 34 years and 152 days, and was on the losing side in a constitutional case only once, in *Ogden v. Saunders* (1827). Even so, that case is only notable today mostly because of his partial dissent in which he laid out his general principles of constitutional interpretation. At the beginning of Marshall's tenure as chief justice, the Court still didn't have a building, even after Congress established the new capital district of Washington, DC. Congress was at least nice enough to let the Court use various rooms in the Capitol building. After the British burned parts of the Capitol down during the War of 1812, they met in some random dude's house. However, thanks to Marshall's bidding, the Court secured a chamber in the newly restored Capitol building beginning in 1819. Today this is known as the Old Supreme Court Chamber.

Early in his tenure, Marshall gave the opinion of *Marbury v. Madison* (1803), which formalized the Court's power of judicial review, which means they could declare laws unconstitutional and therefore single-handedly throw them out. I will go into more detail about the *Marbury* decision later, but it's the most important Supreme Court decision in history because it dramatically elevated the power of not only the Court but the entire judicial branch. While today there's little debate about the courts' power, it was a controversial decision at the time. In 1804, Jefferson wrote to Abigail Adams in response to the Marbury decision:

The Constitution…meant that its coordinate branches should be checks on each other. But the opinion which gives to the judges the right to decide what laws are constitutional and what not, not only for themselves in their own sphere of action but for the Legislature and Executive also in their spheres, would make the Judiciary a despotic branch.

Partially due to Jefferson's disgust with Marshall, Congress increased the size of the court to seven in 1807 to give him an extra appointment to the bench.

Yet, John Marshall still had the last laugh. Not only does the *Marbury* decision still stand, but Marshall oversaw several important decisions that expanded the Court's role regarding federalism after 1807. Marshall took a broader interpretation of the Constitution and the federal government's powers. This is commonly called a "loose construction." A literal interpretation of the Constitution is called a "strict construction." With the Marshall Court's new loose construction approach, they interpreted broad federal government powers in the interstate commerce clause and Necessary and Proper Clause of the Constitution. The Marshall Court expanded the role of the federal government and made several decisions that restricted the role of state governments. Multiple decisions confirmed the supremacy of federal laws over state laws. As powerful as the Marshall Court was, states did not always comply. One infamous example of this is *Worcester v. Georgia* (1832), in which the Court said Georgia couldn't pass laws controlling the Cherokee Nation. Georgia simply ignored the decision, and even the president, Andrew Jackson, sided with the state.

Marshall's tenure as chief justice was a time of remarkable unity in the Court—there was hardly ever any fighting. It was also a time of stability; several of Marshall's associate justices served for over twenty years. Throughout much of Marshall's tenure, the Court met only two months out of the year—the first Monday in February through the third week in March. When they met, they boarded together in the same house and avoided outside socializing. Decisions were often made in a few days. During the Marshall Court, justices usually didn't get written briefs, so they had to listen intently to oral arguments. Finally, there is some evidence that John Marshall established the tradition of justices wearing black robes.[8]

After Marshall died in 1835, he left big shoes to fill. Who filled them was perhaps the most notorious of all American chief justices, Roger Taney. Compared to Marshall, Taney believed the federal government's powers were less broad. Therefore, he often preferred constraint over action for the Court. In 1837, the Democrat-led Congress increased

8   onlinelibrary.wiley.com/doi/abs/10.1111/jsch.12255

the Supreme Court to nine justices to give President Jackson a chance to appoint two new justices.

Easily the most controversial and, in my opinion, the worst decision of the Taney Court was in *Dred Scott v. Sandford* (1857), commonly referred to as the *Dred Scott Decision*. I will go into more detail about the *Dred Scott Decision* later, but it ruled that African Americans were not and could not ever become citizens of the United States. This ruling was met with outrage from abolitionists, and it's the only Supreme Court case that played a significant role in *causing a war*, the American Civil War, of course.

During that war, Congress expanded the Court to ten justices to guarantee a pro-Union majority on the bench. President Abraham Lincoln appointed Salmon Chase as chief justice. Just like Marshall, Chase was one of the few people in American history to have served in all three branches of the federal government. He was incredibly ambitious and even ran for president while sitting on the bench.

After the Civil War ended, Congress increased the size of the Court to nine—one chief justice and eight associate justices—and it's been that way ever since.

Around that same time, Congress passed and the states ratified the Fourteenth Amendment, arguably the part of the Constitution most interpreted by the Supreme Court in American history. While the amendment was meant to primarily deal with citizenship in the aftermath of slavery ending, its meaning has dramatically expanded ever since. It said that all people born in the United States (except for Native Americans not taxed) were citizens and would be given full and equal benefit of all American laws.

The Fourteenth Amendment included three main parts:

1.  State and federal citizenship is guaranteed to all persons, regardless of race or skin color. This part is known as the Citizenship Clause.

2.  State and local government can't prevent people from life, liberty, or property, without certain steps to make everything fair. This part is known as the Due Process Clause.

3.  All people are guaranteed equal protection under the laws. This part is known as the Equal Protection Clause.

For the rest of the 1800s, the Supreme Court had a mostly strict construction interpretation of the Fourteenth Amendment. In the *Slaughterhouse Cases* (1873), the Court ruled that a monopoly didn't go against the Fourteenth Amendment because that amendment was about giving equality to former slaves. In the *Civil Rights Cases* (1883), the Court ruled that Congress couldn't stop racial discrimination by private individuals under the Fourteenth Amendment. By the time of those cases, Morrison Waite was now the chief justice, and he felt he had to narrowly interpret the Fourteenth Amendment to unite the country and attempt to be as apolitical as possible while on the bench.

After Waite died from pneumonia in 1888, Melville Fuller took over as chief justice. Fuller was right-leaning on the political spectrum and almost always was on the side of capitalism, big business, and states' rights. Under his leadership, the Court infamously ruled in the case *Plessy v. Ferguson* (1896) that the Equal Protection Clause did not prevent racial segregation in public places, as long as those public places were equal. This led to the now notorious phrase "separate but equal." Many Americans don't realize that the *Plessy* decision was 8–1. Only John Marshall Harlan dissented. Interestingly, the Fuller Court sometimes expanded how the Fourteenth Amendment was interpreted, as with the case *United States v. Wong Kim Ark*, which affirmed that all people born on American soil are automatically United States citizens.

In the early 1900s, the United States was in the midst of what we now call the Progressive Era, a period of widespread reform and activism. However, the Court was late to the party. At a time when most Americans favored more rights for workers, the Supreme Court kept overturning many federal and state laws designed to help workers. Probably the most famous (or infamous) example of this was in the case *Lochner v. New York* (1905), in which the Court struck down a New York law limiting the number of hours bakers could work each week.

After Edward White took over as chief justice after the death of Fuller, the Court continued its more conservative ways and increasingly seemed to be not only out of step but out of touch with many Americans. Like Fuller, White often ruled on the side of capitalism, big business, and states' rights. However, under White's leadership the Court had slowly begun to lean more to the left. While the White Court ruled that the federal government couldn't ban child labor in the case *Hammer v. Dagenhart* (1918), they also upheld a federal law that mandated a maximum eight-hour shift for railroad workers in the case *Wilson v. New* (1917). White wrote the majority opinion in that case. By the time he died in 1921, White had seemed to broadly support the federal government regulating business and expanding civil rights.

The guy who took over as chief justice after White was the same guy who first nominated White to *become* chief justice: William Howard Taft. Taft is the only president in American history to also serve on the Court, and he enjoyed his time there more than his time in the White House. As you might expect, since Taft and White were political allies, their interpretations of the Constitution were similar, and the Court continued to lean to the right throughout the 1920s. However, one notable case that suddenly pivoted the Court in a left-leaning direction was *Gitlow v. New York* (1925), in which the Court ruled that the Bill of Rights could also restrict state governments, not just the federal government. And what did they use to justify this decision? The Fourteenth Amendment.

In the early years of the presidency of Franklin Delano Roosevelt, his biggest obstacle was often the Supreme Court. Congress largely sided with his New Deal legislation, but later the Court would rule some of that legislation unconstitutional. Throughout Roosevelt's time in office, the Court had three solidly left-leaning justices and four right-leaning justices. The other two justices—the "swing" justices—were Owen Roberts and chief justice Charles Evan Hughes, who had taken over after Taft retired in 1930. The media called those right-leaning justices the "Four Horsemen," an allusion to the Four Horsemen of the Apocalypse, figures referenced in the Christian Bible. These Four Horsemen—Pierce Butler, James McReynolds, George Sutherland, and Willis Van Devanter, consistently opposed Roosevelt's New Deal agenda, and were often successful at swaying Roberts and Hughes to their side. One example was *United States v. Butler* (1936), in which the Court declared the Agricultural Adjustment Act unconstitutional. The press called the three left-leaning justices the "Three Musketeers." The Three Musketeers were Louis Brandeis, Benjamin Cardozo, and Harlan Stone. Roosevelt became so frustrated with the Four Horseman that he proposed the Judiciary Reorganization Bill, which would have increased the size of the Supreme Court by adding a justice for each incumbent justice who had reached the age of 70.5 and refused retirement. In addition, the bill said appointments of new justices could continue until the Court reached a maximum size of fifteen justices. Well, the bill soon created a big, bipartisan backlash, with opponents accusing Roosevelt of trying to "pack the Court."

Roosevelt didn't need that bill to push his agenda forward after all. Afterward, the tide had turned, as Roberts began to consistently vote with the left-leaning wing of the Court. It seemingly began with *West Coast Hotel Co. v. Parrish* (1937), in which the Court ruled that a Washington state law that set a minimum wage was, in fact, constitutional. It was a turning point, and the media took note. The writer Cal Tinney famously called Owen's pivot "the switch in time that saved nine." Historians often refer to this case as the end of the Lochner Era, a period in American legal history marked by the Court being more friendly to big business. After Justice Butler died and Van Devanter and Sutherland retired, Roosevelt got his nominations on the Court, and by the end of 1941, he had appointed seven Supreme Court justices. After Hughes retired, he promoted Harlan Stone to chief justice.

For much of Franklin Roosevelt's presidency, the Supreme Court overturned many convictions of African Americans in Southern courts, beginning with *Powell v. Alabama* (1932). While World War II raged on, back home the Supreme Court tackled "white primaries," which, as the name suggests, were primary elections, held in former Confederate, Southern states, in which only citizens of European descent were allowed to vote. In *Smith v. Allwright* (1944), the Court banned white primaries, which led to more Blacks being able to vote in former Confederate states for the first time since the 1890s.

After the death of Harlan Stone, President Harry Truman appointed Fred Vinson as chief justice. Like John Marshall and Salmon Chase before him, Vinson was another chief justice who had served in all three branches of the federal government. However, Vinson was less ambitious during his time on the bench. By the end of the 1940s, the Court had splintered into two sides again, with one faction led by Justice Hugo Black, and the other led by Justice Felix Frankfurter, but overall the Court had shifted by this time to favor more and more federal government intervention whenever injustice happened at the state or local level.[9]

In 1953, President Dwight Eisenhower did one of the most consequential things in United States Supreme Court history. He nominated Earl Warren, the governor of California, as chief justice. The Senate confirmed the appointment on March 1, 1954, and Warren became the most influential chief justice in American history besides John Marshall. The Marshall Court handed down landmark ruling after landmark ruling that dramatically changed criminal procedure, voting representation, and how the Fourteenth Amendment ought to be applied.

Warren also united the Court on these big decisions, like his first major decision, and perhaps most famous of all, *Brown v. Board of Education* (1954). Under Warren's leadership, the Court unanimously ruled that segregation in public schools was unconstitutional, thus reversing the "separate but equal" doctrine of Plessy. It's worth noting that Warren often got William Douglas, one of the most left-leaning justices in American history, on the same page with the most right-leaning justices on the Court, Felix Frankfurter and John Marshall Harlan II (the grandson of the elder Justice Harlan).

But the Warren Court didn't stop there. Other landmark cases decided during Warren's tenure include *Engle v. Vitale* (1962), in which the Court said officially sanctioned prayer in public schools was unconstitutional; *Mapp v. Ohio* (1961), in which the Court ruled that illegally seized evidence couldn't be used in a trial; *Gideon v. Wainwright*

9　openyls.law.yale.edu/bitstream/handle/20.500.13051/3522/Fred_Vinson_and_the_Chief_Justiceship.
pdf?sequence=2&isAllowed=y

(1963), in which the Court said states had to provide lawyers to those who couldn't afford them; *Reynolds v. Sims* (1964), in which the Court said all state legislative districts have to have an approximately equal population; *Miranda v. Arizona* (1966), in which the Court ruled that the police have to inform suspects of their Fifth and Sixth Amendment rights; *Griswold v. Connecticut* (1965), in which the Court established the right to privacy; and *Loving v. Virginia* (1967), in which the Court ruled that interracial marriage bans were unconstitutional. Whew. And those were just the major cases!

On June 13, 1967, President Lyndon Johnson nominated the same civil rights lawyer who argued for Brown in the *Brown v. Board of Education* case for the Supreme Court. That lawyer was Thurgood Marshall. The Senate confirmed him on August 30 by a vote of 69–11, thus making him the first African American in history to serve on the bench.

At the time, several of the Warren decisions were controversial in the United States, but over time they have received widespread support from folks who lean to the left and right. However, after Warren stepped down from the Court in 1969, there was a notable backlash against his accomplishments. Many law schools and think tanks have helped foster a resurgence in what is known as "originalism," or an interpretation of legal texts (including the Constitution) with their *original* meaning in mind.

Regardless, after the right-leaning Richard Nixon nominated Warren Burger as chief justice, the Court continued interpreting the Bill of Rights to intervene when states went against them. Some of the most left-leaning decisions in American history were handed down under the Burger Court. The most famous of these cases was *Roe v. Wade* (1973), in which the Court ruled that abortion was a constitutionally protected right in some circumstances. In *Lemon v. Kurtzman* (1971), the Court created the "Lemon Test" to determine if something goes against the Establishment Clause of the First Amendment. *Miller v. California* (1973) created the "Miller test" to figure out whether a law that obscenity went against the First Amendment's freedom of speech clause.

Ironically, the Burger Court also played a big role taking down President Richard Nixon after his revealed role in the Watergate Scandal. In *United States v. Nixon* (1974), the Court ruled that no one, not even the president, is completely above the law. Nixon resigned shortly after the ruling.

The Burger Court was also one of the most impactful eras in Supreme Court history. It mostly affirmed the Warren Court's rulings, but this was often because of the influence of the left-leaning justices Marshall, William Brennan, and John Paul Stevens.

On August 19, 1981, President Ronald Reagan nominated Sandra Day O'Connor as an Associate Justice of the Supreme Court to replace the retiring Potter Stewart. The

Senate confirmed with a vote of 99–0, and O'Connor became the first female Supreme Court justice in American history. It took 192 years for this to happen. Since then, five additional women have made it to the highest court, and *four of them are currently serving*.

During the 1980s, the country was leaning more and more to the right politically, and soon the Court would too. By the time Reagan nominated William Rehnquist to replace Burger as chief justice after his retirement in 1986, the Court overall was fairly moderate politically, and would remain so over the next three decades. That said, Rehnquist leaned to the right and thought the federal government's role should be diminished.

Under Rehnquist's leadership, the Court became more divided. This seemed to culminate with *Bush v. Gore* (2000), the only Supreme Court case in American history to essentially decide a presidential election. While the Court decided strictly based on the Equal Protection Clause of the Fourteenth Amendment, the five right-leaning justices ended a recount of votes, thus securing victory for the right-leaning George W. Bush. As president, Bush would go on to nominate three right-leaning justices.

However, it wasn't always divided along partisan or ideological lines under the Rehnquist Court, as seen with the landmark case *Texas v. Johnson* (1989), which argued that burning an American flag was a form of speech protected by the First Amendment. In *Lawrence v. Texas* (2003), the Court said laws prohibiting sodomy were unconstitutional, and the right-leaning O'Connor and moderate Justice David Souter joined the left-leaning bloc of the Court.

After the death of Rehnquist in 2005, President Bush nominated John Roberts as chief justice, and he has been in the role ever since. The Roberts Court has been even *more* divided than the Rehnquist, which is no surprise if you look at the political dynamics in the United States since the presidential election of 2000.

The Roberts Court has also been more consequential. In fact, other than the Marshall and Warren courts, no other Court has been as consequential in American history, shifting the Court dramatically to the right, especially in recent years. For much of this period, the influence of Justice Antonin Scalia has been undeniable. Scalia, who proudly proclaimed himself an originalist, played a big role in cases like *DC v. Heller* (2008), where the Court ruled that the Second Amendment protects a citizen's right to own a firearm for self-defense. The *Heller* case was the most significant Second Amendment case since the 1870s, and it was expanded on later in *McDonald v. City of Chicago* (2010). Scalia also had tremendous influence over the Court's infamous decision in *Citizens United v. FEC* (2010), which said laws that prevented corporations and unions from using revenue for political advertising went against the First Amendment's guarantee of freedom of speech.

In 2009, Sonia Sotomayor became the first Hispanic American to serve on the Supreme Court after being nominated by President Barack Obama. During the Obama years, the Court became more diverse than it ever had been. During this time, Anthony Kennedy became a key swing justice. He played a major role in legalizing same-sex marriage with his opinion in *Obergefell v. Hodges* (2015).

After Justice Scalia died in 2016, the right-leaning Senate refused to consider *any* nomination for his replacement by the left-leaning President Obama. After the right-leaning President Donald Trump took office the next year, he would go on to nominate three justices who all praised Scalia and subscribed to originalism to one degree or another. After the death of Ruth Bader Ginsburg in 2020, right-leaning justices now had a clear majority on the bench.

Some of the most consequential Supreme Court decisions happened in 2022, the year I wrote this book. Notably, with *Dobbs v. Jackson Women's Health Organization*, in which the Court argued that the Constitution does not protect a right to an abortion. The decision reversed the *Roe* decision and *Casey v. Planned Parenthood* (1992) and has sent shockwaves throughout the country. Another controversial case decided was *West Virginia v. EPA*, in which the Court said the Environmental Protection Agency did *not* have the authority to establish emissions caps to fight climate change. Yet another controversial case is *Kennedy v. Bremerton School District*, where the Court said an individual could engage in a religious observance at a public school. This case overturned the Lemon Test of *Lemon v. Kurtzman*. The firestorm caused by these decisions has led to a dramatic decline in American approval of the Court.[10]

Today, the United States is arguably more controversial than ever. When Americans vote for a president every four years, they are often indirectly "voting" for Supreme Court justices. In other words, they only vote for a presidential candidate they assume will nominate a Supreme Court justice they approve of. With the political polarization of the United States Congress, the Senate has now approved a simple majority vote to approve justice nominations instead of a supermajority. The Court is also arguably more powerful than ever, which is why, according to one poll, two out of three Americans now favor term limits for justices.[11]

To be honest, I'm just happy more people are finally paying attention to the Supreme Court.

---

10 www.pewresearch.org/politics/2022/02/02/publics-views-of-supreme-court-turned-more-negative-before-news-of-breyers-retirement

11 apnews.com/article/abortion-ketanji-brown-jackson-us-supreme-court-government-and-politics-only-on-ap-8adc9a08c9e8001c8ef0455906542a60

# How I Came Up with a Hundred Supreme Court Cases You Should Know About

The United States Supreme Court has delivered over 35,000 decisions, but almost all will be forgotten. However, historians and legal scholars often recognize that a *few* should stand out. You could call them *landmark* decisions.

In the United States, a "landmark court decision" creates precedents that guide a new legal principle *or* concept or dramatically changes how we all ought to interpret an existing law. A precedent is a new standard set by a previous legal case. Whenever a judge interprets the law, they would immediately be called out if they ignored precedent. Rule number one of interpreting laws might just be "don't ignore precedent." That'd be ignoring the wisdom of generations of judges who came before you.

Put another way, a landmark court decision is a freaking important Supreme Court decision, and yes, what makes a decision a "landmark" is also open to interpretation. According to the Supreme Court Historical Society, there are twenty landmark Supreme Court cases in American history.[12] According to the National Constitution Center, there are at least seventy.[13] According to Wikipedia, there are 423 landmark cases.[14] However, if you take the Advanced Placement US Government and Politics exam, you just have to know fifteen cases.

So why did I pick a hundred cases? First, for obvious reasons, one hundred is a nice round number that makes this a reasonably sized book. That said, I combined the *Insular Cases* and *Civil Rights Cases* to help get this nice round number. Second, one hundred is a good middle ground based on the various sources I've researched that list the most important Supreme Court decisions. I wanted to make sure that I focused on *every* part

12  www.landmarkcases.org/
13  constitutioncenter.org/education/constitution-101-curriculum
14  en.wikipedia.org/wiki/List_of_landmark_court_decisions_in_the_United_States

of the Constitution, and therefore was a more balanced look at the entire American legal framework. Often, historians and judges can get too caught up in specific parts of it. For example, I think the First Amendment has gotten far too much attention from the courts. I don't mean to undermine its importance—it's one of the most important, if not *the* most important parts of the Constitution—but it has been interpreted ad nauseam.

In contrast, the Second Amendment, which some argue is even *more* important than the First Amendment, has gotten considerably less interpretation by the Court historically. How is it that there are dozens of so-called landmark First Amendment Supreme Court cases but *four* landmark Second Amendment Supreme Court cases? I should add that *half* of those landmark cases have been decided since 2007. Since the mid-1900s, the Court has largely focused on First Amendment rights, voting rights, federalism, criminal law, and the Equal Protection Clause of the Fourteenth Amendment. While all of those legal concepts are admittedly most important to me, if we take an unbiased approach, we must admit that most of the Constitution is often ignored.

Whenever I could combine precedents, I did. For example, I attempted to avoid covering cases that were overturned. Obviously, there are exceptions to this. There's no way I could have ever felt comfortable not covering *Plessy v. Ferguson* (1896), for example. However, after the recent *Dobbs v. Jackson Women's Health Organization* case, I felt it unnecessary to include *Casey v. Planned Parenthood* (1992), as I could easily reference it explaining the *Dobbs* decision. As is common practice, several cases are combined if the decisions are strongly linked, i.e., the *Slaughterhouse Cases*, *Civil Rights Cases*, and *Insular Cases*.

As mentioned earlier, I spent twelve years in the classroom teaching American government to middle schoolers and juniors and seniors in high school. I know which cases resonated with them and which cases did not. I know which cases were relevant to them. In fact, these interactions in the classroom have profoundly influenced how I decide to make videos for my Supreme Court Briefs series. Speaking of which, several of the cases I have covered in Supreme Court Briefs didn't make the cut for this book.

That said, most of these cases revolve around civil rights and civil liberties, making the Court most relevant to us. Because of that, most cases deal with interpreting the Bill of Rights and the Fourteenth Amendment. Besides emphasizing our rights and liberties, this book also dedicates significant portions to cases dealing with federalism and the proper role of government. In particular, the balance between federal power and state power.

It's probably no surprise that most of these cases are from the past hundred years. This reflects the growing power of the Court in recent years.

In conclusion, the way I chose which cases for this book was not random. These are the decisions that represent all of the Constitution. These decisions have impacted how the Constitution is interpreted and how new laws are passed. These decisions will continue to impact how future laws are passed. Many of these decisions have changed American culture. I chose them because they are most relevant to you, even if you are not an American citizen, as the Court's decisions often impact the entire world. We will look at them chronologically.

# 1. Chisholm v. Georgia (1793)

This case began in Savannah, Georgia, on October 31, 1777. On that day, the Executive Council of Georgia said Georgia's state government could buy clothing, cotton, linens, and blankets from Robert Farquhar for the soldiers stationed in Savannah. At this point, the American War of Independence had been raging for a year and a half, and the soldiers there were desperate for supplies. Due to the war, Georgia's government was a bit strapped for cash, though, and they promised to pay Farquhar for the goods later, presumably when the war ended. They ended up owing him $169,613.33.

Well, the war ended in 1783 with a United States victory, but by the time Farquhar died a year later, Georgia still hadn't paid him a dime. After Farquhar's death, a dude named Alexander Chisholm took over his estate. Chisholm patiently awaited Georgia to pay him, but they never did. When he filed a claim for the debt with the Georgia legislature in 1789, they said they wouldn't pay him. Chisholm had had enough. He sued Georgia in the US Circuit Court for the District of Georgia, and they agreed to hear the case in October 1791.

However, Georgia argued that the circuit court lacked jurisdiction. Georgia governor Edward Telfair said Georgia was a "free, sovereign and independent State…[and] cannot be drawn or compelled…to answer, against the will of the said State of Georgia, before any justices of the federal Circuit Court for the District of Georgia or before any justices of any Court of Law or Equity whatsoever." Dang, Telfair. Nathaniel Pendleton and James Iredell, who also was a Supreme Court justice, heard the case. Both agreed they lacked jurisdiction to rule in this case based on the Judiciary Act of 1789. However, Iredell said perhaps the Supreme Court could hear the case, writing, "The Constitution…seems to provide, that in the cases where a state is a party, the Supreme Court shall have original jurisdiction."

Chisholm was disappointed that the circuit court dismissed his lawsuit but simultaneously hopeful after hearing Iredell's suggestion that the Supreme Court could hear the case. In 1792, he filed a new suit before the Supreme Court, and they agreed to hear the case in August 1792. However, Georgia sent no representative for their side, viewing the whole ordeal as illegitimate. Chisholm's lawyers, which included Founding Father Dude and *the* Attorney General of the United States Edmund Randolph, decided to give Georgia some more time and push back the arguments to February 1793, but come February, Georgia still didn't show up. Despite Georgia sending no one, the Supreme Court proceeded to hear

Randolph's arguments for Chisholm anyway on February 5, 1793. Georgia sent a letter stating it had "sovereign immunity," meaning a government is *immune* from lawsuits.

## The Big Questions in this case:

- Can a citizen sue a state government in a federal court?
- Does the Constitution give power to the federal courts to hear cases involving citizens and states?

The Court said yes to both questions. It announced its decision on February 18, 1793. In a 4–1 decision, they sided with Chisholm. Ironically, it was only Iredell who dissented. Speaking for the majority, Justice James Wilson (another Founding Father Dude) took a jab at the entire idea of "state sovereignty." Wilson argued that because the federal union of states was based on popular consent for all, a state couldn't claim it had state immunity just to get out of something.[15] Chief Justice John Jay went further, arguing that state sovereignty maybe wasn't a real thing. He said the citizens had sovereignty, writing, "Sovereignty is the right to govern...here it rests with the people."[16] The Court made it clear that yes, the Constitution gave the federal courts the power to hear cases involving citizens and states, not just lawsuits within states.

In Iredell's dissent, he argued states had independent sovereignty, basing it on the English common law tradition carried over from when each state used to be a British colony. Iredell said the Constitution didn't say the Court could step in on this case, and he had a good point. Most state governments generally condemned the Court's decision and agreed with Iredell. In fact, Iredell's dissent ultimately led to the passing of the Eleventh Amendment to the Constitution two years later, preventing a state from being sued in federal court without that state's consent. It was the first of only two notable times in American history when the states agreed to change the Constitution based on a Supreme Court decision.

*Chisholm v. Georgia* is the first historically significant Supreme Court case. Even though the Eleventh Amendment squashed this Supreme Court's decision, Chisholm continued fighting to get his estate reimbursed for the rest of his life. After he died in 1810, Farquhar's son-in-law Peter Trezevant kept the case alive on behalf of the estate. Finally, in November 1847, the Georgia General Assembly passed a bill to pay back the money owed to Farquhar's estate. By that time, Trezevant was seventy-nine years old, and the family had been fighting to get their owed money for fifty-eight years.[17]

---

15   www.nps.gov/articles/000/chisholm-v-georgia.htm
16   founders.archives.gov/documents/Jay/01-05-02-0251
17   www.trezevantfamilyproject.com/generation-4/peter-trezevant-1768-1854elizabeth-willoughby-farquhar-1772-1845/

# 2. Marbury v. Madison (1803)

This case began in the District of Columbia on March 2, 1801. On that day, President John Adams, who had just two days left in office, made several last-minute appointments for his Federalist Party friends to important positions. It was a mad rush to get all his allies into the executive branch before the new president, his archenemy Thomas Jefferson, took over.

He nominated twenty-three justices of the peace, who were judges in lower courts, in Washington County. One of those nominated was a dude named William Marbury. Like Adams, Marbury was a Federalist who had talked a lot of trash about Jefferson when he ran against Adams in the months before the presidential election of 1800.

Even though Adams nominated Marbury along with the other twenty-two folks, and even though the Senate approved their nomination the next day (March 3), and even though later that day Adams signed the commissions, which were the final orders so they could get to work, several of them didn't get the job. Why not? Well, John Marshall, the acting Secretary of State for President Adams, did not deliver those commissions on time. At noon the next day (March 4), Thomas Jefferson officially took over as president. He instructed his Secretary of State, James Madison, to only deliver those commissions to *some* of the nominees. You know, the ones *Jefferson* liked. One of the people who never got his commission was William Marbury. Jefferson did not like Marbury.

Marbury was obviously upset. He felt he was promised that job and was only denied it now due to his political beliefs. He wanted to force Madison to deliver that commission, and he petitioned the Supreme Court to help do just that. The Court agreed to look into it, and they heard arguments on February 11, 1803. But guess what? By this time, John Marshall was chief justice of the Supreme Court. Even though it was probably inappropriate for Marshall to make a judgment on this case due to his link to the commissions and the Adams administration, he decided to sit in on arguments anyway.

The Big Questions in this case:

- Should Marbury and the other justice of the peace nominees get the jobs they were promised?
- Could the aforementioned justice of the peace nominees use the court to get their jobs?
- Does the Supreme Court have the authority to say they could have their jobs?

The Court said yes to the first two questions but no to the last one. It announced its decision on February 24, 1803. All four justices involved with the case sided with Marbury. They thought Marbury deserved that position and believed he should be able to fight in court to get it. *However, they also sided with Madison.* Why? Well, the law that enabled Marbury to take Madison to court to begin with, the Judiciary Act of 1789, was *unconstitutional* because it gave the Supreme Court more power than the Constitution allowed.[18]

In other words, the Supreme Court effectively decided to weaken its power, at least in the short term. However, I would argue that John Marshall knew that, in the long term, the Court was strengthening its power with this decision. While the Court gave up power by declaring the Judiciary Act of 1789 unconstitutional, they gained far greater power, that of being *judicial review.* Again, judicial review is the process by which the judicial branch can determine whether the actions of the executive and legislative branches are constitutional. So if the Court could declare the Judiciary Act of 1789 unconstitutional, they could declare *any* law Congress passed unconstitutional. Just like that, John Marshall, along with justices Samuel Chase, Bushrod Washington, and William Paterson, had made the Supreme Court kind of a big deal.

Because of this, *Marbury v. Madison* is the most important Supreme Court case in American history. In fact, it dramatically elevated the power of not only the Court, but the entire judicial branch.

# 3. Fletcher v. Peck

# (1810)

This case began in the Yazoo lands in 1795. The Yazoo lands, named after the Yazoo Nation, were the central and western portions of Georgia that today mostly make up the states of Alabama and Mississippi. The Georgia legislature divided up the Yazoo lands into four tracts and then sold each tract to a different land development company for $500,000 each, which ended up being about a penny per acre, or about thirty-two cents per acre adjusted for inflation. I'd say that was a good deal.

Anyway, whistleblowers later revealed that Georgia politicians, including the governor himself, George Mathews, only sold all this land so cheaply because they were bribed! Once voters found out about the bribes, they voted out anyone remotely involved in the scandal and demanded the new legislature repeal the law that approved of the land deal. The new legislature voided the land deal, declaring all claims made under it no good. The new legislature even burned almost all remaining copies of the original land deal. Dang, that was dramatic.

Regardless, the whole ordeal was not over. While Georgia had refunded money to its citizens who had already bought portions of the Yazoo lands, some straight up refused the money, preferring to hold on to their land. However, Georgia no longer recognized their claims, and this created a mess in the courts for several years.

Enter two veteran land speculators named Robert Fletcher and John Peck. The two conspired together to challenge the legal system to profit from some of the portions of the Yazoo lands they were holding onto. They both agreed that Fletcher would sue Peck, with Fletcher claiming that when he had bought the tract of land in the Yazoo lands from Peck in 1795, he was misled to believe that Peck owned the land. Therefore, the sale was invalid since the land deals had been repealed the following year.

Fletcher's lawsuit against Peck didn't happen until 1803. In the suit, Fletcher argued the United States owned the land due to the presence of Native Americans in the region. Peck argued Georgia owned the land. So where did the collusion come in? Well, no matter how the courts decided, they needed to prove that Native Americans didn't legally own the land. In other words, it didn't matter whether Georgia or the United States owned the land, as long as it wasn't Native Americans. More importantly, both Fletcher and Peck wanted to establish that they could own their land.[19]

The Federal Circuit Court for the District of Georgia ruled in favor of Peck, and so Fletcher appealed to the Supreme Court. The Court heard oral arguments throughout 1809 and 1810. High-profile lawyers came in to argue for Peck, like future Supreme Court Justice Joseph Story and future President John Quincy Adams. Fletcher, who, again, wanted to lose this case, brought in an elderly lawyer named Luther Martin, who delayed arguments multiple times because he kept showing up drunk.[20]

## The Big Question in this case:

- Could the contract between Fletcher and Peck be invalidated by Georgia's legislature?

The Court said no. It announced its decision on March 16, 1810. In a 4–1 decision, the Court sided with Peck. They argued that yes, Georgia owned the land, but no, it could not repeal its previous land grants because that went against Article 1, Section 10, Clause 1 of the United States Constitution, which is also known simply as the Contract Clause. Therefore, the sale between Fletcher and Peck was a binding contract and Georgia had to recognize it. Now, the Court did acknowledge that the fraud underlying the land grants was bad, but it said Peck was an innocent third party who got the land in good faith. After all, *he* wasn't one of the dudes accepting bribes.

*Fletcher v. Peck* was the first case in which the Supreme Court ruled a state law unconstitutional. The decision also established a strong precedent for the importance of contracts. More specifically, the decision further cemented the protection of property rights. Over the next several decades, it established a big obstacle for the state regulation of private companies. Unfortunately, the decision also introduced another precedent—Native Americans did not hold the complete title to their lands.

19   Banner, Stuart (2005). *How the Indians Lost Their Land: Law and Power on the Frontier.* Cambridge: Harvard. pp. 171–172.
20   fas-history.rutgers.edu/clemens/constitutional1/fletcher.html

# 4. Martin v. Hunter's Lessee (1816)

This case began in Northern Virginia during the American War of Independence. In 1781, Denny Martin, who was British, inherited land from his uncle, a Loyalist. In case you forgot, in the American War of Independence, the colonies were fighting for freedom from Britain, and the Loyalists during that war were the ones still *loyal* to Britain.

Well, as the war wound down as American victory became imminent, the Virginia legislature said that the land grant to Denny Martin was no good and transferred the land back to Virginia. The land ultimately ended up being owned by a dude named David Hunter. However, when the war *did* end, the United States and Great Britain signed the Treaty of Paris (the one signed in 1783), which, among other things, said the confiscated property had to be returned to the previous owners. Therefore, Martin had the authority to sue to get his land back.

Martin didn't do this, though, until 1791. He sued David Hunter in Virginia state court. In fact, he took Hunter to court many times, and each time lost.[21] Meanwhile, this entire time, Martin was confiscating parts of the land and selling it off anyway, even while Virginia was *also* selling off parts of it! Interestingly, future Chief Justice John Marshall and his brother were among those who bought tracts of the land from Martin.[22]

Martin and Virginia fought over this land for several years when finally Martin realized he needed to settle this once and for all in 1813. The plan was to appeal all the way to the Supreme Court, knowing that all of Virginia's courts would vote against him. The Supreme Court agreed to hear the case, officially known as *Fairfax's Devisee v. Hunter's Lessee* (Martin was also referred to as Fairfax, as it was his family name). Now, because John Marshall and his brother had bought some of Martin's land, Marshall had to excuse himself from the case. On February 27, 1813, the Court announced that it unanimously sided with Martin, stating that the Martin land titles were legit, thus reversing the ruling of the Virginia Court of Appeals. It cited the Supremacy Clause of Article 6 of the Constitution to back up that it was okay that a federal treaty superseded a state law.

The United States Supreme Court ordered the Virginia Supreme Court to carry out its ruling. However, at this time, the Virginia Supreme Court legitimately didn't think it

---

21 F. Thornton Miller, "John Marshall Versus Spencer Roane: A Reevaluation of *Martin v. Hunter's Lessee*," *Virginia Magazine of History and Biography* 96 (July 1988): 297–314.

22 edge.sagepub.com/clca/resources/a-short-course/3-the-judiciary/cases/martin-v-hunters-lessee

had to listen to the United States Supreme Court and ultimately it did not comply. Not only that, but it also declared Section 25 of the Judiciary Act of 1789 unconstitutional. That part of the law granted the United States Supreme Court appellate review over state court cases as long as it involved federal laws. Dang, Virginia Supreme Court, way to get feisty.

And so, Martin appealed again, and the Court heard oral arguments again in March 1816. Again, John Marshall stayed out of it due to it being a conflict of interest.

## The Big Question in this case:

- Was Section 25 of the Judiciary Act of 1789 unconstitutional?

The Court said no. It announced its decision on March 20, 1816. They again sided with Martin, and it was again unanimous. Again, the Supremacy Clause of Article 6 of the Constitution, combined with Article 3 of the Constitution giving the Court appellate jurisdiction, both justify federal courts reviewing state court decisions that interpret federal laws. In effect the Court argued that federal courts superseded state courts. Justice Joseph Story wrote the majority opinion: "The constitution of the United States was ordained and established, not by the states in their sovereign capacities, but emphatically, as the preamble of the constitution declares, by 'the people of the United States,'" going on, "The constitution was not...necessarily carved out of existing state sovereignties, nor a surrender of powers already existing in state institutions."

*Martin v. Hunter's Lessee* was the first case in which the Supreme Court asserted its authority to review state court decisions regarding federal law. It was also the first major case to justify the Supremacy Clause, which gave the federal government more power over the states. Although his legal battle lasted twenty-five years, Denny Martin finally had complete, legal ownership of his inherited land, but he needed the federal government to step in to guarantee it.

# 5. Dartmouth College v. Woodward (1819)

This case began in Concord, New Hampshire, in June 1816, when the state's legislature passed a law to make Dartmouth College a public university run by the state. In doing so, however, it would break a forty-seven-year-old charter traced back to King George III. That charter guaranteed that twelve trustees would always have full power to run the college. This new law would take away the power of the trustees and have New Hampshire run it. Sure, Dartmouth would still have trustees, but they'd be appointed by the state's governor.

Politics was a major factor in this attempt to convert a private college into a public university.[23] By 1816, New Hampshire's legislature was mostly Democratic-Republicans. However, most of Dartmouth's trustees were Federalists. These trustees wanted the school to remain more religious-based. The legislature wanted it to be more secular.[24]

With the support of professors and students, the trustees rebelled, ignoring the New Hampshire law and still running Dartmouth privately. In addition, with the help of US Representative and Dartmouth alumnus Daniel Webster, they sued William Woodward, the guy sent by the state to take control over important documents and other college property. The trustees said the state law was unconstitutional because it broke a private contract. Well, that sounds familiar, doesn't it?

New Hampshire's state supreme court, perhaps predictably, ruled against Dartmouth College, and so the trustees appealed to the Supreme Court, and the Court agreed to hear oral arguments in March 1818. Specifically, the justices considered Article 1, Section 10 of the Constitution, which includes the Contract Clause, which says state governments can't pass laws that undermine contracts. Webster eloquently argued for Dartmouth, famously saying, "It is...a small college and yet there are those who love it."[25]

## The Big Question in this case:

- Was it constitutional for the New Hampshire legislature to take control of a privately funded college?

23  scholarship.law.duke.edu/cgi/viewcontent.cgi?article=6721&context=faculty_scholarship
24  www.mtsu.edu/first-amendment/article/729/dartmouth-college-v-woodward
25  250.dartmouth.edu/highlights/dartmouth-college-case-decided-us-supreme-court

The Court said no. They announced their decision on February 25, 1819. They sided with the trustees of Dartmouth, 5–1. The Court said the New Hampshire legislature broke the law when it took control of the college by going against the Contract Clause of the Constitution. Even though the charter that created Dartmouth was created by a king, it still qualified as a contract between two private parties. It's important to note, however, that Chief Justice John Marshall stressed that the term "contract" specifically referenced transactions regarding property rights and didn't relate to "the political relations between the government and its citizens."[26] Dartmouth would remain a private college and still is today.

*Dartmouth College v. Woodward* marked a turning point. After it, with cases like *Terrett v. Taylor* (1815) and *Philadelphia Baptist Association v. Hart's Executors* (1819), states could no longer just take over a private corporation if they wanted to. There was now a sharp line dividing public and private institutions. In fact, historians have noted that this case was responsible for the dramatic rise of American corporations, and it's responsible for American capitalism as we know it today.[27]

26  supreme.justia.com/cases/federal/us/17/518
27  Newmyer, R. K. (2001). *John Marshall and the heroic age of the Supreme Court.* Baton Rouge: Louisiana State University Press.

# 6. McCulloch v. Maryland
# (1819)

This case began in the District of Columbia in February 1816. The United States Congress created the Second Bank of the United States. I like to call it the Bank of the US 2.0. The bank's main purpose was to handle all monetary transactions for the federal government. Most who supported its creation thought it was needed to stabilize the economy. They were tired of wildly fluctuating markets prices. Critics of the new national bank viewed it as a threat to state sovereignty and private banks. Regardless, President James Madison signed the charter that made the Bank of the US 2.0 a done deal on April 10, 1816.

The next year, it opened in Philadelphia, and everything was mostly groovy until later that same year the feds tried to open another branch in Baltimore, Maryland. In 1818, Maryland's state legislature passed a law that said all banks in Maryland not chartered by them had to pay an annual tax of $15,000. This was, of course, meant to hurt the national bank's operations within the state.

A cashier at the national bank's Baltimore branch, James McCulloh, refused to pay the tax, and rebelled against it by issuing unstamped bank notes. Once the state of Maryland found out about these shenanigans, it sued him. In state court, McCulloh said the tax was unconstitutional. However, Maryland argued that the Constitution says nothing about the federal government having the right to create a national bank. Therefore, *any bank of the United States* was unconstitutional. Oh snap!

Maryland won the case, but McCulloh appealed the case to the Maryland Court of Appeals. It agreed with the lower court, arguing that, again, the Constitution didn't say one word about Congress having the right to create a national bank. But McCulloh appealed again, this time to the Supreme Court, and it agreed to hear oral arguments in February and March of 1819.

## The Big Questions in this case:

- Did Congress have the authority to establish a national bank?
- Did Maryland have the authority to interfere with congressional powers?

The Court said yes to the first question and no to the second one. It announced its decision on March 6, 1819. The Court sided with McCulloch (by this time his name was misspelled in official court documents) and it was unanimous. Folks, this was a big one. The Court ruled the federal government *did* have the authority to create a national bank. Chief Justice John Marshall argued that there was precedence for a national bank. After all, the First of the United States came before the Second.

However, more importantly, Marshall argued that just because the Constitution does not explicitly say the federal government can create a bank, doesn't mean it *can't*. He brought up what's now known as the Necessary and Proper Clause of Article 1, Section 8 of the Constitution, which says Congress has the power to "make all laws which shall be necessary and proper" to help the country. Marshall said the federal government had *several* powers that weren't specifically listed in the Constitution but still were *implied*.[28]

Not only that, but the Court also said Maryland couldn't tax the national bank because the Supremacy Clause of Article 6 of the Constitution says federal laws overrule state laws. You know, they are the "supreme Law of the Land." Finally, the Court argued Maryland's tax also violated constitutional sovereignty by penalizing *all* Americans in favor of the people of one state. And just like that, McCulloh took on an entire state in a big way.

*McCulloch v. Maryland* was the first major Supreme Court decision to justify the idea of "implied powers." After this case, the Necessary and Proper Clause meant the federal government had powers beyond what was explicitly stated in the Constitution. The decision dramatically increased the power of the United States Congress, especially in relation to state legislatures. The decision also justified the Supremacy Clause, giving the federal government *even more* power over the states. I would argue that no other Supreme Court case has done more to strengthen the federal government compared to the state governments than this one.

# 7. Gibbons v. Ogden (1824)

This case began in Albany, New York, in 1808. The New York state legislature granted Robert Livingston and Robert Fulton exclusive privileges to operate their steamboats on the rivers of the state. If those names sound familiar, it's because Livingston was a Founding Father Dude, and Fulton built the first working steamboat. With those exclusive privileges, no one else could do business on New York rivers unless they got special permission from them. This meant Livingston and Fulton had no competition on those rivers, meaning they held a monopoly over them.

Competitors tried to kill this monopoly, but whenever they did this Livingston and Fulton would just buy the competition and issue franchises. Two dudes who bought a franchise from Livingston and Fulton to operate steamboats in New York were Thomas Gibbons and Aaron Ogden, even though they hated Livingston and Fulton's monopoly and initially had tried to get around it.

Three years later, Gibbons and Ogden's partnership ended. However, Gibbons kept sending his steamboats from New Jersey to New York, despite no longer having the license to do so. Gibbons argued that he could do this because he had a federal license from Congress, thanks to an obscure law regulating trade along the coast passed in 1793.[29] Gibbons, you sneaky person, you.

Ogden, the former governor of New Jersey, was angry about this, as his former partner was taking away business from him by skirting past a state law. Ogden made a complaint in the Court of Chancery of New York, asking them to stop Gibbons from operating steamboats there.

Gibbons got a lawyer to defend him who, by this time, had become somewhat famous, thanks to being a US Representative and a high-profile lawyer in the *Dartmouth College v. Woodward* case. That lawyer was Daniel Webster, who also later became one of the most celebrated US Senators and Secretary of State in American history. Webster argued that the United States Congress had the final say over buying and selling stuff across state lines thanks to Article 1, Section 8, Clause 3 of the Constitution. Also known as the commerce clause, it says that Congress can "regulate Commerce with foreign Nations, and among the several States, and with the Indian Tribes." However, the Court of Chancery and Court of Errors of New York said "nope," siding with Ogden and forcing Gibbons to stop his steamboat operations in the state.

And so, still with the help of Webster, Gibbons appealed to the Supreme Court. The Court heard arguments in February 1824.

## The Big Question in this case:

- Was New York able to regulate commerce within its borders, even if that commerce depended on commerce in other states?

The Court said no, announcing its decision on March 2, 1824. They unanimously sided with Gibbons. The Court agreed with Webster's argument, that Congress's power overruled New York's due to the commerce clause, but they argued that the *Supremacy Clause* of the Constitution *also* guaranteed this.[30]

Chief Justice John Marshall defined the word "commerce," which included navigation on interstate waterways. Heck, he even defined the word "among," saying "among the several states" meant the states mixed together. Therefore, whenever state laws conflicted, both Congress and the Supreme Court could step in.

*Gibbons v. Ogden* was the most pivotal Supreme Court decision regarding opening the door for the federal government to get more involved with the expansion and growth of the national economy. Afterward, the federal government could build national roads, canals, and telegraph and railroad lines more easily since they didn't have to worry as much about state interference.[31] Specifically, more than nearly every other Supreme Court decision, it broadened the power of Congress, and that trend has continued to the present day.

---

30  caselaw.findlaw.com/us-supreme-court/22/1.html
31  www.archives.gov/milestone-documents/gibbons-v-ogden

# 8. Worcester v. Georgia (1832)

This case began in Milledgeville, Georgia, during the 1820s. The Georgia legislature was increasingly concerned with the Cherokee Nation, which held territory within Georgia's borders, as well as in North Carolina, Alabama, and Tennessee. The Cherokee were also increasingly concerned, as their sovereignty was threatened by the increasing number of Americans trespassing and stealing their land to mine and farm. Unfortunately for the Cherokee, Georgia Governor George Rockingham Gilmer, as well as most of the Georgia legislature, had also made it clear they wanted the Cherokee out of the state.

In 1827, the Cherokee Nation formally established a constitutional government and declared themselves a sovereign state, meaning American laws didn't apply to them. This, of course, angered Governor Gilmer and most of the legislature, and they responded by annexing *all* Cherokee land in the state, dismantling the Cherokee government, and redistributing most of the Cherokee's land to "white" citizens. Not only that, but three years later Congress passed and President Andrew Jackson signed the Indian Removal Act, which gave the president the power to negotiate treaties to remove Native Americans from their lands.

While all of this was happening, American missionaries had been working with the Cherokee Nation to help them defend their sovereignty and continue resisting the Georgia laws kicking them off their own land. The Georgia legislature didn't like this so much, so they passed a law that specifically banned "white persons" from living with the Cherokee without special permission from the state.

However, several of these missionaries were rebels, you could say. They refused to leave. Two of them who refused to leave were Elizur Butler, a doctor from Connecticut, and Samuel Worcester, a minister from Vermont. The state militia arrested Butler and Worcester for "residing within the limits of the Cherokee Nation without a license" and "without having taken the oath to support and defend the constitution and laws of the state of Georgia."[32] They were convicted and sentenced to "hard labor" for four years as punishment.

Worcester and Butler appealed the decision, with the help of lawyers paid for by the Cherokee Nation, and their case went directly to the Supreme Court. The Court agreed to hear arguments in February 1832. Georgia refused to send lawyers as it believed the Constitution said the Supreme Court didn't have the authority to hear the case. Worcester and Butler's main argument was that Georgia couldn't force the Cherokee Nation to do whatever it said because, according to the Constitution, only *Congress* could make treaties and deals with Native American tribes.

## The Big Question in this case:

- Does Georgia have the authority to regulate deals between citizens of its state and members of the Cherokee Nation?

The Court said no. On March 3, 1832, it announced it had sided with Worcester and Butler, voting 5–1 in their favor. Chief Justice John Marshall delivered the majority opinion. He said the Georgia law was unconstitutional. He also said it *got in the way* of the federal government's authority, saying, "The Cherokee Nation, then, is a distinct community occupying its own territory in which the laws of Georgia can have no force. The whole intercourse between the United States and this nation, is, by our constitution and laws, vested in the government of the United States." In other words, he and the majority of the Court recognized the Cherokee as an independent nation.[33] Georgia couldn't pass laws controlling Spain or France, so why could they pass laws controlling the Cherokee?

So what did Georgia do in response to this decision? They ignored it, and Worcester and Butler stayed imprisoned. Predictably, President Andrew Jackson also didn't force Georgia to follow the Supreme Court decision, and instead said the Cherokee Nation had two choices: get out of Georgia or fall in line with their laws. Eventually Georgia released Worcester and Butler from prison, but only after both promised to stop helping the Cherokee resist Georgia laws. In 1835, a faction of Cherokees broke away and secretly signed the Treaty of New Echota, which gave up Cherokee lands in Georgia in exchange for money. This group claimed to represent all of the Cherokee, but they were not. In 1838, the US Army forced almost all remaining Cherokees in Georgia off their lands and marched them around 1,000 miles (1,600 km) to Indian Territory in present-day Oklahoma. This was a horrible journey, known today as the Trail of Tears. The relocated Native Americans suffered from disease, exposure, and starvation as they traveled through harsh conditions. Thousands died on the way.

While *Worcester v. Georgia* led to the Trail of Tears, it led to a long-term win for Native American tribes. It was an important decision because it clarified the relationships Native

33  www.umass.edu/legal/derrico/marshall_jow.html

American tribes had with state and federal governments. Ultimately, it strengthened tribal sovereignty in the United States. The Court made it clear that, even though they reside within the borders of the United States, Native American tribes govern themselves and thus can have their own laws.

Still, Georgia's state government and the president chose to disregard the decision, which is why it was mostly ignored for almost two hundred years.

# 9. Barron v. Baltimore (1833)

This case began in Baltimore, Maryland, in 1815. John Barron owned a deep-water wharf that was among the most profitable in Baltimore Harbor. A wharf is a safe area for a ship to dock and unload or load. However, that year, Baltimore began a big renovation project to modernize the city's infrastructure. The city began paving streets, building embankments, and diverting waterways to prevent flooding.

While the city was better off after these improvements, John Barron and his wharf business were not. These improvements caused lots of sand to wash down into Baltimore Harbor. After seven years, so much sand had accumulated in the harbor that the waters around Barron's wharf were now too shallow for most ships to dock. His business was failing.

Desperate, Barron sued the city of Baltimore to compensate for his losses. He claimed the city had violated his Fifth Amendment rights. Specifically, the Takings Clause of the Fifth Amendment, which says that private property will not be taken for public use without "just compensation." The government taking private property for public use is also commonly known as "eminent domain." Barron said the city's destruction of his wharf fell under eminent domain, and he sued for $20,000, or about $421,000 today. He won the case, but Baltimore County Court gave him $4,500, or $105,000 in today's money.

The city appealed to the Maryland Court of Appeals, and it reversed the decision, siding with Baltimore. So Barron appealed again, but this process took years. Finally, the Supreme Court agreed to take on the case, hearing oral arguments in February 1833.

## The Big Questions in this case:

- Does the Fifth Amendment prevent local governments from taking private property for public use without just compensation?
- Did the Bill of Rights as a whole even apply to state and local laws, or did it apply only to federal laws?

The answer to both questions, as it turns out, was no. On February 16, 1833, the Supreme Court unanimously sided with Baltimore. Not only does the Fifth Amendment not apply to the states, but *none* of the Bill of Rights did. Chief Justice John Marshall wrote the majority opinion of this decision, and he struggled with it. Marshall argued that the Bill of Rights authors specifically tried to stop potential abuses by the *federal* government, not state and local governments.

*Barron v. Baltimore* was significant because it stated that the Bill of Rights did not restrict whatever state and local governments did. This decision single-handedly prevented *many* state cases from ever making their way to federal courts. It reversed a trend of major Supreme Court decisions during the Marshall era that had generally increased the federal government's power. The state governments finally had a big win.

After the American Civil War, the decision was a big influence on the creation of the Fourteenth Amendment,[34] which future Court justices referenced when justifying that the Bill of Rights could restrict what state and local governments did.

# 10. United States v. The Amistad (1841)

This case began in Havana, Cuba, on June 27, 1839. On that day, a Spanish ship called the *Amistad* left for the Province of Puerto Principe, another part of Cuba. On board were fifty-three illegally purchased African slaves. On July 2, one slave broke free and freed others on the ship. Soon there was an uprising. After a big struggle resulting in the deaths of the captain of the ship and at least three others, the slaves had taken over the ship, forcing two dudes named José Ruiz and Pedro Montez to redirect the ship across the Atlantic Ocean to Africa.

Ruiz and Montez deceived the Africans, however, and instead ended up sailing the *Amistad* up the East Coast of the United States, dropping anchor just off the coast of Long Island, New York, on August 26, 1839. The United States Revenue Cutter Service, which was basically the US Coast Guard before the US Coast Guard existed, was there to meet them. Led by the Americans Thomas Gedney and Richard Meade, the Revenue Cutter Service arrested the Africans after they reached the shore and took custody of the *Amistad*. Gedney and Meade made sure the Africans were brought to Connecticut, since slavery was still technically legal in that state.

After President Martin Van Buren found out about them, he thought they should be sent back to Cuba to go on trial. Spain, who controlled Cuba at the time, agreed. After all, the *Amistad* was a Spanish ship and Ruiz and Montez were Spanish citizens. Great Britain chimed in, though, since they had a deal with Spain prohibiting the slave trade south of the equator and said that this slave uprising at sea fell under international law. That said, abolitionists were ultimately able to pressure the United States government to keep the Africans in the country, and they got the Africans a trial in the District of Connecticut. Keep in mind that at the time, the slave trade was illegal in the United States. The United States charged the Africans with mutiny and murder.

In court, a lot of people were involved and wanted stuff. First, Ruiz and Montez argued the Africans were slaves and their property. Therefore, they had a right to regain control of them. Next, a lawyer representing Spain argued the slaves either rightfully be returned to Ruiz and Montez *or* be sent back to Africa. The Africans, represented by an abolitionist group called the Amistad Committee, argued that they were born free in their native Africa and unlawfully kidnapped to be sold as slaves. Plus, they landed in New York, where slavery was illegal. The Amistad Committee accused Ruiz and Montez of assault, kidnapping, and false imprisonment. Next, Gedney and several others helped Ruiz and Montez "rescue" the "cargo," also known as Africans, arguing *they* deserved a piece of the pie. They argued that they helped Ruiz and Montez get their slaves back, so maybe they could have a few slaves as well. Finally, another Spanish dude named Antonia Vega wanted the captain's personal slave, claiming he was his rightful owner. Whew. What a mess of a case.

The US District Court ruled that the Africans aboard the *Amistad* were unlawfully kidnapped and ordered the federal government to return them to Africa. In response, President Van Buren ordered the US attorney, Henry Gilpin, to appeal the case to the Circuit Court for the Connecticut District, and some of the other dudes appealed for their piece of the pie. The United States argued it was legally obligated to return the *Amistad* and everything and everyone on it to Spain.

Oh, and the United States made another silly argument. Believe it or not, they argued the Africans violated the American laws that said the slave trade was illegal. You know, like they were voluntarily trying to import themselves into the United States as slaves or something? Cue an eye roll here. Anyway, the Circuit Court for the Connecticut District agreed with the lower court, so the United States appealed again to the Supreme Court.

By this time, it seemed like the entire country was watching this case with fascination. It opened a lot of eyes about slavery and fired up a bunch of abolitionists. The Court heard oral arguments on February 23, 1841. Former president and son of another former president John Quincy Adams represented the Africans in front of the Supreme Court, passionately arguing for their freedom.[35]

## The Big Question in this case:

- Were the Africans aboard the Amistad the property
  of Ruiz and Montez?

The Court said no. On March 9, 1841, it announced it had sided with the Africans, 7–1. The Court said the Africans were never citizens of Spain, and were illegally taken from their homes in Africa, where they were free people. In addition, Africans aboard the *Amistad* were trying to go home. Justice Joseph Story wrote the majority opinion for the case and called the whole thing "peculiar and embarrassing." The Court ordered the

35  www.gilderlehrman.org/history-resources/spotlight-primary-source/john-quincy-adams-and-
    amistad-case-1841

Africans to be sent to the president and ordered the president to send them back to Africa as soon as possible.

The Amistad Committee helped care for the Africans until they could raise enough money to return them home. In 1842, the thirty-nine surviving Africans, and a few missionaries, sailed to Sierra Leone.

*United States v. The Amistad*, also known as *The Amistad Case*, was one of the most important Supreme Court cases involving slavery in American history. It helped the abolitionist movement grow, putting the slavery issue front and center for many Americans for the first time. Twenty-four years after the decision, the United States abolished slavery by passing the Thirteenth Amendment. However, this only came after a bloody and destructive civil war and another, more significant Supreme Court decision that was a major cause of that war, which we will learn about next.

# 11. The Dred Scott Decision (1857)

This case began in St. Louis, Missouri, sometime between 1830 and 1833.[36] During that time, Dr. John Emerson, a United States Army surgeon, bought a slave named Dred Scott. Due to his work in the military, Emerson moved around a lot, but he always took Scott with him.

In 1836, Emerson moved to Fort Armstrong, Illinois, again taking Scott. At the time, Missouri was a state where slavery was legal, but in Illinois it was not. The next year, Emerson moved again, this time to the territory of Wisconsin (in an area that is now the modern-day state of Minnesota), where slavery was also illegal. While there, Dred Scott fell in love and married Harriet Robinson, another slave owned by a dude named Lawrence Taliaferro.

Emerson ended up moving back to Missouri again shortly after this, leaving Dred and Harriet behind and leasing them out to other army officers. Well, guess what? Emerson fell in love, too. He met Eliza Irene Sanford, who went by Irene, after he moved down to Louisiana, and soon after their marriage requested Dred and Harriet to join him again. By this time, Harriet was pregnant and had the baby on the trip down, somewhere between Illinois and Wisconsin, where slavery was illegal. In other words, that child was born free. Regardless, the Scotts returned, and a couple of years later they followed the Emersons as they moved back to Missouri.

John Emerson died in 1843, and Irene inherited his estate, which included the Scott family. However, for the next three years, Dred and Harriet Scott were hired out to different people. Dred and Harriet had had enough. They wanted freedom. At first, the Scotts tried to buy that freedom, but after that didn't work, they sought help from legal advisors and ultimately sued Irene Emerson on April 6, 1846. By this time, they had two kids. What's crazy is the Scotts could pay for legal aid only because the family of Dred Scott's previous owner had given them money. The Scotts went through three lawyers over fourteen months, but ultimately lost the case in the Circuit Court of St. Louis County due to a technicality. Dred and Harriet Scott could not prove they were Irene Emerson's slaves. However, the Scotts' lawyers got them a second trial. Due to a major fire, a cholera epidemic, and several other delays, that trial didn't begin until January 1850. In it, they

36  www.sos.mo.gov/archives/resources/africanamerican/scott/scott.asp

proved that they were Emerson's slaves. The jury favored the Scotts, granting them their freedom.

However, this story doesn't have a happy ending. Emerson continued to fight. After all, Emerson would lose four slaves worth a lot of money. First, her lawyers asked for a new trial, but they were denied. Next, Emerson appealed to the Missouri Supreme Court, who reversed the decision, arguing the Scotts were still slaves due to residing in Missouri, adding that they should have sued for freedom when they had the chance back when they lived in a free state. The Scotts were still slaves.

Nevertheless, the Scotts kept fighting for their freedom. On November 2, 1853, Dred Scott sued again, this time in federal court. For this suit, a lawyer named Roswell Field agreed to help free of charge. By this time, it's worth noting, Scott was not suing Irene, but her brother, John Sanford, who now claimed ownership of him. Scott also alleged that Sanford had assaulted his family. The judge went with Sanford because of the previous Missouri Supreme Court decision that said the Scotts were still slaves. Field was determined to get this one to the Supreme Court, though. The Supreme Court did agree to hear the case, but not until February 1856. Keep in mind that this was *ten years* after the Scotts first sued for freedom. Just Dred officially filed, with the implication his family would also be freed if they sided with him. The case became known as *Dred Scott v. Sandford*. Wait...*Sandford*? Even though John Sanford's name was Sanford, a clerk misspelled his name on court records, and it stayed that way. This was not easy for the Supreme Court justices. After hearing oral arguments, they argued.

## The Big Question in this case:

- Did living in a free state or territory permanently free a slave?

The Court said no. On March 6, 1857, it announced it had sided with Sanford, 7–2. One final time, Dred Scott and his family were denied their freedom. The Court ruled the Constitution said that Scott's case shouldn't have been even heard since he wasn't a citizen. The Court also had a lot to say about the Missouri Compromise, a law passed by the US Congress in 1820 which, among other things, banned slavery north of 36°30′ parallel. Well, the Court said that the law was unconstitutional because Congress lacked the power to ban slavery in US territories. It was only the second time the Court had ruled something Congress did as unconstitutional up to that point.

Justice Roger Taney wrote the majority opinion, and this quote is harsh so hold onto your butts. "In the opinion of the court, the legislation and histories of the times, and the language used in the Declaration of Independence, show, that neither the class of persons who had been imported as slaves, nor their descendants, whether they had become free or not, were then acknowledged as a part of the people." Dang, Taney, that's messed up. The Court also ruled slaves as "property," adding that the Fifth Amendment prevents Congress from taking property away from individuals without just compensation.

Although Taney hoped this ruling would finally settle the slavery controversy, it worsened things. It even caused one justice, Benjamin Robbins Curtis, to quit the court. The abolitionist movement in the North dramatically grew much bigger due to this ruling. The decision further divided the country, ultimately proving to be a major cause of the Civil War. So yeah, if anyone ever asks you if a Supreme Court decision caused a war, tell them yes.

Many historians say that what is more commonly known as the Dred Scott Decision is the worst Supreme Court decision in American history. They especially tend to talk trash about Roger Taney, who came across as a horrible racist with this one. Following the American Civil War, the Thirteenth, Fourteenth, and Fifteenth Amendments, and the Civil Rights Act of 1866 all directly overturned the decision.

However, Dred Scott never lived to see that. Although, it's not completely a sad ending for him and his family. The Scotts were freed soon after the Supreme Court's decision. Scott got a job working at a St. Louis hotel, where he made *money*. Unfortunately, though, he didn't get long to enjoy his freedom, as he died the next year.

# 12. Ex parte Milligan (1866)

This case (kind of) began in Cincinnati, Ohio, in the spring of 1863. The American Civil War had been raging for two years, and it had not been going so well for the Union. Many Americans were tired of the fighting and wanted the Union to let the Confederate States of America exist. One such American was Clement Vallandigham, a former US Representative from Ohio who was outspoken about his opposition to the war.

In response to these antiwar protestors like Vallandigham, President Abraham Lincoln declared martial law and suspended the writ of habeas corpus, meaning people detained in jail no longer had the right to appear before a civil court to know why they were being detained. This led to all kinds of random arrests in the name of suppressing Union dissenters. And yep, that included the arrest of Vallandigham. Union soldiers arrested him on May 5, 1863, after he gave a speech talking trash about the war and Lincoln. Now, while he did get a trial, it was before a military commission. A jury found him guilty of the public expression of sympathy for the Confederacy, and a judge sentenced him to prison for the rest of the war. In response, Vallandigham tried to get the Supreme Court to chime in, arguing that he, as a civilian, shouldn't be tried for a crime before a military tribunal. Well, the Supreme Court denied Vallandigham's request. But President Lincoln overrode that and exiled him to the Confederate States of America.

Flash forward to the next year, and Union soldiers arrested a bunch of other Confederate sympathizers. This included a lawyer and farmer based out of Huntington, Indiana, named Lambdin P. Milligan. The US Army charged him with conspiring against the federal government, helping the Confederacy, trying to start insurrections, "disloyal practices," and "violation of the laws of war." Specifically, they accused Milligan and others of trying to free Confederate prisoners of war. Even though he was *also* a civilian, he faced a military commission, which found him guilty on December 10, 1864. His punishment? Death by hanging, scheduled for May 19, 1865.

But nine days before this execution, Milligan's lawyer, Jonathan Gorden, formally requested that the Circuit Court of the United States for the District of Indiana in Indianapolis hear his case. Gorden argued that Milligan was never formally indicted and should therefore be freed. In other words, Milligan wanted freedom through a writ of habeas corpus, and Gorden argued his military trial was unconstitutional. However, the

Circuit Court of the United States for the District of Indiana in Indianapolis couldn't agree on how to proceed, so they requested that the Supreme Court look at it. The Court, now headed by Chief Justice Salmon Chase, agreed to hear oral arguments in March 1866.

## The Big Questions in this case:

- Can civilians be tried in military courts?
- Does a civil court have jurisdiction over a military trial?
- Should Milligan even get a writ of habeas corpus?

The Court answered no to the first two questions and yes to the third one. On April 3, 1866, it announced it had sided with Milligan unanimously. The Court said civilians *cannot* be tried in military courts, so Milligan never should have faced a military commission. Milligan should have been given a writ of habeas corpus. Chief Justice Chase, a former Secretary of the Treasury for Abraham Lincoln, wrote the majority opinion, saying during the suspension of the writ of habeas corpus, civilians may only be detained without charges, not faced with a military trial.[37] More broadly speaking, the Court had concluded that both the president and the military had exceeded their legal powers to hurt people who were hurting the war effort.

*Ex parte Milligan*, as this became known, helped expand liberty for ordinary citizens during wartime. It established that both the president and the military couldn't do whatever they wanted during a war.

The Court ordered Milligan's release from prison, and he returned home to Indiana to continue practicing law. In 1868, Milligan sued his home county for thousands of dollars to pay for the business losses caused by his being detained and fighting in the courts. He ultimately won the lawsuit, but only got five dollars and money to cover court costs.

# 13. Texas v. White (1869)

This case began in Austin, Texas, in 1851, when the US Congress paid the state of Texas ten million dollars in bonds, as promised in the sweeping federal legislation known as the Compromise of 1850. Flash forward to February 1, 1861, when Texas citizens and members of the Texas state legislature voted for the state to secede, or leave the United States, and join the Confederate States of America. This decision occurred, of course, right before the American Civil War began. Notably, Sam Houston, the governor of Texas, refused to swear allegiance to the Confederate States of America and therefore was removed from office.

In 1862, as the war became increasingly destructive and Texas fought on the side of the Confederate rebels, the state ran out of money. Due to this, the Texas legislature cashed in its remaining bonds to buy war supplies. To make sure the bonds wouldn't be purposely made worthless by the US Treasury, since Texas was now part of a foreign nation at war against them, the Texas legislature hid where the bonds came from.

Two brokers named George W. White and John Chiles bought 136 of those bonds. After the Confederates surrendered and the Civil War ended, the Union forced Texas, and all other former rebel states, to create a new state constitution and state government loyal to the United States. That new state government found out about those bonds sold to White and Chiles, and now wanted them back. And so, they sued them. Oh, and check this out. Texas wasn't messin' around. They took White, Chiles, and the rest of the bondholders directly to the highest court in the land, the Supreme Court.

White and Chiles argued that the Texas government had no right to sue them in the Supreme Court because Texas wasn't a part of the United States when they bought the bonds! However, the Texas government argued that they never left the Union. Sure, Texas seceded, but no governor ever officially approved of it.

But wait, there's more! White and Chiles also argued that looking at this case was out of the Supreme Court's jurisdiction since Texas residents, at the time anyway, were still under military rule and thus had no representation in Congress or any constitutional rights.

The Court heard oral arguments in February 1869. Believe it or not, one major consideration of the Court was whether Texas was a state at the time since it was ruled by the federal military.

The Big Questions in this case:

- Could Texas reclaim those bonds?
- Was Texas even eligible to be seeking those bonds with the Supreme Court?

The Court said yes to both questions. It announced its decision on April 12, 1869, voting 5–3 in favor of Texas. The Court argued Texas had the right to sue for those bonds. They also argued that, when the Texas legislature voted to secede from the Union during the Civil War, um....yeah....*that didn't count*. Throughout the war, the Court argued Texas was still a state and they couldn't have seceded if they wanted to. Chief Justice Salmon Chase wrote, "When, therefore, Texas became one of the United States, she entered into an indissoluble relation." Chase did say that while Texas still *owned* the bonds, it messed up by letting go of them. It would have to pay White and Chiles to make up for their troubles.[38]

Justice Robert Grier wrote the dissent, arguing that Texas wasn't a state during the rebellion, and that *Congress* should determine this anyway, not the Court.[39]

However, later in the case *Williams v. Bruffy* (1877), the Court clarified that secession *is* constitutional, but only if the state seceding is military successful in seceding. Texas was not successful, and if any state wanted to secede, they'd better plan on winning a likely violent rebellion.

Still, *Texas v. White* is that Supreme Court case that is brought up when talking about how states can't secede from the rest of the country. Many argue that the Constitution doesn't let states secede, and this case often backs up their claims, but *Williams v. Bruffy* backs up claims that, outside of the law, of course states can secede. Legally speaking, though, even though the majority of Texans wanted Texas as part of the Confederate States of America, an entirely new country, and despite the fact that Texans fought against and killed Union soldiers during the Civil War, they never technically left the United States. Sure, they thought they were, but they lost, so no, they weren't. I guess that's why historians today call it a *civil war* and not a *war of independence*.

38   www.americanthinker.com/articles/2013/01/on_secssion.html
39   www.law.cornell.edu/supremecourt/text/74/700

# 14. The Slaughterhouse Cases (1873)

This case began in New Orleans, Louisiana, in 1867. That year, around three thousand residents had died from cholera, a horrible disease characterized by having violent diarrhea until you're seriously dehydrated. How did they get cholera? From drinking the water. This is not surprising, as New Orleans water at the time was filthy. The president of the Board of Health testified, "When the river is low, it is not uncommon to see intestines and portions of putrefied animal matter lodged immediately around the pipes." You read that correctly. Animal guts were in the drinking water, and citizens were dying horrible deaths after drinking it.[40]

So how did the animal guts get in the drinking water in the first place? Just outside the city, around 1,000 butchers regularly gutted more than 300,000 animals per year. New Orleans begged the Louisiana state legislature to do something about it. They passed a law granting a monopoly to the Crescent City Livestock Landing and Slaughtering Company, saying that only *it* could run a slaughterhouse in New Orleans. Now, the company would not actually butcher animals, but instead rent space to other butchers in the city for a fee.

As it turns out, the Crescent City folks had bribed the Louisiana legislature to give them the monopoly, and a bunch of butchers didn't like this so much. More than four hundred butchers of the Butchers' Benevolent Association joined to sue the Crescent City Company, saying that their monopoly created involuntary servitude, which went against the Thirteenth Amendment of the Constitution. They also argued the monopoly prevented them from getting property and hurt their freedom to make money, bringing up the Privileges or Immunities Clause of the recently ratified Fourteenth Amendment.

There were many lawsuits, and the butchers lost every one of them. However, six butchers appealed to the Louisiana Supreme Court, which agreed with the lower courts. And so, the butchers appealed again, this time to the Supreme Court, and they agreed to look at their cases, hearing oral arguments in January and February 1873.

Remember, the Fourteenth Amendment had passed less than five years prior, and the Court was still trying to figure out its implications. John A. Campbell, who

40   *The Slaughterhouse Cases: Regulation, Reconstruction, and the Fourteenth Amendment*, Ronald M. Labbe and Jonathan Lurie (Lawrence: The University of Kansas Press, 2003), pp. 17–37.

represented the butchers and was a federal judge but stepped down due to his former Confederate loyalties, argued that the Fourteenth Amendment should be interpreted broadly to protect equality not just for the recently freed slaves, but *all* Americans. Matthew H. Carpenter, who represented Louisiana, argued the monopoly of the Crescent City Company was justified to protect public health and safety.

### The Big Question in this case:

- Did Louisiana's creation of a monopoly go against the Thirteenth and Fourteenth Amendments?

The Court said no. It announced its decision on April 14, 1873. They narrowly sided with Louisiana, 5–4. The Court held the monopoly did *not* go against the Thirteenth and Fourteenth Amendments because the Thirteenth was about ending slavery and the Fourteenth was about giving equality to former slaves. In other words, you couldn't expand those two amendments to all groups of people.

Justice Samuel Miller wrote the majority opinion. He wrote that no, the butchers' "privileges or immunities" were *not* violated, and went back to Article 4, Section 2 of the Constitution for context when looking at the Privileges or Immunities Clause of the Fourteenth Amendment. Miller said the two clauses protected two different bundles of rights. Article 4, Section 2 was about protecting the rights of *state* citizenship, while the Fourteenth Amendment was about protecting the rights of *national* citizenship. Miller said the Privileges or Immunities Clause only applied *in areas controlled by the federal government*, like ports and waterways.

This was the opposite of what the dude who *wrote* the Fourteenth Amendment had in mind. That dude, US Representative John Bingham, had explained on the House floor after he wrote it that the Privileges or Immunities Clause was meant to give the federal government power to enforce the Bill of Rights against the states. Oops.

Miller gave a narrow interpretation of the Fourteenth Amendment, making the Privileges or Immunities Clause meaningless. In a dissenting opinion, Justice Stephen Field said Miller made the Fourteenth Amendment a "vain and idle enactment." Well, that was a bit salty there, Justice Field.

Regardless, the *Slaughterhouse Cases* weakened the Fourteenth Amendment. However, years later the Supreme Court would return to the Fourteenth Amendment time and time again, using the Due Process Clause and Equal Protection Clause instead to expand civil rights and liberties.

The Crescent City Company kept its monopoly until 1879, when Louisiana banned slaughterhouse monopolies. Finally, despite its shadiness, the monopoly had a positive impact on the drinking water of New Orleans. Soon after its formation, animal guts no longer filled the streets and got into the drinking water. Yay!

# 15. Munn v. Illinois (1876)

This case began in Springfield, Illinois, in 1871. At the time, a railroad monopoly made it so farmers had to pay unreasonable fees to store and transport their grains. And so, farmers across Illinois united as part of the larger Granger movement. These farmers begged the Illinois state legislature to step in. And the legislature stepped in, passing a law that set maximum prices that private companies could charge for storing and transporting agricultural products in the state. This government practice is commonly referred to as "price controls."

The Chicago-based grain warehouse company Munn and Scott didn't like that. It decided to ignore the new law. In response, the state's attorney general ordered Munn and Scott to be fined. Well, things were delayed due to the Great Chicago Fire of 1871, but the next year Munn and Scott were found guilty in a state trial court and ordered to pay a fine of $100, or around $2,400 in today's money.[41]

Munn and Scott appealed to the Illinois State Supreme Court, arguing the law was unconstitutional since it deprived them of their property without due process of the law, and thus violated the Due Process Clause of the Fourteenth Amendment. However, the Illinois State Supreme Court agreed with the lower court, so Munn and Scott appealed again, this time to the Supreme Court, which heard oral arguments in January 1876. Whereas the *Slaughterhouse Cases* mostly looked at the Privileges or Immunities Clauses of the Fourteenth Amendment, for *this* case the Court decided to focus on the Due Process Clause and Equal Protection Clause of the Fourteenth Amendment.

## The Big Question in this case:

- Did Illinois's price controls go against the Due Process Clause and Equal Protection Clause of the Fourteenth Amendment?

The Court said no. On October 1, 1876, the Court announced it had sided with Illinois, 7–2. Chief Justice Morrison Waite, nominated by President Ulysses Grant two years prior, wrote the majority opinion. He argued that state governments could regulate private

41   Kitch, E. W., & Bowler, C. A. (1978). The Facts of *Munn v. Illinois*. *The Supreme Court Review*, 1978, 313. www.jstor.org/stable/3109535.

industries in the name of protecting the public interest. Because grain storage warehouses affected public use, they could be subject to public regulation, saying, "When private property is devoted to a public use, it is subject to public regulation." In other words, those grain storage facilities were public utilities.

Justice Field, who argued for the dissent, said it shouldn't matter that the public interest was affected by what Munn and Scott did with their company—their freedoms to do business as they pleased were hindered by government interference. He added, "The defendants were no more public warehousemen...than the merchant who sells his merchandise to the public and is a public merchant, or the blacksmith who shoes horses for the public is a public blacksmith."[42]

*Munn v. Illinois* is a little-known but important case that became pivotal in the struggle over government regulation over private enterprise in the coming decades. In fact, in the following decades governments began to regulate private industries more and more.

42   Ibid.,314.

# 16. Strauder v. West Virginia (1880)

This case began in Wheeling, West Virginia, on April 18, 1872. That's when a man named Taylor Strauder, an African American and former slave, brutally murdered his wife. Strauder's stepdaughter, Fannie Green, witnessed the murder. Before Strauder decided to flee the scene, he threatened Fannie, telling her that if she told anyone about the murder he would kill her, too.

A week later, local authorities in Pittsburgh, Pennsylvania, found Strauder and arrested him and returned him to Wheeling. He appeared before the circuit court for West Virginia's Ohio County. A grand jury, or jury of citizens to help court proceedings and see whether criminal charges should be brought up, decided to indict, or formally charge Strauder with first-degree murder. However, Strauder's lawyers argued that the "all-white" grand jury was biased against Strauder. In fact, Blacks were excluded from being on the grand jury!

The circuit court ignored these complaints and proceeded with the trial anyway. The trial lasted three days. On the third day, an all-white jury returned a guilty verdict, and the judge sentenced Strauder to death by hanging, scheduled for July 8, 1873.

However, West Virginia had just created a new state constitution that changed criminal procedures in the state. Due to that, after appealing to the Supreme Court of Appeals of West Virginia, Strauder got a new trial, this time with the Ohio County court, not the circuit court. Again, a new all-white grand jury also indicted Strauder with first-degree murder. Again, Strauder's lawyers argued that the all-white grand jury was biased against Strauder so the indictment was no good. The county court also ignored these complaints and proceeded with the trial anyway. On November 6, 1874, the all-white jury found Strauder guilty of murder and the judge sentenced Strauder to death by hanging, scheduled for January 9, 1875.

Well, Strauder wasn't dying yet. His lawyers appealed again to the Supreme Court of Appeals of West Virginia, and they agreed to hear the case on June 27, 1876. Strauder's lawyers argued that the Equal Protection Clause of the Fourteenth Amendment said that citizens of any state ought to be protected against any "unjust legislation by their own State." Well, long story short, the Supreme Court of Appeals of West Virginia agreed with the lower court, but as Strauder awaited resentencing, his lawyers appealed again, this time to the Supreme Court, who agreed to hear the case, along with two related cases, *Virginia v. Rives*, and *Ex parte Virginia*.

The Court finally heard oral arguments in October 1879.

## The Big Questions in this case:

- Does the Constitution say citizens have the right to a trial by a jury selected that won't be biased against the defendant based on their skin color?
- If the answer to the first question is yes, can the federal courts hear the case based on the Fourteenth Amendment?

The Court answered yes to both questions. On March 1, 1880, they announced they had sided with Strauder, 7–2. The Court argued that prohibiting African Americans from jury service violated the Equal Protection Clause of the Fourteenth Amendment. Justice William Strong wrote the opinion, stating that denying citizen participation in court solely on racial grounds is "practically a brand upon them, affixed by law; an assertion of their inferiority, and a stimulant to that race prejudice which is an impediment to securing to individuals of the race that equal justice which the law aims to secure to all others."[43]

That said, the Court *didn't* strike West Virginia's law that banned Blacks from serving on juries as unconstitutional, as Strauder's lawyers hadn't aimed for that. In other words, the Court argued federal courts could step in for this specific case. The Court sent the case back to the Supreme Court of Appeals of West Virginia to look at again.

Ultimately, though, the federal government released Strauder from their custody, and Strauder was rearrested and went through state courts again. However, the state courts ruled that they didn't have jurisdiction. On May 3, 1881, nine years after first being arrested, Strauder was a free man. There is no record of what happened to him after that, but apparently he found work and integrated back into society.[44]

*Strauder v. West Virginia* was a big win for the rights of Black defendants and one of the most important civil rights Supreme Court cases in American history. However, this case wasn't just a victory for African Americans. After this case, federal courts could step in if *any* citizen felt a state violated their rights guaranteed by the Equal Protection Clause of the Fourteenth Amendment.

43  www.oyez.org/cases/1850-1900/100us303
44  www.archivingwheeling.org/blog/the-case-of-taylor-strauder

# 17. The Civil Rights Cases (1883)

The catalyst for these cases was Congress passing the Civil Rights Act of 1875, also known as the Enforcement Act, which granted everyone equal treatment in public accommodations, public transportation, and jury selection. "Public accommodations" meant facilities generally used by the public, like retail stores, movie theaters, and recreation centers. The Enforcement Act granted equal treatment in public accommodations even if the facilities were privately owned. First and foremost, the law was meant to protect African Americans, most of whom had just been freed from slavery ten years prior.

Well, many governments throughout the country did not enforce the Enforcement Act. Blacks still faced widespread discrimination in facilities all over the country. Often, "white" owners of facilities would simply not let Black customers enter their establishments. Racial segregation laws were quickly becoming more common throughout the country, especially in Southern states, since the federal government no longer stopped these laws from happening. These segregation laws were like flashing a middle finger to the Enforcement Act.

In response, several African Americans sued businesses across the country for discrimination. Specifically, they sued two dudes for refusing to allow people of color to stay at their hotels. They also sued two other dudes for refusing to allow people of color into their theaters. Finally, an African American family sued the Memphis & Charleston Railroad after they were denied first-class accommodations traveling through Tennessee in 1879. Together, these lawsuits later became known as the *Civil Rights Cases*.

The Supreme Court decided to take on all five cases, consolidating them since they were all similar. They heard oral arguments on March 29, 1883. Undoubtedly, the justices understood that discrimination was taking place. In every case, a Black person was denied the same accommodations as a white person. However, they debated whether the federal government truly had the authority to prevent private companies from discriminating against customers. They were looking at both the Tenth Amendment and the Due Process Clause and Equal Protection Clause of the Fourteenth Amendment. If the Fourteenth Amendment didn't apply, then the Tenth Amendment, which says all powers not granted to the national government goes to the states or the people, would.

The Big Question in this case:

- Did the Civil Rights Act of 1875 go against
  the Tenth and Fourteenth Amendments of
  the Constitution?

The Court said yes. On October 15, 1883, they announced they had sided with the discriminating businesses, 8–1. You read that right. First, the Court distinguished government and private action. They said according to the Fourteenth Amendment, the federal government couldn't regulate stuff that was the result of conduct by private individuals, not state law or action. Justice Joseph Bradley wrote the majority opinion. "Positive rights and privileges are undoubtedly secured by the Fourteenth Amendment; but they are secured by way of prohibition against state laws and state proceedings affecting those rights and privileges, and by power given to Congress to legislate for the purpose of carrying such prohibition into effect."[45] Sure, Blacks were discriminated against, but the federal government's hands were tied. Because of this, the Court said that parts of the Civil Rights Act of 1875 were unconstitutional, and therefore, the Tenth Amendment applied.

Justice John Marshall Harlan was the only one on the Court who disagreed. He later gained the nickname "The Great Dissenter" since he often was the lone dissenter. He argued that the rest of the Court's interpretation of the Fourteenth Amendment was too narrow for these cases. He said that hotels, theaters, and railroads, though privately owned, were effectively still in the public realm. Besides, he wrote, "The one underlying purpose of congressional legislation has been to enable the black race to take the rank of mere citizens. The difficulty has been to compel a recognition of their legal right to take that rank, and to secure the enjoyment of privileges belonging, under the law, to them as a component part of the people for whose welfare and happiness government is ordained." Harlan may have been ahead of his time, but he wasn't convincing anyone else on the Court back then.

The *Civil Rights Cases* led to lots of protests around the country. It almost single-handedly led to Congress no longer actively trying to protect the civil rights of African Americans and further led to the spread of racial segregation in housing, employment, and public facilities. Over the next eighty years, African Americans would be treated like second-class citizens. Only after the Civil Rights Act of 1964 and the subsequent Supreme Court case *Heart of Atlanta Motel v. United States* (1964) would these cases finally be overturned.

45  supreme.justia.com/cases/federal/us/109/3/

# 18. United States v. E.C. Knight Co. (1895)

This case began in March 1892 in Philadelphia. The American Sugar Refining Company, which already dominated the sugar industry, had bought E.C. Knight Company. With this purchase, the American Sugar Refining Company now held 98 percent of all sugar processing in the country. It was a monopoly.

In response, President Grover Cleveland ordered the federal government to sue E.C. Knight Company, arguing that the deal went against the Sherman Antitrust Act. Passed by Congress two years prior, the law was meant to control the growth of gigantic businesses and prevent monopolies. The federal government argued that this monopoly on the sugar refining industry would cause sugar prices to skyrocket, affecting almost everyone, since pretty much everyone bought sugar. The government argued it had the authority to break up the monopoly because of the Sherman Antitrust Act and the Interstate Commerce Clause of the Constitution.

That said, the Circuit Court of the United States for the Eastern District of Pennsylvania sided with E.C. Knight Company. The federal government appealed to the US Circuit Court of Appeals for the Third Circuit but agreed with the lower court. So the federal government appealed again, this time to the Supreme Court, which heard oral arguments on October 24, 1894.

## The Big Questions in this case:

- Does the contract between the American Sugar Refining Company and E.C. Knight Company create an unlawful monopoly that violates the Sherman Antitrust Act?
- Is the Sherman Antitrust Act unconstitutional?

The Court said no to both questions. On January 21, 1895, in another 8–1 decision, the Court announced they had sided with E.C. Knight Company. Sure, the Sherman Antitrust Act was constitutional, but the Court argued that the Constitution's Interstate Commerce Clause does not grant Congress the authority to regulate manufacturing. The Court interpreted this case narrowly, saying the Sherman Antitrust Act was meant to prevent conspiracies or combinations that hurt commerce between states or foreign countries. That said, the Court made the distinction between *manufacturing* sugar and *selling* sugar. The federal government could regulate how sugar was sold but not how it was manufactured. Chief Justice Melville Fuller gave the majority opinion, writing, "The fact that an article is manufactured for export to another State does not of itself make it an article of interstate commerce, and the intent of the manufacturer does not determine the time when the...product passes from the control of the State and belongs to commerce."

Justice John Marshall Harlan was the lone dissenter and didn't buy this distinction between manufacturing and selling, saying that if you're going to say the Constitution can't regulate manufacturing, you could also easily say it can't regulate commerce.

*United States v. E.C. Knight Co.* exempted manufacturing companies from the Sherman Antitrust Act. In the decades following the decision, more mergers created more monopolies, concentrating power in most markets with a few corporations. While this case has never officially been overturned, the Supreme Court later held that Congress could regulate manufacturing in *Swift & Co. v. United States* (1905).

# 19. Pollock v. Farmers' Loan & Trust Co. (1895)

This case began in the District of Columbia on August 27, 1894, when Congress voted for the Wilson-Gorman Tariff Act. In addition to reducing the federal government's tariff rate, the law created a 2 percent tax on any income over $4,000, around $131,000 today. This income could even include interest from investments, like stocks and bonds and rents from real estate. Those who supported this law believed it could help pay off the country's debt but also, in a small way, help reduce wealth inequality, which was bad during this time. They thought an income tax on the super-wealthy was more fair than higher tariffs, which hurt those in poverty more than those who were richer. A tariff, by the way, is a tax on imports or exports.

Many people did *not* support the Wilson-Gorman Tariff Act, especially those who suddenly had to pay an income tax for the first time. One of those folks was a stockholder named Charles Pollock. Pollock sued the bank that held his stocks, the Farmers' Loan & Trust Company, to prevent them from paying the tax. Other stockholders joined him in the suit. Their argument? The Wilson-Gorman Tariff Act was unconstitutional because Congress couldn't directly tax individuals if the tax wasn't divided proportionally to how Congress represented them. Specifically, they said it went against Article 1, Section 9 of the Constitution. Pollock got Joseph Hodges Choate, one of the most well-known Wall Street lawyers, to represent him.

Choate must not have impressed the Circuit Court of the United States for the Southern District of New York. It ruled in favor of Farmers' Loan & Trust Company, so Pollock appealed to the Supreme Court, which heard oral arguments on March 7, 1895. Choate called the income tax "socialistic" and "communistic" and an assault on capitalism.[46]

## The Big Question in this case:

- Was an income tax a direct tax in violation of Article 1, Section 9, of the Constitution?

Although this was a difficult question, the Court ultimately said yes. On April 8, 1895, it announced it had sided with Pollock, 5–4. The Court argued the income tax imposed by the Wilson-Gorman Tariff Act was unconstitutional because it directly taxed individuals and wasn't apportioned properly among the states. The Court explained that a tax on *income* from land and investments was essentially the same as a tax on the land and investments itself. Therefore, an income tax was a direct tax.

The dissenting justices, John Marshall Harlan, Howell Jackson, Edward White, and Henry Brown, were upset with the majority. First, Harlan disagreed that taxing the income from land was the same thing as taxing the land itself. He accused the Court's majority of randomly using their power on behalf of the super-wealthy. Brown said the decision was a "surrender of the taxing power to the moneyed class."[47] He even accused the Court's majority of voting against the income tax simply because they disliked the idea.

*Pollock v. Farmers' Loan & Trust Co.* was an extremely unpopular decision with the public. It added extra fuel to Populism, a political movement of the decade that called for sweeping reforms to reduce the power of plutocrats, or people who get their power from becoming rich. In fact, it led to an even larger, broader series of movements over the following two decades that today we call the Progressive Era. Almost immediately after the *Pollock* decision, Populist politicians called for a constitutional amendment to make it okay for Congress to collect income taxes without apportioning them back to the states based on population. Fast forward to February 3, 1913, and the states approved such an amendment, the Sixteenth Amendment, effectively overruling the *Pollock* decision. Today, most Americans pay a tax on their income.[48]

47   www.oyez.org/cases/1850-1900/157us429
48   www.cnbc.com/2022/03/25/57percent-of-us-households-paid-no-federal-income-tax-in-2021-study.html

# 20. Plessy v. Ferguson (1896)

This case began in New Orleans, Louisiana, on June 7, 1892. On that day, Homer Plessy bought a first-class ticket and boarded a train headed to Covington. He sat in a vacant seat in a "whites-only" train car. You wouldn't think Plessy would draw any attention since he was seven-eighths white and one-eighth Black. While there are no known pictures of Homer Plessy, records describe him as a "white man." Yet the conductor *knew* he was one-eighth Black, and he told Plessy that he had to get up and move to the "blacks-only" train car. After Plessy refused to leave his seat, almost immediately a detective, Christopher Cain, arrested him.

You might be wondering, *How did this detective know Plessy was one-eighth Black?*

Well, this was all planned. Plessy acted on behalf of a civil rights group called the Citizens' Committee. They had carefully planned for this exact moment to protest the Separate Car Act, a law recently passed by the Louisiana legislature that required "equal but separate" train cars for Blacks and Whites and defined what it meant to be "black" and "white."

The Citizens' Committee not only had let the railroad company know ahead of time that Plessy would be boarding the "whites-only" car, but they also hired the private detective, Christopher Cain, to make sure he arrested him for breaking the Separate Car Act and not vagrancy or some other crime. The folks who owned the railroad company also hated the Separate Car Act because they had to spend more on additional train cars, which cut into their profits. So it all went according to plan.

Plessy eventually appeared in the Criminal District Court for New Orleans, arguing that the Separate Car Act denied him his rights protected under the Thirteenth and Fourteenth Amendments of the Constitution. The judge, a dude named John Ferguson, ruled that Louisiana had the right to regulate railroad companies as long as they ran within state boundaries. In response, Plessy filed a petition against Ferguson at the Louisiana Supreme Court. The Louisiana Supreme Court, however, sided with Ferguson, citing a precedent that came before the Thirteenth and Fourteenth Amendments. They got him on a technicality!

And so, Plessy appealed again, this time to the Supreme Court, and it heard oral arguments on April 13, 1896. Justice David Brewer wasn't there to hear the arguments due to the death of his daughter, so he did not participate in the case. The Court focused on the Equal Protection Clause of the Fourteenth Amendment.

## The Big Question in this case:

- Did the Separate Car Act go against the Fourteenth Amendment?

The Court said no. On May 18, 1896, they announced they had sided with Ferguson and upheld the law, 7–1. Justice Henry Brown wrote the majority opinion, saying that while the Fourteenth Amendment guaranteed equality for all Americans regardless of skin color, a law requiring separate treatment didn't mean that Blacks were inferior to whites. As evidence, Brown stressed how there wasn't a meaningful difference in quality between the "whites-only" and "blacks-only" train cars. In other words, segregation didn't automatically mean discrimination.

The Court said *all* segregated facilities based on skin color were fine, as long as both facilities were the same quality. This became known as the infamous "separate but equal" doctrine.

John Marshall Harlan, the only one in dissent and the only voice of reason in this case, said, "Everyone knows that the statute in question had its origin in the purpose, not so much to exclude white people from railroad cars occupied by Blacks, as to exclude colored people from coaches occupied by or assigned to white persons... The thing to accomplish was, under the guise of giving equal accommodation for whites and Blacks, to compel the latter to keep to themselves while traveling in railroad passenger coaches. No one would be so wanting in candor as to assert the contrary."

Because I am so impressed with Harlan's dissent, here's more for you. "Our constitution is color-blind, and neither knows nor tolerates classes among citizens. In respect of civil rights, all citizens are equal before the law."

Harlan predicted that this decision would go down in history as one of the worst ever, up there with the *Dred Scott Decision*. And guess what? He was right. In fact, fifty-eight years later, the Supreme Court overturned the case in *Brown v. Board of Education* (1954), the landmark case that made *all* racial segregation illegal.

Today, *Plessy v. Ferguson* is known as one of the worst Supreme Court decisions in American history. It ended up justifying and strengthening Jim Crow laws, or racial segregation laws that caused African Americans to be treated as second-class citizens. However, at least the *Plessy* decision *did* help fuel the creation of the National Association for the Advancement of Colored People, or NAACP. In fact, it eventually helped fuel the entire Civil Rights Movement.

So whatever happened to Homer Plessy? He faded into obscurity. However, there's a cool, modern twist to this story. In 2009, Keith Plessy, a descendant of Homer, and Phoebe Ferguson, a descendant of John Ferguson, united to form the Plessy and Ferguson Foundation for Education and Reconciliation, an organization whose main mission is to teach the history of *Plessy v. Ferguson* and why the case is still relevant today.

# 21. Holden v. Hardy
# (1898)

This case began in Salt Lake City, Utah, in March 1896. Utah had recently become a state, and, that month, its legislature passed a law mandating a maximum eight-hour workday for miners and workers in smelters, or factories that get metal out of rocks.

A few months later, Salt Lake County Sheriff Harvey Harden arrested Albert Holden, the owner of Old Jordan Mine, for breaking that law. He charged him with forcing two of his workers to work longer than eight hours. While Holden admitted to making his workers work longer hours, he also argued that the Utah law was unconstitutional because it prevented individuals from making contracts with each other. In addition, Holden argued that the law prevented him from having property and liberty without due process. The law also singled out managers in the mining industry, preventing them from equal protection of the laws. Holden was found guilty and fined fifty dollars, which he refused to pay so he ended up serving a jail sentence of fifty-seven days.[49]

Meanwhile, Holden appealed the case to the Utah Supreme Court, focusing on the part of the Utah Constitution that protected the freedoms of labor. Holden argued the Utah legislature had no right to pass any law restricting how many hours people could work in a day. The Utah Supreme Court disagreed with him, siding with the legislature and explaining that mining and smelting were dangerous, writing, "prolonged effort day after day...will produce morbid, noxious, and often deadly effects in the human system."[50] Therefore, limiting hours of this work was necessary.

Holden then appealed to the US Supreme Court, which agreed to hear oral arguments on October 21, 1897. Before the Court, Holden argued that the Utah law went against the Equal Protection Clause and Privileges or Immunities Clause of the Fourteenth Amendment.

## The Big Question in this case:

- Did the Utah law regulating work hours in the mining industry go against the rights of citizens protected under the Fourteenth Amendment?

---

49  tile.loc.gov/storage-services/service/ll/usrep/usrep169/usrep169366/usrep169366.pdf
50  edge.sagepub.com/conlaw/resources/a-short-course/10-economic-substantive-due-process/cases/holden-v-hardy

The Court said no. On February 28, 1898, the Court announced it had sided with the Utah legislature, 7–2. It argued the Utah legislature *did* have the power to regulate work hours within its state. In fact, the Court called it a "police power," the ability of a state to control behavior and enforce order within its borders to promote general welfare. Justice Henry Brown wrote the majority opinion, stating, "The legislature has also recognized the fact, which the experience of legislators in many states has corroborated, that the proprietors of these establishments and their operatives do not stand upon an equality... the proprietors lay down the rules, and the laborers are practically constrained to obey them. In such cases self-interest is often an unsafe guide, and the legislature may properly interpose its authority."[51]

*Holden v. Hardy* marked the first time the Supreme Court approved a law limiting working hours. Partially inspired by the decision, progressive legislators in other states would pass more laws to protect worker safety. Business owners would continue to fight back against the worker safety laws in the coming decades, but more of them would lose their court battles, and it all traces back to this case.

51   edge.sagepub.com/conlaw/resources/a-short-course/10-economic-substantive-due-process/cases/
     holden-v-hardy

# 22. United States v. Wong Kim Ark (1898)

This case began in San Francisco, California, when Wong Kim Ark was born. That may have been 1868, 1871, or perhaps 1873. For this story, though, it doesn't matter what year he was born. It matters that he was born in the United States.

His parents, Wong Si Ping and Wee Lee, were immigrants from China, *not* United States citizens. According to the Naturalization Law of 1802, the two could never become citizens because they weren't "white" (whatever that means). Due to the Chinese Exclusion Act discriminating against them, the Wongs moved back to China when Kim Ark was around nine years old. However, a few years later, Kim Ark came back to California because he wanted to make more money. This shouldn't have been a problem for Kim Ark because, thanks to the Citizenship Clause of the Fourteenth Amendment, he was automatically an American citizen.

In 1890, Wong went to China to visit his parents, and he came back home to the United States with no troubles. However, four years later when he went back to China to visit them, he was denied reentry upon his return at the port of San Francisco. He pleaded with them, explaining that he was born in the United States and had a home there, but because he couldn't prove it, they didn't believe him. During the five months when Wong fought for reentry into the country, what is today known as US Customs kept him confined on different ships off the coast of San Francisco.

Fortunately for Wong, he got support from an organization called the Chinese Six Companies to help him fight for his citizenship. He went to federal district court. The judge focused on the Citizenship Clause of the Fourteenth Amendment. He specifically zoomed in on the different interpretations of the phrase "subject to the jurisdiction thereof." The judge wondered if it covered when a child was born in the country to parents who were not citizens. Wong's lawyers, of course, argued yes. They had been waiting to test the Citizenship Clause for a while, and here was their chance. Henry Foote, a former Confederate soldier, represented the United States, calling Wong an "accidental citizen." That's not the term you usually hear today. Today that derogatory term is "anchor baby."

On January 3, 1896, the district judge announced he had sided with Wong, declaring him a citizen since he was born in the United States. The federal government appealed the decision directly to the Supreme Court, which heard oral arguments on March 5, 1897.

**The Big Question in this case:**

- Could the federal government deny citizenship
  to people born in the United States in
  any circumstance?

The Court said no. On March 28, 1898, it announced it had sided with Wong, 6–2. The Court said that any child born in the country to parents of a foreign country is automatically a citizen. There were exceptions. The Court noted citizenship could be denied if the parents are foreign diplomats, if the baby is born on a public ship, or if the parents are nationals of a foreign enemy country trying to take over the United States. Otherwise, if you're born in the United States, you're automatically a citizen. It's that simple.

The Court relied on English common law tradition as much as it relied on the Citizenship Clause of the Fourteenth Amendment for this one. Leading the dissent was Chief Justice Melville Fuller, joined by Justice John Marshall Harlan, of course. They argued that the history of American citizenship broke with the tradition of English common law after it declared independence in 1776. They wondered about the part of the Citizenship Clause that said, "subject to the jurisdiction thereof." Wouldn't that also mean not subject to any foreign power? They argued Wong was still under the control of China due to his parents being under their control.

Of all US Supreme Court decisions in history, *United States v. Wong Kim Ark* is the strongest at protecting that Citizenship Clause, no matter the situation with the parents. Over the years, millions of Americans have owed their citizenship to this single case.

So how did the story end for Wong Kim Ark? While Wong was fighting for citizenship in the courts, he had started a family back in China. He had a wife and kids back there. After the Supreme Court decision, Wong went back and forth, but for the rest of his life, he never fully enjoyed the benefits of citizenship. Every time he went home to China and came back, he got hounded by US Customs, always having to show extra documentation like the signatures of European Americans vouching for him. After Wong's oldest son tried to move to the United States, the federal government wouldn't let him. However, Wong's three youngest sons *were* able to move to the country as citizens, although it wasn't easy for them. One of those sons later served in World War II. Eventually, however, Kim Ark stopped trying to be an American. In the 1930s, at the age of sixty-two, he went to China and decided to never return.

# 23. The Insular Cases (1901)

These cases all began in Paris, France, on December 10, 1898, the day the United States and Spain signed the Treaty of Paris, ending the Spanish-American War. It's often a war that gets glossed over in history books. The one thing many of us seem to remember about it is future American President Theodore Roosevelt's service with the Rough Riders. However, the war is more influential than you might realize. The main reason why is the Treaty of Paris saw the loser of the war, Spain, hand over its territories of the Philippines, Guam, and Puerto Rico to the victor, the United States. Meanwhile, the United States had also, independently, taken over Hawaii, using the war as political cover. The United States government had no idea how to determine the political and legal implications of all these folks living in shiny new territories.

While the United States was experienced in dealing with new territory throughout its history of purchase and conquest, controlling the faraway islands of Puerto Rico and the Philippines would be a lot more difficult than deciding the fate of say, Kansas and Nebraska, for example. Puerto Rico and the Philippines were colonies, after all, not soon-to-be states. All the US government had to go off of was these two stipulations:

1.  Article 9 of the Treaty of Paris, which said, "The civil rights and political status of the native inhabitants of the territories hereby ceded to the United States shall be determined by Congress."

2.  The little-known part of the *Dred Scott Decision* said that, besides getting new states, there was no constitutionally given power the US government could use to maintain colonies.

However, that wouldn't stop President William McKinley and his buddies in Congress from going about it *their* way. In 1900, Congress passed and McKinley signed the Foraker Act, which set up a government in Puerto Rico, with specific Puerto Rican citizenship for the island's residents. Notably, this law did *not* give them US citizenship. It also had numerous caveats relating to tariffs on imported Puerto Rican goods.

Overall, though, there were still more questions than answers regarding how the federal government should handle these new territories it gained, questions often answered by the Supreme Court in a series of cases known as the *Insular Cases*. The word "insular" comes from the fact that the territories were all located on islands and under the day-to-day control of the Bureau of Insular Affairs. While historians have labeled at least sixteen cases as part of the *Insular Cases*, I have focused on the four that left the biggest impact. As it turns out, all of the cases I picked deal with Puerto Rico. I will go in chronological order.

## DeLima v. Bidwell (1901)

In 1899, the DeLima Sugar Importing Company wanted to get back what they paid in tariffs on Puerto Rican sugar they imported to New York. The company sued the Collector of the Port of New York, George Bidwell, reasoning that because Puerto Rico was part of the United States, New York couldn't slap tariffs on imported stuff from Puerto Rico. An appeals court ruled in favor of DeLima, stating that, for tax purposes, Puerto Rico was a US territory and not a foreign country. In addition, it said Congress didn't have to write a whole new law to work out tariffs for Puerto Rican trade, so DeLima Sugar *could* get their money back. New York appealed, and the Supreme Court heard oral arguments in January 1901.

### The Big Question in this case:

- Did American companies have to pay tariffs on goods imported from Puerto Rico?

The Court said no. On May 27, 1901, it announced that it had sided with DeLima, agreeing with the appeals court in a 5–4 decision. In the majority opinion, Justice Henry Brown wrote that, regarding tariff laws, Puerto Rico was not a foreign country. Therefore, tariffs were not required under the law. Because Congress had never made a law deciding the exact status of Puerto Rico for tax purposes, the United States couldn't get away with issuing tariff rules on Puerto Rico for domestic consumption by saying the territory was a foreign country.

## Downes v. Bidwell (1901)

As it turns out, Bidwell's name was on *another* case *decided on the same day*, May 27, 1901. A dude named Samuel Downes of the S.B. Downes & Company was in a similar situation as the DeLima Sugar Importing Company, as he had to pay New York tariffs on oranges from Puerto Rico. Downes said that the Foraker Act still allowed for a special temporary tariff on imports for Puerto Rico, which was unconstitutional because Article 1, Section 8 of the Constitution says that "all duties, imposts, and excises shall be uniform through the

United States." Puerto Rico couldn't be the only part of the country with tariffs like those on their oranges since all states have to have the same tariff laws on domestic trade. The Supreme Court heard oral arguments for this case at the same time as *DeLima v. Bidwell.*

## The Big Question in this case:

- Does the Constitution apply to territories?

The Court said no. Well, it also said yes. Interestingly, in *this* case the Court sided with *Bidwell,* 5–4. Although the Court said Puerto Rico was not a foreign country for tax purposes, the island was not fully part of the United States. However, certain constitutional protections were guaranteed for inhabitants of the island territory. Only when Congress "incorporates" a territory could the people living there get *all* the protections under the Constitution. It's important to note "territorial incorporation" doesn't mean a legal process Congress uses to suddenly make Puerto Rico, Guam, or another territory a full part of the country. Instead, it's a general agreement that certain US territories are more connected to the country than others. Clear as mud?

Justice John Harlan wrote the dissent (because of course he did), arguing that incorporation was too abstract, and that Congress should give Puerto Rico residents full rights. He added that Congress was restricted to following what was in the Constitution. Incorporation made it so that Puerto Ricans didn't live within the jurisdiction of the Constitution, which was a problem because Congress could only do things based on what the Constitution says.

This is where the question "Does the Constitution follow the flag?" originated. Does the Constitution apply to everywhere the American government controls? According to the Supreme Court, the answer is *not really*. If a territory like Hawaii at that time was incorporated, that meant that Hawaiians got full protection under the Constitution. However, the residents of territories like Puerto Rico and the Philippines, which were "unincorporated," did not.

# González v. Williams (1904)

*Downes v. Bidwell* left one significant question unanswered: If Puerto Rico isn't a foreign country, but it's not fully covered by the Constitution, what kind of rights do its residents have? The Court attempted to answer that question in another *Insular Case.* It began with a young woman named Isabel González, a native Puerto Rican, who went to New York City from Puerto Rico in 1902 to be with her fiancé. To her surprise, federal authorities labeled her as an "alien immigrant" who would be a "public discharge," meaning she couldn't come to New York as a citizen or United States resident. She could also be turned away if she was determined to be a burden on the public welfare system. Given that she was pregnant and unmarried at the time, this might be a real possibility.

After being detained, González appealed to the local board, which ruled against her. Representing the other side was the federal commissioner of immigration for the Port of New York, William Williams. Yes, that was his actual name. González then petitioned the United States Circuit Court for the Southern District of New York, which upheld the board's decision. When González took the case to the Supreme Court, Federico Degetau, the first resident commissioner of Puerto Rico in the House of Representatives (a representative with no voting power), and Frederic René Coudert, Jr., who was on the anti-tariff side of *Downes v. Bidwell*, joined forces with her. The Court heard oral arguments in December 1903.

**The Big Question in this case:**

- Are Puerto Ricans full citizens of the United States?

The Court said yes. Well, kind of. On January 4, 1904, the Supreme Court announced it sided with *both*. The case was unanimous. The Court said González was *not* an alien *nor* a United States citizen. She, and all other Puerto Ricans, could enter the country as "noncitizen nationals," essentially a status somewhere between a full citizen and not a citizen at all. In case you were wondering, González was already a US citizen by that point because she had married her fiancé and became a citizen through marriage.

Puerto Ricans eventually gained citizenship as part of the Jones Act of Puerto Rico, signed by President Woodrow Wilson in 1917. However, this did *not* give Puerto Ricans full rights as US citizens.

# Balzac v. Porto Rico (1922)

This one began a few years later, when Puerto Rican newspaper editor Jesús Balzac got sued by Puerto Rico's local government for libel, written defamation. Defamation is the action of hurting someone's reputation. The Puerto Rican government wasn't happy that Balzac wrote a negative article that indirectly mentioned Puerto Rican colonial governor Arthur Yager. Even though Puerto Ricans had United States citizenship by this time, Balzac didn't get a jury trial, guaranteed under the Sixth Amendment of the Constitution! So without a jury, the District Court of Puerto Rico found him guilty. In 1920, Balzac's appeal was rejected by the Puerto Rican Supreme Court, which cited earlier cases to say that, regardless of the Jones Act that guaranteed citizenship, parts of the Bill of Rights still did not apply to Puerto Ricans. Balzac appealed to the Supreme Court, who heard oral arguments on March 20, 1922.

### The Big Question in this case:

- Are Puerto Ricans guaranteed Bill of Rights protections?

The Court said no. On April 10, 1922, it announced it had sided with Puerto Rico. It was unanimous. Chief Justice William Howard Taft's majority opinion stated that, since Puerto Rico was not incorporated into the country (not designated as ready for statehood), Congress had free rein in deciding how the Constitution applied to Puerto Ricans. It didn't matter that Puerto Ricans were US citizens, since they previously lived under Spanish law; they would not be ready for the American court system of trial by jury. According to Taft, territories like Puerto Rico and the Philippines "should be permitted themselves to determine how far they wish to adopt this institution of Anglo-Saxon origin, and when." Yes, that was a *big* setback for Puerto Ricans wanting to expand their rights.

Also, while I've been focusing on Puerto Rico–specific cases, they all represent a larger point of the *Insular Cases*. Today, most American territories and their citizens remain in this weird limbo status where they are fully part of the United States for *some things*, like taxes and citizenship, but they can't take advantage of *other things*, like full representation in Congress. While Puerto Ricans now have rights in court, they still can't vote in presidential elections or have voting members in Congress. The island has been discussed as a possible fifty-first state, but not all Puerto Ricans are fully on board with that idea, and like with the possibility of the District of Columbia also being a state, today it's a highly contentious issue in Congress. Puerto Rico today officially remains an unincorporated territory of the United States.

What about the other American territories gained after the Spanish-American War? The Philippines won its independence in 1935, but only after years of persecution and violence. Hawaii became the fiftieth state in 1959. Like Puerto Rico, Guam, the North Mariana Islands, and the US Virgin Islands remain unincorporated US territories. Many today argue that the *Insular Cases* were decided simply as a sneaky way to justify racism and imperialism.[52]

# 24. Jacobson v. Massachusetts (1905)

This case began in Cambridge, Massachusetts, in 1902. Henning Jacobson, a local minister, refused to be vaccinated for smallpox by the city's board of health. It's worth pointing out that smallpox is one of the most devastating diseases in human history. Even though Edward Jenner had discovered a vaccine to help prevent smallpox in 1796, in 1902 the average mortality rate for the disease was as high as 30 percent. In fact, between around 1902 until when it was finally eradicated thanks to the World Health Organization in the late 1970s, smallpox killed an estimated 300 million people around the world.

As much of a threat as smallpox still was in 1902, Jacobson didn't think it was worth it to get vaccinated. Today, folks would likely call him an "anti-vaxxer." Jacobson grew up in Sweden, where they had a law that required all children to get vaccinated for smallpox, and yes, as a child, Jacobson got the vaccine. However, he later claimed the smallpox vaccine caused him "great and extreme suffering" that he had to deal with permanently. Later, he claimed his son also went through "adverse effects" after getting the vaccine as a child. Based on these experiences, Jacobson and his wife were done with vaccines.

Meanwhile, Massachusetts had passed a law saying city boards of health could force their citizens to get vaccinated "when necessary for public health or safety." Cambridge, which had seen a surge in smallpox outbreaks in June, forced everyone to get the smallpox vaccine or face a fine of $5, around $150 today. Now, the vaccine was not guaranteed to last your entire life, so adults who were vaccinated as children had to get vaccinated again. Despite many of his neighbors dying from smallpox, Jacobson still refused to get vaccinated again, and the city fined him.

Others also refused and appeared in court together in July. Jacobson argued the vaccine was an "invasion of his liberty." Well, they made him pay the fine anyway. He and others appealed to the Massachusetts Supreme Court, but it agreed with Cambridge. So Jacobson appealed again, this time to the Supreme Court, which heard oral arguments on December 6, 1904. Jacobson and his lawyers brought up the almighty Fourteenth Amendment, saying the Massachusetts law requiring vaccination overstepped personal liberty, and could lead to more government control of individual behaviors.

**The Big Question in this case:**

- Did a mandatory vaccination law go against the Fourteenth Amendment?

The Court said no. On February 20, 1905, it announced it had sided with Massachusetts, 7–2. While the Court agreed that individual liberties were important, public safety and the state's obligation to get rid of smallpox were *more important*. Those who did not get vaccines endangered the lives of others, and the Court ultimately decided that forced vaccinations were a legitimate way to protect the lives of citizens.

Justice John Marshall Harlan gave the opinion and acknowledged that there could be exceptions. Harlan said certain folks might be harmed by forced vaccinations and therefore should be exempt. However, Jacobson couldn't prove that he fell into this category. Harlan also pointed out that citizens could never be forced to be vaccinated. They could be *fined* but not forced.[53]

*Jacob v. Massachusetts* set a precedent that sometimes the freedom of the individual has to be limited in the name of general welfare, and sometimes states could use their police power in the name of public safety. Courts across the country have upheld compulsory vaccination ever since.

The anti-vaccine movement, however, only grew after this case, with the founding of the Anti-Vaccination League of America three years later. Today, there is still a vocal group opposed to vaccines of various kinds. In 2021,, a prominent organization declared the anti-vaccine movement as one of the top ten global health threats. What was that organization? The same one that eradicated smallpox forty-three years ago: The World Health Organization.

53   www.ncbi.nlm.nih.gov/pmc/articles/PMC1449224/

# 25. Lochner v. New York (1905)

This case began in Utica, New York, in 1899. That year, New York authorities fined an immigrant baker named Joseph Lochner for letting one of his employees work more than sixty hours in one week. New York's Bakeshop Act made it illegal for bakeries to employ workers more than ten hours a day or sixty hours a week. The New York state legislature passed the law after it was revealed that these bakeries were often horrifying places to work. They weren't Paneras. Bakeshops, today more commonly known as "bakeries," back then were often hot, dark, filthy places with no ventilation. Before the Bakeshop Act, a typical baker worked seventy-four hours a week and would be exposed to all kinds of dangerous stuff.[54]

Lochner technically wasn't making his bakers work ten hours a day or sixty hours a week. While most bakeries hired workers to work separate shifts during the day, Lochner only had one crew at his bakery. One crew was often all smaller bakeries could afford. They would arrive in the evening to prepare the bread dough, sleep for several hours in a dorm at the bakery, and then wake up early in the morning to bake loaves of bread. Lochner *paid his bakers to sleep*. He counted their time sleeping in the dorm as "working hours."

Regardless, the Oneida County Court fined Lochner $25 for breaking the Bakeshop Act. That's about $850 in today's money. Two years later, and Lochner hadn't learned his lesson, because he still had at least one baker working more than sixty hours a week. Local authorities arrested him. Eventually Lochner got a trial, where he refused to plead guilty or not guilty. He didn't even try to defend his actions. The Oneida County Court fined him $50 this time, or around $1,700 in today's money, and after Lochner refused to pay the fine, they sent him to jail.[55]

Lochner appealed to the Appellate Division of the New York Supreme Court, where he finally had a lawyer, William Mackie, who offered a defense. Mackie argued that the Bakeshop Act interfered with the right to pursue a lawful profession and earn a living. The Appellate Division of the New York Supreme Court disagreed, upholding the Bakeshop Act, so Lochner appealed again, this time to the New York Court of Appeals. It agreed with the lower courts, so Lochner appealed to the Supreme Court. By now, Lochner was

54    www.britannica.com/event/Lochner-v-New-York
55    tile.loc.gov/storage-services/service/ll/usrep/usrep198/usrep198045/usrep198045.pdf

done with Mackie and had found a new lawyer to help him out named Henry Weismann. Weismann was an interesting choice. First, he'd never passed the bar exam, so many questioned whether he was qualified to argue before the Court. Second, Weismann was kind of a traitor to bakers. At one point, he had been a lobbyist for the Journeyman Bakers Union and was even the editor of their newsletter. He was a big reason why the sixty-hour work week for bakers happened in the first place! By 1905, he was firmly on the side of Lochner and bakery owners. He had changed his mind after opening a bakery, and through that experience became vocal about his regret for helping get the Bakeshop Act passed.

Weisman argued that the Bakeshop Act went against the Constitution's protection of "liberty of contract," protected in the Fourteenth Amendment's Due Process Clause. In other words, he argued the law hurt a person's freedom to contract their labor.[56] The Court heard oral arguments in February 1905.

**The Big Question in this case:**

- Did the Bakeshop Act go against the Due Process
  Clause of the Fourteenth Amendment?

The Court said yes, although this was a close one. On April 17, 1905, it announced it had sided with Lochner, stating that the Bakeshop Act was unconstitutional, 5–4. Justice Rufus Peckham wrote the majority opinion, stating that the Bakeshop Act hurt the right of contract between employers and employees, and therefore went against the Due Process Clause of the Fourteenth Amendment. Peckham wrote, "The right to purchase or to sell labor is part of the liberty protected by this amendment unless there are circumstances which exclude the right."[57] In addition, the Court argued that limiting how many hours workers could work was not a police power of the state of New York. New York could only have such police power if it could prove that a maximum-hours law had a close connection to public health. The Court concluded it had not.

Yet again, Justice John Marshall Harlan wrote a dissent, joined by justices Edward White, William Day, and Oliver Wendell Holmes, Jr. Harlan argued that Lochner and bakery owners should prove that working conditions were safe, not the government. As he saw it, there *was* a close connection to public health, so New York *could* regulate the employees' hours.

Holmes' dissent is one of the most famous dissents in Supreme Court history. In it, he criticized the Court's majority for favoring cutthroat, laissez-faire capitalism over

56   constitutioncenter.org/blog/lochner-v-new-york-fundamental-rights-and-economic-liberty
57   law2.umkc.edu/faculty/projects/ftrials/conlaw/lochner.html

human rights. He wrote, "The liberty of the citizen to do as he likes so long as he does not interfere with the liberty of others to do the same, which has been a shibboleth for some well-known writers, is interfered with by school laws, by the Post Office, by every state or municipal institution which takes his money for purposes thought desirable, whether he likes it or not." Holmes added that American laws restricting a person's freedom of contract was nothing new.

*Lochner v. New York* remains one of the most controversial Supreme Court decisions of all time. The case marked a shift in how the Court began interpreting laws regulating working conditions. After this, the Court increasingly struck down state and federal laws that regulated labor. More broadly speaking, this case marked the beginning of a period that lasted more than three decades in which the Court generally erred more on the side of individual freedom instead of government power. In fact, historians today call this period the "Lochner Era." Crazy enough, the Lochner Era overlapped with the Progressive Era, a time when reformers worked overtime to eliminate social and economic injustice. These reformers viewed the *Lochner* decision as one that favored employers over employees.

# 26. Bailey v. Alabama
## (1911)

This case began in Alabama in 1907. The Alabama legislature was still mostly racist back then, and often sought ways to make African Americans second-class citizens. One way of doing this was peonage laws. Peonage is a system in which an employer can force a worker to pay off a debt with work. Wait, doesn't that sound like slavery? Wasn't slavery outlawed with the Thirteenth Amendment? Well, peonage was a sneaky way around the Thirteenth Amendment. Anyway, in 1907, the Alabama legislature amended a law previously passed that said:

> Any person who, with intent to injure or defraud his employer, enters into a contract in writing for the performance of any act of service, and thereby obtains money or other property from such employer, and with like intent, and without just cause, and without refunding such money, or paying for such property, refuses or fails to perform such act or service, must on conviction be punished.

In other words, if you sign a contract to work, you best fulfill that contract or pay your way out of it.

On December 26, 1907, an African American named Alonzo Bailey signed a contract agreeing to do farming work with the Alabama-based Riverside Company for one full year. They would pay him $12 a month, or about $370 a month in today's money. He also got a signing bonus of $15, or $460 a month in today's money. After working for over a month, Bailey decided he didn't want to work for Riverside anymore and quit, thus breaking the contract. He didn't pay back his signing bonus.

Soon after that, local authorities arrested and charged him with fraud. At his criminal trial, a jury found him guilty of defrauding his employer, and the judge required him to pay back the $15 signing bonus, and an additional fine of $30. If Bailey couldn't pay the money, then he would have to work for it—the judge sentenced him to 136 days of "hard labor."[58]

Bailey appealed to the Alabama Supreme Court, but it agreed with the lower court. He then appealed again, this time to the Supreme Court, which agreed to hear oral arguments in October 1910. Bailey and his lawyers argued that Alabama's peonage law went against the Thirteenth Amendment, that it was a form of slavery.

58   www.oyez.org/cases/1900-1940/219us219

**The Big Question in this case:**

- Did the Alabama peonage law go against the
  Thirteenth Amendment?

The Court said yes. In a 7–2 decision, it announced on January 3, 1911, it had sided with Bailey. The Court argued that the peonage law violated the Thirteenth Amendment because it was essentially indentured servitude. Justice Charles Evans Hughes wrote the majority opinion, explaining it was fine to punish someone for fraud and make them pay money for committing it. However, forced labor as a punishment crossed the line.

Justice Oliver Wendell Holmes dissented, but not because he agreed Bailey should have got the punishment of forced labor. In fact, he argued that the Court's majority was unwittingly making the peonage law *stronger*. If you take away forced labor, then fines will likely become stricter, and if the convicted can't pay the fines, then they most certainly will go to prison.[59] The Thirteenth Amendment says slavery and involuntary servitude are fine "as a punishment for crime whereof the party shall have been duly convicted." Holmes was concerned that the Court's majority had paved the way for more African Americans to go to prison in the South.

*Bailey v. Alabama* didn't do much to limit systemic racism against African Americans. In fact, Alabama's state legislature would just continue its racist shenanigans with future laws. One of those laws, which said a convict must pay off debt through forced labor but allowed others to pay off the fines instead, was also struck down by the Supreme Court just three years later.

---

# 27. Schenck v. United States (1919)

This case began in Philadelphia, Pennsylvania, in 1917, shortly after the United States government had decided to enter World War I. Charles Schenck, the general secretary of the Socialist Party, had printed and mailed more than 15,000 copies of pamphlets to men drafted into the military to fight. "Drafted" meaning that, under the Selective Service Act, they *had* to enlist, whether they wanted to or not. The pamphlets instructed men to resist the draft, adding that it was no different than slavery, which the Socialist Party argued went against the Thirteenth Amendment. If it wasn't obvious by now, Schenck, and generally the entire Socialist Party, was *strongly* against the war, claiming it was only fought to benefit Wall Street investors who could make money from selling stuff to the military.

As it turns out, by distributing these pamphlets, Schenck was *breaking the law*. The US federal government had just passed the Espionage Act, and parts of that law said it was illegal to try to cause people enlisted in the military to disobey orders. More pertinently, the law also made it illegal to interfere with the draft or military recruitment. The federal government arrested Schenck and charged him with violating the Espionage Act. They also arrested his colleague, Elizabeth Baer, for helping him.

Schenck and Baer argued that the First Amendment protected their freedom to distribute those pamphlets. Specifically, they argued it was their freedom of speech! The US District Court for Pennsylvania disagreed, explaining that it didn't think the First Amendment applied in this case. They found Schenck and Baer guilty of conspiracy to violate the Espionage Act.

Schenck and Baer appealed to the Supreme Court, and it agreed to hear oral arguments over two days in January 1919. By that time the war was over. Regardless, Schenck and Baer wanted the Espionage Act gone to prevent this from happening in future wars.

## The Big Question in this case:

- Did the Espionage Act go against the First Amendment with respect to Schenck and Baer's freedom of speech?

The Court said no. On March 3, 1919, it announced it had sided with the United States. It was unanimous. The Court argued that the First Amendment did *not* protect speech that encouraged enlisted folks to disobey their military orders. Justice Oliver Wendell Holmes, Jr. wrote the opinion. He admitted that, during normal times, Schenck and Baer would have been fine distributing the pamphlets. However, this was during a war, and these pamphlets greatly hurt the war effort.

This was also the case in which Holmes delivered this famous line:

> The most stringent protection of free speech would not protect a man in falsely shouting fire in a theatre and causing a panic…The question in every case is whether the words used are used in such circumstances and are of such a nature as to create a clear and present danger that they will bring about the substantive evils that Congress has a right to prevent. It is a question of proximity and degree.[60]

The famous "shouting *fire* in a crowded theater" analogy for the limitations of free speech was thus born. What became known as the Clear and Present Danger doctrine was also born, which the Court used for decades to determine when there are First Amendment limitations. Later the Court replaced the doctrine with the Brandenburg test in the case *Brandenburg v. Ohio* (1969).

Interestingly, Holmes changed his tone a few months later in the case *Abrams v. United States* (1919), saying the Court was already misinterpreting his Clear and Present Danger doctrine.

Regardless, *Schenck v. United States* is one of the most important Supreme Court cases in history dealing with how to interpret the First Amendment. It's almost the first thing most of us even think of when explaining that freedom of speech doesn't always mean you get to say anything you want at any time.

One thing is certain. Don't yell, "Fire!" in a crowded theater, okay? That might get you into some trouble.

# 28. Gitlow v. New York (1925)

This case began with the assassination of President William McKinley in Buffalo, New York, on September 6, 1901. The man who assassinated McKinley, Leon Czolgosz, was a self-proclaimed anarchist, or someone who believes no government is justified. In response, New York state legislators passed the Criminal Anarchy Law, making it illegal to promote "the doctrine that organized government should be overthrown by force or violence, or by assassination...or by any unlawful means."[61]

Flash forward to July 1919, when a socialist leader, Benjamin Gitlow, published a document called "Left Wing Manifesto" in a newspaper he helped run in New York City called *The Revolutionary Age*. The document called for "the proletariat revolution and the Communist reconstruction of society." He called for workers to take over where they worked. This freaked out a bunch of factory owners and politicians. Heck, it seemed to freak out most people. This was the height of the Red Scare, after all, a time marked by widespread fear of ideas related to communism, socialism, and anarchism. After Gitlow distributed around 16,000 copies of the Left Wing Manifesto throughout New York City, local authorities arrested him and charged him with breaking the aforementioned Criminal Anarchy Law.

Newspapers nationwide publicized his trial, which lasted from January 22 to February 5, 1920. Gitlow chose to defend himself at the trial, arguing that he published the Left Wing Manifesto as a historical analysis, not a literal call for people to overthrow any government. In addition, he argued that no revolutionaries *did* anything in response to his document after its publication, proving that it was harmless and thus protected under the First Amendment. The jury was not convinced and found him guilty. On February 11, the judge sentenced him to up to ten years in prison. Gitlow served over two years at Sing Sing, a maximum-security prison about thirty miles north of New York City. While in prison, Gitlow repeatedly tried to appeal his case. Finally, on December 13, 1922, a judge granted his motion to appeal, and he was released from prison on bail.

However, the Supreme Court of New York agreed with the lower court. Fortunately for Gitlow, his next appeal, this time to the New York Court of Appeals, went a lot quicker.

---

61  moses.law.umn.edu/darrow/documents/NEW%20YORK%20CRIMINAL%20ANARCHY%20ACT_Harv_L_
Rev.pdf

Unfortunately for Gitlow, the New York Court of Appeals *also* agreed with the lower courts. That said, by this time Gitlow's case had caught the attention of the recently formed American Civil Liberties Union, or ACLU. The ACLU had primarily formed in response to the Red Scare's effect on freedom of speech and the First Amendment. Its goal was to protect protestors and whistleblowers from all levels of government.

After the ACLU lawyer Walter Pollak agreed to help Gitlow out, they got the Supreme Court to take on the case, and it heard oral arguments on April 13, 1923. However, the Court couldn't make up its mind and decided to hear oral arguments again on November 23.

## The Big Question in this case:

- Does the First Amendment prevent a state from making laws that prohibit political speech that calls for the overthrow of the government?

The Court said no. On June 8, 1925, it announced it had sided with New York, 7–2. It argued that New York's Criminal Anarchy Law was fine since it only restricted speech that could potentially lead to violence. Justice Edward Sanford wrote the opinion, citing *Schenck v. United States* (1919) and *Abrams v. United States* (1919) as precedents for this case. Sanford wrote that Gitlow's Left Wing Manifesto had "the language of direct incitement" and was not "the expression of philosophical abstraction." In other words, the Court thought it was reasonable to believe Gitlow's words *could* lead to a violent overthrow of the government.

The ACLU and Gitlow viewed this decision as a victory since the Court also effectively reversed *Barron v. Baltimore* (1833) by firmly establishing that the Bill of Rights could also be applied to states.[62] How did it justify this? The Court argued that the magical Fourteenth Amendment had extended the First Amendment's protections to state governments.

Just like in *Abrams v. United States* (1919), Justices Oliver Wendell Holmes and Louis Brandeis dissented with similar reasoning. Holmes wrote that Gitlow had *not* violated his Clear and Present Danger doctrine because his call to action was too abstract.

Regardless, *Gitlow v. New York* remains one of the most important Supreme Court decisions in history because it was the first major case to apply the Bill of Rights to state legislatures, which legal scholars call the Incorporation of the Bill of Rights. The *Gitlow* decision opened the floodgates. After it, the Court would increasingly use the Fourteenth Amendment to limit state laws that hurt civil rights and civil liberties.

After the decision, Benjamin Gitlow was forced to finish his original court sentence. However, on December 11, 1925, Governor Al Smith pardoned Gitlow, making him a free man.[63] Gitlow spent the next several years of life running for public office with the Workers Party of America and the Communist Party.

Crazily enough, later in life Gitlow changed his political views, becoming an outspoken anti-communist.[64]

63   www.nytimes.com/1925/12/12/archives/gitlow-is-pardoned-by-governor-smith-as-punished-enough-executive.html
64   www.journals.uchicago.edu/doi/abs/10.1086/218771

# 29. Buck v. Bell (1927)

This case began in Madison Heights, Virginia, on September 10, 1924, when a doctor, Albert Sidney Priddy who was in charge of the Virginia State Colony for Epileptics and Feebleminded, requested to sterilize an eighteen-year-old patient, Carrie Buck. According to Dr. Priddy, Buck had the "mental age" of a nine-year-old and argued that if she was allowed to have children, this would be dangerous for society. He wanted to force her to go through a procedure that made it so she could never give birth to kids, and this was only due to her genetics. Priddy was part of a disturbingly mainstream movement of the time that promoted eugenics, or the promotion of selective breeding of human populations to improve their genetic quality.

However, if we go back further, this story is even more messed up than this. Carrie Buck was the daughter of Emma Buck, who the local government had previously taken away from Carrie and her siblings when Carrie was a kid. The government claimed that Emma was taken from her kids for prostitution, immorality, and having syphilis. The state then confined Emma to the Virginia State Colony for Epileptics and Feebleminded. After this, Carrie grew up with foster parents, who often treated her like a slave. When Carrie was a teenager, her foster parents sent her to the Virginia State Colony for Epileptics and Feebleminded for being sexually promiscuous, "bad behavior," and "feeblemindedness."[65] Before her foster parents sent her there, Carrie had been raped by her foster mother's nephew. This resulted in Carrie getting pregnant, but because the state had declared her mentally incompetent to raise her child, her former foster parents adopted the baby. At seven months old, that baby, Vivian, would also be declared "feebleminded."

Before Dr. Priddy attempted to sterilize Carrie Buck, he wanted to make sure it was legal. The state *had* passed a law called the Virginia Sterilization Act of 1924, allowing doctors to forcibly sterilize patients who supposedly had genetic traits that would be damaging to society if passed on to the next generation. However, the law had yet to be tested in court. The Virginia State Colony for Epileptics and Feebleminded got the first test going. After ordering Buck sterilized, their board appointed a dude named Robert Shelton as her guardian. He was already the guardian of several of the institution's patients and got paid for it. Buck's lawyer was a dude named Irving Whitehead, a eugenics fan and supporter of the Virginia Sterilization Act. He was also on the board, helping request Buck's

65  Cohen, Adam (2016). *Imbeciles: The Supreme Court, American Eugenics, and the Sterilization of Carrie Buck.* New York: Penguin Press. ISBN 978-1594204180.

sterilization. Oh, and one more thing. He was good friends with Albert Priddy and Aubrey Strode, who represented Priddy in court. Talk about a conflict of interest! Predictably, Whitehead made no effort to challenge the accusations that Buck was feebleminded.

Shelton first got the case to the Circuit Court of Amherst County, who agreed the sterilization should take place. However, since eugenics was increasingly controversial, Shelton knew he'd have to attempt to get the case to the Supreme Court to prevent any issues. He first appealed the case to the Supreme Court of Virginia, which also agreed that it was fine for the sterilization to take place. The next appeal was the Supreme Court, which had been looking to chime in on eugenics for a while.[66] The Court heard oral arguments on April 22, 1927. By this time, Priddy had died and his successor, Dr. John Bell, now represented the Virginia State Colony for Epileptics and Feebleminded.

Even though the Court didn't hear much of a defense of Buck, it had to consider her right to have kids as protected by the Due Process Clause and Equal Protection Clause of the Fourteenth Amendment.

## The Big Question in this case:

- Does a law that permits forced sterilization go against the right to due process of the law and the equal protection of the laws, as protected by the Fourteenth Amendment?

The Court didn't take long to think about the question. It said no. On May 2, 1927, it announced it had sided with Bell, saying the Virginia Sterilization Act was constitutional. Surprisingly, it was 8–1. The lone dissenter was Justice Pierce Butler, who did not write an opinion, but his devout Roman Catholic beliefs likely influenced how he decided.[67]

The Court concluded that, in this instance, public welfare was more important than the welfare of one person's body. It was a classic "greater good" argument, and the Court compared sterilization to forced vaccinations. Justice Oliver Wendell Holmes wrote the opinion, saying that Buck and Buck's mother and daughter were "feebleminded" and "promiscuous," and it was in Virginia's interest to get her sterilized. Holmes argued that the case *Jacobson v. Massachusetts* (1905) provided a precedent for this case, writing, "It is better for all the world, if instead of waiting to execute degenerate offspring for crime, or to let them starve for their imbecility, society can prevent those who are manifestly unfit from continuing their kind. The principle that sustains compulsory vaccination is

66   www.npr.org/2017/03/24/521360544/the-supreme-court-ruling-that-led-to-70-000-forced-
      sterilizations
67   scholarship.law.stjohns.edu/cgi/viewcontent.cgi?article=2507&context=tcl

broad enough to cover cutting the Fallopian tubes." He now infamously concluded, "Three generations of imbeciles are enough."[68] Wow, Holmes.

*Buck v. Bell* further legitimized eugenics laws throughout the United States, and several states passed *new* eugenics laws afterward. Thirty states had some sort of sterilization law, and states ultimately forced up to around 70,000 Americans to be sterilized at some point. Most of those sterilized came from poor or working-class backgrounds, and many were sterilized without knowing about it. At the Nuremberg trials after World War II, Nazi doctors specifically cited Holmes' opinion in defending themselves. The Holocaust mostly ended any momentum the eugenics movement still had. *Buck v. Bell* remains one of the most hated Supreme Court decisions in history.

Believe it or not, the *Buck* decision was never overturned, and still technically stands. That said, the Court's decision in *Skinner v. Oklahoma* (1942) weakened it. Seventy-five years after *Buck v. Bell*, Virginia Governor Mark Warner formally apologized for his state's participation in eugenics, and after this some called for reparations to all sterilization victims. Reparation is a way to correct a mistake of the past, usually through a monetary payment.

So whatever happened to Carrie Buck? On October 19, 1927, a few months after the Supreme Court decision, Dr. John Bell performed the operation that prevented her from ever having children again. She was the first person in Virginia sterilized under the new law. To make sure the *entire family* couldn't reproduce, Carrie's sister, Doris, was also later sterilized after she was hospitalized for appendicitis. No doctor ever told Doris about the sterilization. Doris and her husband attempted for years to have children. Only in 1980 did Doris find out why they had been unsuccessful. Carrie's supposedly "feebleminded" daughter, Vivian, later did well in school, even making the honor roll. However, she unfortunately died from an infection when she was eight years old.

As it turns out, there was never any evidence that Carrie Buck was "feebleminded." Most accounts later describe her as having average intelligence. People who knew her recalled how nice she was to everyone and how much she enjoyed reading books. She lived a long life, dying on January 28, 1983, at the age of seventy-six. Today she's buried in Charlottesville, near Vivian, her only child.[69]

68   supreme.justia.com/cases/federal/us/274/200/
69   encyclopediavirginia.org/entries/buck-carrie-1906-1983/

# 30. Near v. Minnesota
# (1931)

This case began in Minneapolis, Minnesota, in 1927. That year, two dudes named Jay Near and Howard Guilford began publishing a newspaper called the *Saturday Press*. They devoted much of the newspaper's content to attacking people with baseless accusations influenced by xenophobia, racism, and anti-Semitism. The newspaper claimed Jewish gangs ran the city and that local politicians were doing shady stuff. Near and Guilford liked to target two politicians, in particular: George Leach, the mayor of Minneapolis, and Floyd Olson, the Hennepin County attorney and future Minnesota governor.

Many people were upset with the *Saturday Press*. Shortly after its first issue came out, someone shot Guilford, nearly killing him. However, the *Saturday Press* did more than make up nasty rumors—it also led to a gang leader being convicted of extortion.[70]

Regardless, the newspaper was so controversial that some people tried to prevent its future publication. Floyd Olson was one of these people. He filed a complaint against Near and Guilford under the Minnesota Gag Law, which made it illegal to create a "public nuisance" by publishing, selling, or distributing a newspaper that viciously hurt folks' reputations. In other words, this censorship law was meant to prevent defamation. Censorship is the act of preventing stuff from getting published. As you hopefully recall, defamation is the action of hurting someone's reputation. Judge Matthias Baldwin of the Hennepin County District Court agreed with Olson that the *Saturday Press* was a "public nuisance," and he ordered it to stop publishing.

In response, Near appealed to the Minnesota Supreme Court. Near's lawyer argued that the Minnesota Gag Law went against the Freedom of Press Clause of the First Amendment, and, thanks to the *Gitlow v. New York* (1925) decision, the Fourteenth Amendment *also* protected a citizen's speech if a state government tried to restrict it. However, the Minnesota Supreme Court disagreed, upholding the Minnesota Gag Law and arguing that the newspaper created a nuisance and endangered public safety. The case returned to Hennepin County District Court, and again that court upheld the law, and so Near and Guilford appealed again to the Minnesota Supreme Court, arguing that they now had no right to publish *any* newspaper. The Minnesota Supreme Court agreed with

70   Lewis, Anthony (1991). *Make No Law: The Sullivan Case and the First Amendment*. New York: Random House. pp. 90

the lower court, saying that Near and Guilford could publish another newspaper as long as it was "in harmony with the public welfare."[71]

Near and Guilford appealed again to the *United States* Supreme Court, which agreed to hear oral arguments on January 30, 1930.

### The Big Question in this case:

- Does the Minnesota Gag Law go against the Freedom of Press Clause of the First Amendment?

The Court said yes. On June 1, 1931, it announced it had sided with Near. This was a close case, with a 5–4 majority. The Court ruled that censorship almost always went against the First Amendment, and it used the Incorporation of the Bill of Rights doctrine, under the Fourteenth Amendment, to justify that state legislatures also can't make censorship laws.

Chief Justice Charles Hughes wrote the majority opinion, arguing that even if freedom of the press leads to inflammatory and malicious stuff getting printed, that doesn't mean censorship is okay. He wrote, "a more serious evil would result if (public) officials could determine which stories can be published."[72] Hughes said individuals could still sue Near and Guilford for defamation.

Justice Pierce Butler wrote the minority opinion, mainly arguing that the Fourteenth Amendment did *not* allow federal courts to declare a state censorship law unconstitutional.

*Near v. Minnesota* made prior restraint, meaning courts suppressing media because it hurts society, *much* more difficult. It was the first major case to tackle attempts to limit what gets published. It was a win for freedom of the press, but it's also why many media outlets publish fake news today.

After winning the case, Near went back to publishing fake news in the *Saturday Press*. Guilford also stayed in journalism, continuing to talk trash about gang leaders. This ultimately led to his getting murdered in a drive-by shooting on September 6, 1934.

71   supreme.justia.com/cases/federal/us/283/697/
72   Ibid.

# 31. The Scottsboro Boys Cases (1932)

This case began in Jackson County, Alabama, on March 25, 1931. On that day, a group of Black teenage boys got into a fight with six "white" teenage boys on a freight train that they had all illegally hitched a ride on. After the fight, the six white males were kicked off the train because they had started it. These six boys didn't like that, so they went to the nearby town of Paint Rock to tell everyone they could that they were assaulted.

Soon a mob of people gathered and caught up with the train; it stopped and every African American boy on board was arrested. Yep, they arrested *every* African American boy on that train.[73] They narrowed the suspects to nine boys. The nine were Clarence Norris, age nineteen; Charlie Weems, age nineteen; Andy Wright, age nineteen; Haywood Patterson, age eighteen; Olen Montgomery, age seventeen; Ozie Powell, age sixteen; William Roberson, age sixteen; Eugene Williams, age thirteen; and Roy Wright, age twelve. William could barely walk due to a severe case of syphilis. Andy and Roy were brothers who had just left their homes for the first time. Olen couldn't see well and hoped to get a job to pay for glasses. Haywood had ridden freight trains for so long that he claimed he could light a cigarette on top of a quickly moving one. Of these nine boys, only four knew each other before getting arrested.

While the boys were in custody, two white women on that train, Victoria Price and Ruby Bates, approached authorities and claimed the boys had raped them after the white boys had been kicked off. A doctor examined Price and Bates for signs of rape but found nothing. Historians have speculated that Price and Bates may have told police they were raped to distract the police from looking at the fact that both had been involved with prostitution in Tennessee.

Regardless, after word got out about *those* accusations, a large mob formed outside the jail. Due to the racism of the time and place, the mob automatically thought that these Black teenage boys were guilty. They demanded the boys be released to be lynched. The authorities did not release the boys. Sheriff Matt Wann stood in front of the jail, blocking the entrance, saying he would kill the first person to come through the door.[74] The Alabama Army National Guard soon came to protect the jail.

73  Linder, Douglas O. (1999). "The Trials of 'The Scottsboro Boys.'" *Famous Trials.* University of Missouri–Kansas City. Archived from the original on December 2, 2016. Retrieved on January 3, 2023.

74  jcsentinel.com/feature_story/article_05e00a4a-7d5d-11e9-ab36-139e57d67569.html

Later journalists referred to the nine boys as the "Scottsboro Boys" since a judge first heard their case in nearby Scottsboro, Alabama. From the beginning, the justice system made these boys seem guilty until proven innocent. Before the trials, they were not allowed to seek legal counsel or even contact their families. The trials were completed in four days. Every day, a huge crowd of spectators booed and hollered. The two lawyers who defended the boys were not given enough time to prepare for the case and didn't even give closing arguments. The only evidence considered was the testimony of Victoria Price and Ruby Bates. The all-white jury didn't need much time to think about it. They found them all guilty, and because rape was punishable by death in Alabama at the time, the eight oldest boys were sentenced to the electric chair, scheduled to die on July 10, 1931. Roy Wright, the youngest of the boys, was spared, not due to his innocence but because the jury couldn't figure out whether to sentence him to death or life in prison, so the judge declared a mistrial.

After word got out about the Scottsboro Boys, a lot of folks protested, including a large group in Harlem, a neighborhood in New York City known for its African American heritage. Both the National Association for the Advancement of Colored People, or NAACP, and the Communist Party USA offered to help the boys out. Ultimately, the boys went with the Communists to save their lives. Lawyer George Chamlee led a team to open a new investigation to prove the boys' innocence and hold off on the executions. He also got an appeal to the Alabama Supreme Court, arguing the boys were not given a fair trial.

However, on March 24, 1932, the Alabama Supreme Court upheld the lower court's ruling on seven of the eight remaining Scottsboro Boys. It granted a new trial for Eugene Williams since he was just thirteen, which they thought was too young to be punished by the electric chair. John C. Anderson, the Chief Justice of the Alabama Supreme Court, gave a strong dissent, saying the boys' trials were sloppy, the defense lawyers in the lower court ineffective, the punishments cruel, and the juries extremely biased.[75]

The Scottsboro Boys appealed again, this time to the *supreme* Supreme Court, which heard oral arguments on October 10, 1932. Because the federal government was now getting involved, the Court had to figure out if the Due Process Clause of the Fourteenth Amendment made it so they could step in to determine whether the boys got fair trials.

## The Big Question in this case:

- Did the trials of the Scottsboro Boys go against the Due Process Clause of the Fourteenth Amendment?

75  dash.harvard.edu/bitstream/handle/1/11226081/Scottsboro.pdf?sequence=2&isAllowed=y

The Court said yes. On November 7, 1932, in a case that became known as *Powell v. Alabama*, the Court announced that it had sided with the Scottsboro Boys, 7–2. The Court reversed the boys' convictions, saying the boys were denied due process and not given a fair trial. The Court said not only were the boys not given enough time to reasonably defend themselves as protected by the Fifth Amendment, they also likely were not given the full opportunity for a right to a lawyer as guaranteed by the Sixth Amendment. They did not declare the Scottsboro Boys not guilty. They said the trials were not legit and ordered a new trial.

So the case went back to the lower court, this time in a new location—Decatur, Alabama—which happened to be near the homes of the victims and deep in the heart of Ku Klux Klan country. The boys got to keep their new lawyers and got a new judge, James Edwin Horton. They also got a new jury, also all white. During the new trial, racist mobs gathered outside the courthouse again, so again the National Guard came to protect the suspects. This time, the defense had a surprise witness. Ruby Bates took the stand to testify that she had *not* been raped by the boys and had made up the story. Despite this, the jury unanimously found them guilty, but Judge Horton said there needed to be new trials as this one again was not fair. He would not be reelected as a judge for doing that.

The new judge for Patterson's trial was heavily biased against him, and while that trial did get one African American on the jury, it still found Patterson guilty. The jury also found Norris guilty at *his* new trial, so both Patterson and Norris returned to death row. Both would appeal their cases again. Meanwhile, the others also still tried to get new trials.

Fortunately for Patterson and Norris, the Supreme Court heard their appeals in February 1935. These cases are now known as *Norris v. Alabama* (1935) and *Patterson v. Alabama* (1935). This time the Court considered that African Americans were still mostly excluded from the juries of their trials.

## The Big Question in these cases:

- Did the new trials of Haywood Patterson and Clarence Norris go against the Equal Protection Process Clause of the Fourteenth Amendment?

The Court said yes. On April 1, 1935, four years after the Scottsboro Boys were arrested, the Court announced its decision, and it was unanimous. They sided with Patterson and Norris, saying the boys did not have a fair trial according to the Equal Protection Clause of the Fourteenth Amendment because their jury pools mostly excluded African Americans. Therefore, the Court argued that Patterson and Norris didn't have a fair shot at proving their innocence. The Court said there needed to be retrials with African Americans on the juries.

Unfortunately, this story doesn't have a happy ending, and it's not over yet. It appears the damage was already done to the Scottsboro Boys.

Haywood Patterson got a fourth trial in January 1936. This time, while Blacks were in the pool of possible jury members, none were picked for the trial. Again, the jury found Patterson guilty of rape. However, this time, instead of the death penalty, they sentenced him to seventy-five years in prison. This was the first time in Alabama history that a Black man had not been sentenced to death for the rape of a white woman. Patterson escaped from prison in 1948. In 1950, the same year he published a book describing what he had gone through, the FBI caught up with him and arrested him in Michigan. However, the governor refused to send him back to Alabama. Patterson was later arrested for stabbing a man in a bar fight and died of cancer in prison in 1952, one year into his second sentence.

What about the others?

First, remember that they were still in jail, waiting for new trials. On the way back to jail after Patterson's seventy-five-year sentence, Ozie Powell, who had suffered from mental illness due to solitary confinement, attacked a guard who had abused him. The guard shot Ozie in the head. Unbelievably, Ozie survived but had trouble speaking, hearing, and remembering stuff for the rest of his life. Ozie wasn't released from prison until June 1946.

In 1937, Alabama dropped all charges against four of the boys—William Roberson, Olen Montgomery, Eugene Williams, and Roy Wright. There is evidence that all four suffered from trauma-induced mental illness for the rest of their lives. Wright served in the army and worked as a merchant marine. In 1959, after coming home from a long trip at sea, he convinced himself that his wife had been cheating on him. He shot and killed her before killing himself.

Roy's brother, Andy Wright, was the last Scottsboro Boy to be freed from prison. After his release in June 1950, he moved to New York City. The next year, he was again accused of rape but quickly was found not guilty, despite once again having an all-white jury.

Charlie Weems, who suffered from permanent eye injuries after being gassed for reading Communist books in prison, was released in 1943 and lived a relatively quiet life afterward.

Clarence Norris, the oldest of the Scottsboro Boys and the only one sentenced to death in the final trial, got out on parole in 1946 and went into hiding. In 1976, Alabama Governor George Wallace, of all people, pardoned him. Norris later also wrote a book about his experiences. As far as we know, he was the last of the Scottsboro Boys to die, on January 23, 1989, at the age of seventy-six.

On November 21, 2013, the Alabama parole board pardoned the rest of the Scottsboro Boys and apologized for the events, even though the boys were all long gone.[76] Today, the story of the Scottsboro Boys is well-known. In fact, Harper Lee's classic book *To Kill a Mockingbird* was partially inspired by their story.[77] There's even a musical about them.

However, few know the complete and shocking real story of the Scottsboro Boys, a group of young men falsely accused of something and victims of an unjust and corrupt Alabama judicial system.

76  www.npr.org/sections/thetwo-way/2013/11/21/246576665/alabama-pardons-scottsboro-boys-in-1931-rape-case

77  nmaahc.si.edu/explore/stories/scottsboro-boys.

# 32. A.L.A. Schechter Poultry Corporation v. United States (1935)

This case began in the District of Columbia on June 16, 1933. On that day, President Franklin Roosevelt signed the National Industrial Recovery Act, or NIRA, a law meant to help workers and consumers during the Great Depression, the worst economic downturn in the history of the industrialized world. The NIRA gave the president broad powers to regulate the industry. Specifically, it said the president could enforce codes of conduct for business groups and boards in certain industries. Some codes included making sure businesses paid their workers fairly and didn't charge consumers too much for products. While Congress overwhelmingly supported the NIRA as part of what became known as the New Deal, those who favored a limited government approach talked trash about it.

Many business owners, like the Schechter brothers, simply ignored it. The Schechter brothers owned a chicken slaughterhouse and sold processed chickens to various grocers in Brooklyn, New York. In 1934, a federal grand jury charged them with going against many of the codes set by the Live Poultry Industry of the Metropolitan Area in New York, including not paying their employees a minimum wage, making their employees work too many hours, letting customers pick out the chickens they wanted to be slaughtered, not reporting all their sales, and selling "unfit" poultry. That last charge got the most media attention, so this whole affair eventually became known as the "Sick Chicken Case." The Schechter brothers let customers pick out their chickens to make it easier for Jews to have their rabbis make sure the chickens they bought were kosher, meaning it didn't go against any Jewish dietary restrictions.[78] The Schechter brothers were Jewish, and "Schechter" means "slaughter" in Yiddish, a language historically spoken by Jews.

The Schechter brothers decided to fight back against the Live Poultry Industry's codes and the NIRA. After all, that law allowed those codes to be enforced in the first place. In the District Court of the United States for the Eastern District of New York, the Schechter brothers argued that the NIRA was unconstitutional because it gave powers supposed to belong to the legislative branch to the executive branch. They also argued it went against the Due Process Clause of the Fifth Amendment and the Interstate Commerce Clause of the Constitution.

78   billofrightsinstitute.org/activities/contribution-the-schechter-brothers-essay

The District Court disagreed, so the Schechter brothers appealed to the US Court of Appeals for the Second Circuit. It dismissed *some* of the charges but agreed with the other charges. After this, the Schechter brothers *and* the Department of Justice appealed to the Supreme Court, which agreed to take on the case, hearing oral arguments in May 1935. Roosevelt and Congress had a close eye on this case, as if the Court overturned the NIRA, it might disrupt *many* of their New Deal ambitions.

## The Big Questions in this case:

- Does the NIRA violate the separation of powers between the legislative and executive branches of government?
- Does the NIRA go against the Fifth Amendment and Interstate Commerce Clause of the Constitution?

The Court said yes to both questions, and it didn't take long to reach this conclusion. On May 27, 1935, it announced that it had unanimously sided with the Schechter brothers. The Court declared the NIRA unconstitutional because it gave the president legislative authority. In other words, it violated the separation of powers between the legislative and executive branches. The Court also argued the NIRA went against the interstate commerce clause, clarifying that Congress could only regulate commerce if it directly affected trade across state lines. Although selling chickens was an interstate industry, the Court said the "stream of interstate commerce" didn't apply in this case since the Schechters only sold their chickens to in-state customers.[79]

Justice Louis Brandeis privately told some of Roosevelt's advisors, "This is the end of this business of centralization, and I want you to go back and tell the president that we're not going to let this government centralize everything."[80] This was a huge blow to Roosevelt's New Deal. A few days after the Court announced the decision, he said the Court had made a big mistake, saying they interpreted the Constitution in an old-fashioned way.[81]

*A.L.A. Schechter Poultry Corporation v. United States* is the most important separation of powers case in American history. It brought in the reins of the executive branch. Even though the legislative branch was okay with the executive branch having more power to enforce regulation on industry, the judicial branch was not. After this, both Roosevelt and Congress would be more pragmatic with their New Deal legislation.

79   publicpolicy.pepperdine.edu/academics/research/faculty-research/new-deal/supreme-court-cases/295us495.htm
80   billofrightsinstitute.org/essays/the-national-recovery-administration-and-the-schechter-brothers
81   Shlaes, Amity. *The Forgotten Man.* New York: HarperCollins (2007), p. 245.

# 33. United States v. Butler (1936)

This case began in the District of Columbia on May 12, 1933. On that day, President Franklin Roosevelt signed a different, sweeping law called the Agricultural Adjustment Act, or AAA. The main goal of the new legislation, which was also part of Roosevelt's broader New Deal goals, was to help farmers by raising agricultural prices. To do this, the federal government would attempt to reduce surpluses by buying livestock to slaughter and paying farmers *not* to plant crops. If that sounds weird, keep in mind that farmers were suffering due to an overabundance of crops leading to extremely low prices that were good for consumers but bad for profits.

Those who favored a more limited government approach didn't like AAA for similar reasons regarding why they didn't like the NIRA—they thought the federal government didn't have the authority to meddle in agricultural markets. More than anything, they didn't like that Congress had created a processing tax on farming commodities, even though these funds would be redistributed to farmers who agreed to plant fewer crops.

William M. Butler, who was helping with the finances of a bankrupt cotton processor called Hoosac Mills, thought the AAA was unconstitutional. When the federal government tried to collect the processing tax on farming commodities from Hoosac, Butler asked the US District Court for the District of Massachusetts to step in to reject the request for more than $81,000 from the federal government, more than $1.8 million today.[82]

The US District Court for the District of Massachusetts disagreed with Butler, ordering Hoosac to pay the taxes it owed. Butler appealed to the US Court of Appeals for the First Circuit, and it *agreed* with Butler, reversing the lower court's decision, and saying that the power to regulate agriculture within state borders was reserved to state governments, as stated in the Tenth Amendment of the Constitution. The United States appealed the case, getting the Supreme Court to hear oral arguments in December 1935. The Court considered the Tenth Amendment and Article 1, Section 8, which explained the spending power of Congress.

The Big Questions in this case:

- Does the AAA go against the Tenth Amendment?
- Does the AAA go against Article 1, Section 8 of the Constitution?

The Court said yes to both questions, and it didn't take them long to reach this conclusion. On January 6, 1936, it announced it had sided with Butler, 6–3. It argued that the AAA was unconstitutional because regulation of agriculture was a state power. In other words, the federal government couldn't force states to follow the law. Justice Owen Roberts wrote the opinion, stating that Article 1, Section 8 allowed Congress to collect money in this way only when it was being used for the general welfare of all citizens in the country. However, this interpretation ultimately *expanded* what Congress could collect money for and regulate in the following decades.

Because of that, *United States v. Butler* is today known as the case that said Congress could not only collect taxes to carry out its powers, but that it could tax any time it is spending that money for the "general welfare."[83] That said, "general welfare" means different things to different people.

While the case was another blow to Roosevelt's New Deal agenda, it's also notable as the last major case that struck down a New Deal law. After this, the Court sided with Roosevelt more often than it had before.

# 34. West Coast Hotel Co. v. Parrish (1937)

This case began in Wenatchee, Washington, in 1932. Elsie Parrish was a housekeeper who worked at the Cascadian Hotel, owned by the West Coast Hotel Company. Elsie and her husband became upset with the West Coast Hotel Company after it didn't comply with a new Washington state law that said every worker should get a minimum wage of $14.50 per forty-eight-hour work week. That's around $320 in today's money. Because Elsie was earning much less than this, she sued the West Coast Hotel Company for an amount that was enough to cover the difference between the state's minimum wage and what they were paying her.

At Elsie's trial in Washington State Court, the judge sided with West Coast Hotel, backing up his opinion with a Supreme Court case, *Adkins v. Children's Hospital* (1923), which said a federal minimum wage law was unconstitutional because it went against freedom to enter contracts. Elsie then appealed to the Washington Supreme Court, which reversed the lower court's decision and sided with her. It ordered West Coast Hotel to pay Elsie what it owed her after the minimum law passed, but the hotel didn't want to, and *it* appealed to the *supreme* Supreme Court, which heard oral arguments in December 1936. The Court considered the Fifth and Fourteenth Amendments. At the time, it was uncertain how the Court would decide in this case. President Franklin Roosevelt watched this one closely. He had been frustrated with the Court consistently striking down his New Deal legislation for the previous three years and had recently even proposed a new law to add more justices to the Supreme Court. If this new bill passed, he almost certainly would get more favorable rulings for his New Deal legislation, which is why many critics trashed his proposal, with one critic even calling it a "court-packing plan."[84]

## The Big Question in this case:

- Did the Washington minimum wage law go against the Due Process Clause of the Fifth Amendment, as applied to the states by the Fourteenth Amendment?

---

84    Epstein, Lee; Walker, Thomas G. (2007). *Constitutional Law for a Changing America: Institutional Powers and Constraints* (6th ed.). Washington, DC: CQ Press, p. 451.

The Court said no. On March 29, 1937, the Court had announced it had sided with Elsie Parrish, 5–4. The Court referenced *Muller v. Oregon* (1908) as a precedent. In that case, the Supreme Court upheld Oregon's limit on the working hours of women because it was in the state's interest to protect public health. In this case, the Court argued Washington establishing a minimum wage was constitutional because it also fell under a state's police power.[85] In other words, it was also in Washington's interest to establish a minimum wage since it protected public health. This decision overturned *Adkins v. Children's Hospital* (1923).

When examining this case, historians often focus on the surprising reversal of judicial interpretation by Justice Owen Roberts. Before this case, Roberts tended to vote with the more right-leaning wing of the Court. Beginning with this case, he tended to vote with the more left-leaning wing of the Court. Historians even conclude that Roberts strategically changed his interpretations of the Constitution to shield the Court's integrity and independence from political pressure, especially after Roosevelt's court-packing plan became public. After all, Roberts was quite aware of how popular Roosevelt was with most ordinary Americans. One writer, Cal Tinney, famously called Roberts' sudden shift as "the switch in time that saved nine." In his dissent, Justice George Sutherland even suggested Roberts had let politics and current events influence his decision to change his interpretation of the Constitution.

Regardless, *West Coast Hotel Co. v. Parrish* was historically significant because it effectively ended the Lochner Era, when the Court often struck down economic regulations and business restrictions to protect contracts. President Roosevelt was happy about the decision. In fact, fifteen months later he'd sign the Fair Labor Standards Act, creating the first federal minimum wage of twenty-five cents an hour. That's $5.50 an hour in today's money.

85   www.oyez.org/cases/1900–1940/300us379

# 35. United States v. Miller (1939)

This case began in Siloam Springs, Arkansas, on April 18, 1938. On that day, Oklahoma and Arkansas state troopers pulled over Frank Layton and Jack Miller, two mobsters from the O'Malley Gang known for robbing places. After the troopers found an unregistered, sawed-off shotgun in the car, they arrested them for breaking the National Firearms Act, or NFA, which Congress had passed in 1934. The law put an excise tax on making, selling, and transporting certain firearms and required people to register any possessed firearms. In addition, the NFA said such gun owners had to report transporting the guns across state lines to the federal government when moving. The gun Layton and Miller had was untaxed and unregistered.

Layton and Miller argued that the National Firearms Act was unconstitutional because it went against not only the Second Amendment but also the Tenth Amendment. The judge for the US District Court for the Western District of Arkansas, Heartsill Ragon, acted like he agreed and dismissed the case, saying the NFA violated the Second Amendment. However, Ragon was cool with the NFA and only ruled that way because he knew Miller had ratted out a bunch of his gangster friends and would have to go into hiding after he was released. As it turns out, Miller wouldn't pay a lawyer to appeal to the Supreme Court anyway.

The United States federal government appealed the case by skipping the appellate courts and going directly to the Supreme Court, which heard oral arguments on March 30, 1939. Just as Ragon had predicted, the defense didn't show up. No arguments were made, and no evidence was presented on behalf of Jack Miller or the Second Amendment. The Court heard lots from the lawyers for the United States, though. They generally had three arguments to justify the existence of the NFA. First, they argued the NFA was mainly a way to collect revenue. Therefore, the Treasury Department had the authority to enforce it. Second, they argued that the defendants, Layton and Miller, transported the sawed-off shotgun from Oklahoma to Arkansas, and thus qualified as interstate commerce. Third, they argued that the Second Amendment only protects having *military-type weapons appropriate for use in an organized militia*. The weapon found in Layton and Miller's car, a double-barrel twelve-gauge Stevens shotgun having a barrel less than eighteen inches, had *never* been used in any militia. The third argument is what the Court decided to focus on the most. They seemed to ignore the fact that short-barreled shotguns had been used in World War I.[86]

## The Big Questions in this case:

- Does the NFA go against the Second Amendment?
- Does the Second Amendment protect the right to keep a sawed-off double-barrel shotgun?

The Court answered no to both questions. On May 15, 1939, the Court announced it had sided with the United States, reversing the lower court's decision and affirming that the National Firearms Act was constitutional. It was unanimous, although the recently appointed Justice William Douglas did not participate in the case since he wasn't present for oral arguments. The Court held that the Second Amendment does *not* guarantee an individual the right to have a sawed-off double-barrel shotgun because that specific weapon was not a reasonable weapon for either a well-regulated militia or self-defense.

Interestingly, *United States v. Miller* was the only Supreme Court case directly dealing with the Second Amendment in the twentieth century. In fact, it'd be more than sixty-nine years later when the Court finally tackled the Second Amendment again, in a case called *DC v. Heller* (2008).[87] During that sixty-nine-year span, gun control advocates and gun rights advocates interpreted the decision as one that helped their "side." Gun control folks said the decision proved that the federal government is justified in regulating certain types of firearms. Gun rights folks said the decision was good because it explicitly and specifically stated that people have the right to own a firearm for self-defense and to form militias. Today *United States v. Miller* doesn't seem to have solved the gun control debate, only further complicated it.

You might be wondering what happened to Frank Layton and Jack Miller. Layton plead guilty, and Ragon placed him on a four-year probation. Miller had a more poetic ending. He died before the Supreme Court made its decision. Authorities found his body in April 1939 with multiple .38-caliber bullet wounds. His gun, a .45 caliber pistol, lay by his side.[88] As it turns out, that gun was legal!

86   www.enterstageright.com/archive/articles/0801/0801usvmiller.htm
87   encyclopediaofarkansas.net/entries/united-states-v-miller-et-al-4742/
88   www.enterstageright.com/archive/articles/0801/0801usvmiller.htm

# 36. United States v. Darby Lumber Co. (1941)

This case began in Statesboro, Georgia, in 1938. Despite the Great Depression, Fred Darby's company, Darby Lumber, was thriving. He had just expanded his operations, hiring more workers and buying more equipment to dramatically increase his company's production. However, that year Darby also got into trouble when he broke the recently passed Fair Labor Standards Act, or FLSA. The law established a federal minimum wage for the first time, a forty-hour workweek with mandatory overtime pay (150 percent of the normal wage of a worker) for all hours in a week worked over that, and the prohibition of most child labor. It was arguably the biggest federal law up to that point dealing with big businesses.

As it turns out, Darby wasn't a fan of the FLSA, and chose to ignore it after he began shipping goods out of Georgia for the first time. Because this fell under interstate commerce, the federal government arrested Darby after it found out he was paying some of his workers less than the federal minimum wage of twenty-five cents per hour ($5.50 today). But that was not the *only* thing he was doing wrong. In the US District Court for the Southern District of Georgia, Darby faced nineteen counts of violations of the FLSA.[89] Oops. Darby and his lawyers argued that, under the commerce clause of the Constitution, Congress only had the power to regulate businesses that had operations across state lines. After all, Darby's company only produced lumber *within* the state of Georgia. Therefore, the Tenth Amendment, which says all powers not reserved for the federal government automatically go to the states or the people, applied in this case.

The US District Court for the Southern District of Georgia agreed with Darby, dismissing his case. The United States federal government appealed the case directly to the Supreme Court, and it agreed to hear oral arguments in December 1940. Two previous cases the Court considered were *Wilson v. New* (1917), which upheld a federal law that mandated a maximum eight-hour shift for railroad workers, and *Hammer v. Dagenhart* (1918), a more infamous case that said the federal government couldn't ban child labor.

89  casetext.com/case/darby-v-united-states-3

The Big Question in this case:

• Did the Fair Labor Standards Act go against the
  Commerce Clause of the Constitution?

The Court said no. On February 3, 1941, it announced it had sided with the United States. Surprisingly, it was unanimous. The Court said the Fair Labor Standards Act was constitutional, adding that Congress may regulate interstate commerce as long as the regulations don't step on any other constitutional protections. In Darby's case, because he *sold* lumber outside of Georgia, it fell under interstate commerce. With this decision, the Court overturned *Hammer v. Dagenhart*, as that decision had made the distinction between *manufacturing* in different states and *selling* in different states.[90] The Lochner Era was over.

*United States v. Darby* upheld the Fair Labor Standards Act and helped strengthen President Roosevelt's New Deal agenda over the previous eight years. The decision was extremely important for the future of nearly all federal legislation that dealt with public welfare. Today, because nearly all businesses are technically involved in "interstate commerce," every business has to abide by the FLSA. However, the law remains incredibly popular and will likely not be challenged soon.

# 37. West Virginia State Board of Education v. Barnette (1943)

To understand this case, we must first go back to Nazi Germany during the 1930s. While most of us are familiar with the Holocaust and the persecution and discrimination of the Jewish people in the years leading up to it, we tend to be less familiar with the persecution and discrimination of Jehovah's Witnesses. Throughout the 1930s, the Nazis arrested thousands of Jehovah's Witnesses across Germany for refusing to salute the Nazi flag. They didn't salute the flag for religious reasons, not political ones. They don't salute any flag. It's against their religion to salute a flag since they believe doing so idolizes the state rather than God.[91]

After the Nazis threw these German Jehovah's Witnesses into concentration camps for not saluting their flag, leaders of the church in the United States called for an end to participation in daily flag salutes that, by that time, had become mandatory in American schools. Because the children of Jehovah's Witnesses refused to salute the American flag and refused to say the Pledge of Allegiance, they often got in a lot of trouble with their teachers. Some administrators even threatened to send these kids to a juvenile detention center or have their parents *arrested*. In 1935, the principal of a school in Lynn, Massachusetts, expelled a nine-year-old named Carlton Nichols for not participating in the Pledge of Allegiance, and the local authorities arrested his dad.[92] This case made headlines across the country and inspired many other Jehovah's Witnesses to also sit down during the pledge.

In Minersville, Pennsylvania, Walter Gobitas had his children not participate in the pledge. By doing so, the entire family was breaking a local law, and they all became marginalized and even physically assaulted by other citizens in town.[93] Residents boycotted the Gobitas family store, and students bullied the Gobitas kids at school. Students threw rocks at one of them.[94] A teacher hurt another one of them after forcing his hand out

91  wol.jw.org/en/wol/d/r1/lp-e/1102008085
92  dailybulldog.com/opinion/from-the-desk-of-the-bulldog-a-lesson-on-patriotism-from-a-9-year-old-boy/
93  www.mcall.com/news/mc-xpm-1988-10-09-2669283-story.html
94  Van Orden, James F. (July 2004). "'Jehovah Will Provide': Lillian Gobitas and Freedom of Religion." *Journal of Supreme Court History.* 29 (2): 136–144.

to salute the flag during the pledge.[95] The school eventually expelled the kids for their pledge boycotts.

However, in 1938 their father, Walter, fought the law that forced students to salute the flag and say the Pledge of Allegiance in the US District Court for the Eastern District of Pennsylvania. Gobitas argued that the law went against the Free Exercise Clause of the First Amendment and the Fourteenth Amendment's Due Process Clause. He and his lawyers said the students were prevented from practicing their religion freely. The District agreed, but the Minersville School District appealed to the Third Circuit of the US Court of Appeals. After it agreed with the lower court, the school board appealed once more to the Supreme Court, which heard oral arguments on April 25, 1940. That case, announced on June 3, 1940, was called *Minersville School District v. Gobitis* (a clerk misspelled Gobitas' name on court records). The Court ruled for Minersville School District, arguing that the law that forced students to say the pledge was *not* a violation of religious freedom. It was 8–1, with Justice Felix Frankfurter, one of the dudes who started the American Civil Liberties Union, ironically, giving the majority opinion.

The *Gobitis* decision was devastating not just for the Gobitas family, but for all Jehovah's Witnesses. They were now glaring targets for continuing to refuse to say the pledge. Nearly 1,500 Jehovah's Witnesses were physically attacked in over 300 cities across the country.[96] In Wyoming, one was tarred and feathered.[97] Some were lynched. Others were forced out of town after having their homes burned to the ground.[98] A Southern sheriff explained it all by saying, "They're traitors; the Supreme Court says so. Ain't you heard?"[99]

This made Supreme Court justices like Frank Murphy feel guilty. Murphy said he regretted his decision in the *Gobitis* case and wanted an opportunity to revisit the issue.

Sure enough, that opportunity came quickly, as Jehovah's Witnesses boldly continued to defy the Pledge of Allegiance and flag salute. On January 9, 1942, the West Virginia State Board of Education ordered all teachers and students in the state to salute the flag and say the pledge. By this time, the United States was at war with both Nazi Germany and the Empire of Japan. Well, this might sound familiar. Another father, Walter Barnett, had his kids not salute the flag nor recite the pledge at Slip Hill Grade School, near Charleston, West Virginia. Predictably, the principal expelled those kids, Marie and Gathie Barnett.

95    Panchyk, Richard (2007). "sidebar: Interview with Lillian Gobitas Klouse." *Our Supreme Court: A History with 14 Activities.* Chicago Review Press, Inc. p. 77.

96    www.cesnur.org/testi/geova_USAtoday.htm

97    www.newspapers.com/clip/27167033/1940-june-24-jw-tarred-feathered/

98    www.journals.uchicago.edu/doi/abs/10.1086/634332?journalCode=ssr

99    Davis, Derek. (2003). *New Religious Movements and Religious Liberty in America.* Baylor University Press. p. 177.

However, on the advice of a lawyer, Walter sent his kids right back to school, where fellow classmates called them "Nazis" and "Japs." Each day, the school would send them home.[100]

The Barnetts sued the West Virginia State Board of Education, taking them to the US District Court for the Southern District of West Virginia, not only for themselves but other families in the area fighting the same thing. The three-judge District Court panel agreed with the Jehovah's Witnesses, arguing it wouldn't normally go against a Supreme Court decision, but recent developments across the country made them reconsider the *Gobitis* decision. The persecution of and violence against Jehovah's Witnesses surely influenced them. The Barnett sisters returned to school, even though by then they were now a half school year behind their classmates.

The West Virginia State Board of Education appealed to the Supreme Court, arguing they had the *Gobitis* decision backing *them* up. The Court seized the opportunity, hearing oral arguments on March 11, 1943. Remember, this was all happening in the middle of World War II. The justices were more conflicted on this one, with perhaps the exception of Frankfurter, who stood firm with his decision in the *Gobitis* case. Frankfurter had argued that a school district's interest in creating national unity was enough to force them to salute the flag. By the time of oral arguments in the *Barnett* case, two new justices had joined the Court who weren't there for the *Gobitis* case—Justice Wiley Blount Rutledge and Justice Robert Jackson. It's important to note that both justices had replaced two of the justices who voted *against* Gobitis three years prior, and both seemed more sympathetic to the arguments of the Jehovah's Witnesses.

### The Big Question in this case:

- Did forcing students in public schools to salute the American flag and say the Pledge of Allegiance go against the First Amendment?

The Court said yes. On June 14, 1943, Flag Day, the Court announced that they had sided with Barnett, 6–3. Rarely in American history does a Supreme Court decision get overturned so quickly. This decision overturned *Minersville School District v. Gobitis*, a decision that occurred just three years prior. Three justices had changed their minds with the *Barnett* decision: Hugo Black, William Douglas, and Frank Murphy, who were a big reason why this case even saw the light of day. What a turn of events.

100   www.nytimes.com/1988/09/11/us/pledge-dispute-evokes-bitter-memories.html

This time, the Court relied heavily on the Free Speech Clause of the First Amendment instead of the Free Exercise Clause of it, which was heavily referenced in the *Gobitis* case.[101] Justice Robert Jackson, still relatively new to the Court, wrote the majority opinion. He wrote, "If there is any fixed star in our constitutional constellation, it is that no official, high or petty, can prescribe what shall be orthodox in politics, nationalism, religion, or other matters of opinion or force citizens to confess by word or act their faith therein. If there are any circumstances which permit an exception, they do not now occur to us."

*West Virginia State Board of Education v. Barnette*—hold up, Barnette? Is it true that a clerk misspelled a Jehovah's Witness's name for the court records again? What are the odds? Well, it's true. It happened. Anyway, *West Virginia State Board of Education v. Barnette* was not only a huge victory for Jehovah's Witnesses across the country but also a big win for the First Amendment protections of the freedom of speech and freedom of religion. To this day, because of this case, students have a right in school not to participate in the Pledge of Allegiance nor be forced to salute the American flag. Are kids still bullied over it? Unfortunately, sometimes they are, but this case set a big precedent that it's quite fine to have a minority opinion. Dissent should be protected.

# 38. Smith v. Allwright (1944)

This case began in Houston, Texas, in 1940. That year, a prominent African American dentist named Lonnie Smith decided to fight back against the Democratic Party there. For years, it had excluded people of color from being allowed to vote in their primaries, in which people typically voted for delegates to represent the party's presidential candidate. Smith thought that was messed up, and he sought to challenge a Texas state law that let political parties establish their own rules.

Fortunately, he had the local branch of the National Association for the Advancement of Colored People, or NAACP, to help him out. After the Democratic Party denied him the right to vote in their 1940 Harris County Democratic Primary, the NAACP helped him sue a person by the name of S.S. Allwright, the election official in charge of the Democratic Primary polls. After the US District Court for the Southern District of Texas dismissed the case, Smith appealed to the US Circuit Court of Appeals for the Fifth Circuit, but it agreed with the lower court. Luckily, the NAACP wasn't done fighting this case, and it hired a young, hotshot lawyer to help Smith named Thurgood Marshall. Marshall became a household name after his leadership in a much more famous case, *Brown v. Board of Education* (1954), and eventually became the first African American Supreme Court justice.

With Marshall's help, Smith appealed again to the Supreme Court, and it agreed to hear oral arguments on January 12, 1944. The Court considered the Texas law that let the Democratic Party discriminate against African Americans and the terrible impact of a series of laws throughout the South that consistently created an outcome of Blacks being treated as second-class citizens. The Court again considered if the Fourteenth Amendment's Equal Protection Clause applied to Smith and other African American voters excluded from participating in primaries.

## The Big Question in this case:

- Did preventing African Americans from voting in primary elections go against the Fourteenth Amendment's Equal Protection Clause?

The Court said yes. On April 3, 1944, it announced it had sided with Smith, 8–1. The Court said that the Texas law let the Democratic Party discriminate against African

Americans in primaries andwent against the Equal Protection Clause of the Fourteenth Amendment. By this time it was common knowledge that the Fourteenth Amendment could be applied to crappy state laws. This decision overturned *Grovey v. Townsend* (1935), which said it was okay for a political party to ban Blacks from voting in primaries. It's notable that this decision also got rid of "whites-only" primaries in several other states.

While *Brown v. Board of Education* gets much more attention, *Smith v. Allwright* arguably was the first case to help launch the Civil Rights Movement. Afterward, African American voter registration got easier and the number of Black voters in the South skyrocketed.[102] It was a big win for African Americans and inspired many to become activists, with the NAACP seeing huge growth in the late 1940s.[103]

Lonnie Smith proudly voted in his first Democratic primary soon after the decision. He eventually served as a Democratic Precinct Committee Member in the same precinct where he was once denied a ballot.

102  www.naacpldf.org/case-issue/landmark-smith-v-allwright/
103  naacp.org/about/our-history

# 39. Korematsu v. United States (1944)

This case began in Pearl Harbor, Hawaii, on December 7, 1941, a day well-known to most Americans even today, as that was the day the Empire of Japan dropped bombs on the American naval base. The bombings killed more than 2,400 Americans and injured more than 1,000 others. In response, the United States declared war on the Empire of Japan, officially entering World War II.

Increasingly, Americans viewed anyone of Japanese heritage suspiciously. Japanese Americans had faced racism and discrimination in the country for nearly a hundred years. After the Pearl Harbor attack, that racism and discrimination went to the next level, as many thought Japanese Americans might be more loyal to Japan than the United States, possibly sharing military secrets with them or perhaps even trying to sabotage the war effort. Despite no evidence whatsoever that this was happening, Japanese American persecution increased. People bought "Jap-hunting licenses." *Life* magazine published an article illustrating how to tell the difference between a Japanese person and a Chinese person by the shape of their nose and height.[104]

In California, the racism and paranoia seemed worse. A barber shop advertised "free shaves for Japs," with a disclaimer that read "not responsible for accidents."[105] A funeral parlor advertised "I'd rather do business with a Jap than an American."[106] Several people called for removing all Japanese Americans from Western states and forcing them to live in concentration camps somewhere else. President Franklin Roosevelt, who had a record of being racist against the Japanese, agreed with this idea. He signed Executive Order 9066, which ordered the roundup of 120,000 Americans of Japanese descent to one of ten concentration camps, officially called "relocation centers." It also said Japanese Americans weren't allowed to be in California or much of Oregon, Washington, and Arizona, unless they were in one of the camps.

Fred Korematsu was one of the Japanese Americans who ignored Executive Order 9066 for two reasons. First, he didn't want to leave his girlfriend in California. She was not Japanese American, and they wouldn't be able to see each other. Second, he thought Roosevelt's order was morally wrong. After his entire family left for one of the camps, he

104   www.vintag.es/2018/02/life-magazine-pearl-harbor-issue-how-to.html
105   Browne, Blaine T. *Mighty Endeavor: The American Nation and World War II*. Rowman & Littlefield. p. 212.
106   Kuznick, Peter. *The Untold History of the United States*. Simon and Schuster. p. 151.

stayed behind, became a welder, and tried not to stand out too much. He changed his name and got a fake ID. Later, he even tried to have plastic surgery on his eyes to look less Japanese. The plastic surgeon didn't do the procedure but took Fred's money anyway.[107] Shortly after this, someone reported him and local authorities arrested him. After his arrest, he never saw his girlfriend again. Eventually, Korematsu was in federal prison.

The American Civil Liberties Union, or ACLU, reached out to him there and offered to represent him in court. Korematsu gladly accepted their help. In the US District Court for the Northern District of California, they argued that Executive Order 9066 went against the Due Process Clause of the Fifth Amendment. While Korematsu's loyalty to the United States never was in question, the US District Court for the Northern District of California found him guilty and upheld Executive Order 9066. It ordered him under five years of probation and sent him to a concentration camp in Utah.

Korematsu appealed to the US Court of Appeals for the Ninth Circuit, but it agreed with the lower court. He then appealed again to the Supreme Court, who surprisingly agreed to hear the case, hearing oral arguments in October 1944. At the time, the war was still raging on. During arguments, the Court considered a similar, recent case, *Hirabayashi v. United States* (1943). That decision upheld Executive Order 9066.

### The Big Question in this case:

- Did the president and Congress abuse their war powers by restricting the rights of Americans of Japanese descent?

The Court said no. On December 18, 1944, it announced that it sided with the United States, 6–3. The Court argued that Executive Order 9066 was justified to keep the country safe. It said the need to protect Americans from espionage was more important than individual rights.

Justice Hugo Black wrote the majority opinion, but today most legal scholars say the opinion is pretty flawed. He wrote, "Korematsu was not excluded from the Military Area because of hostility to him or his race. He was excluded because we are at war with the Japanese Empire." That statement was wrong. Black also wrote, "There is evidence of disloyalty on the part of some (Japanese Americans), the military authorities considered that the need for action was great, and the time was short." You're zero for two there, Hugo.

---

107  www.smithsonianmag.com/history/fred-korematsu-fought-against-japanese-internment-supreme-court-and-lost-180961967/

At that time, there was no evidence of that, either. Justice Felix Frankfurter chimed in that the Constitution gave the president and Congress these war powers.

The three justices who dissented all wrote separate opinions. Justice Frank Murphy passionately argued that the decision was the legalization of racism, and that this racial discrimination went against everything the United States stood for. "All residents of this nation are kin in some way by blood or culture to a foreign land. Yet they are primarily and necessarily a part of the new and distinct civilization of the United States. They must, accordingly, be treated at all times as the heirs of the American experiment, and as entitled to all the rights and freedoms guaranteed by the Constitution."[108] Dang, you tell 'em, Frank.

Fortunately for Korematsu, President Roosevelt had a change of heart. On January 2, 1945, he canceled Executive Order 9066. The camps were shut down, and many Japanese Americans returned home to find their belongings missing or destroyed. Fred Korematsu returned home but did not speak publicly about the case for decades. By the 1980s, most Americans agreed that what the government did to Japanese Americans during World War II was messed up. In 1983, a judge voided Korematsu's original conviction.[109] In 1988, Congress passed the Civil Liberties Act, which formally apologized to the Japanese Americans affected by Executive Order 9066 and awarded $20,000 to each camp survivor, about $50,000 today.

Korematsu *did* speak out in his later years. He died in 2005. In 2009, Fred's daughter founded a nonprofit civil liberties organization called the Fred T. Korematsu Institute. She currently still runs it.

*Korematsu v. United States* is often considered one of the worst Supreme Court decisions in American history. Today most view the case, and the overall treatment of Japanese Americans during World War II, as major tragedies. In *Trump v. Hawaii* (2018) the Court *finally* overruled the *Korematsu* decision.

---

108   supreme.justia.com/cases/federal/us/323/214/#tab-opinion-1938225
109   www.uscourts.gov/educational-resources/educational-activities/facts-and-case-summary-
        korematsu-v-us

# 40. United States v. Paramount Pictures, Inc. (1948)

This case began in Hollywood, California, in 1938. This was the height of Hollywood's "Golden Age," when five major studios dominated the film industry—MGM, Warner Bros., RKO, 20th Century Fox, and Paramount. These five giant corporations, also known as "The Big Five," had overwhelming control over the production and distribution of most films. These corporations often directly or indirectly owned the theaters. Because of this, theater chains showed only the films produced by the studio that owned them, and independent films stood little chance of getting shown.

This caught the attention of the federal government, as this practice created a form of oligopoly, or a market or industry dominated by a small number of producers. Oligopolies often can hurt competition and lead to a worse experience for consumers. The US Department of Justice decided that these corporations' domination of the film industry went against the Sherman Antitrust Act. It sued the "Big Five" film studios and the "Little Three," Universal Pictures, Columbia Pictures, and United Artists. Because Paramount was the largest, it became the primary defendant.

In the District Court for the Southern District of New York, the Justice Department agreed to stop suing the major studios if they agreed to the following:

1. They could no longer force people to watch their short films alongside their feature films in theaters.

2. They could show multiple films together, but that would be limited.

3. Theater owners would have more say over which films got shown in their theaters.

4. An administration board would oversee all of this.

Long story short, the major studios didn't comply with these new standards. In 1943, the Justice Department sued them again. The District Court of the United States for the Southern District, however, sided with the film studios, allowing them to keep their theater chains. The court claimed that separating the theaters from the studios would not make the film industry more fair. The Justice Department disagreed and appealed to the Supreme Court, which agreed to hear oral arguments in February 1948.

**The Big Question in this case:**

- Did film studios owning theater chains and controlling the films these theater chains showed go against the Sherman Antitrust Act?

The Court said yes. On May 3, 1948, it announced it had sided with the United States, 7–1. Justice William Douglas wrote the majority opinion, calling the American film industry a cartel that conspired to shut out competition, and thus hurt the consumer.[110] The Court ordered the eight studios to sign legally binding agreements to stop their anticompetitive practices. Notably, they had to part ways with their theaters. MGM was the last to do so, as it kept fighting in courts over the next several years.

*United States v. Paramount Pictures*, also known as the Hollywood Antitrust Case, effectively ended the Hollywood Studio System and Hollywood's "Golden Age." The studios undoubtedly suffered, and many had to downsize to adjust. However, the *independent* film industry predictably began to thrive.[111]

In 2020, the Department of Justice got the binding agreements overturned, but that didn't mean independent theaters were in jeopardy. Today, the film industry is more fragmented and decentralized than ever, and not due to any antitrust legislation but because of advances in technology. We more commonly watch movies on our TVs or phones. After all, it's highly unlikely the Supreme Court could have predicted streaming services would one day be a thing back in 1948.

---

110   supreme.justia.com/cases/federal/us/334/131/
111   www.promarket.org/2022/12/12/the-paramount-decrees-and-the-deregulation-of-hollywood-studios/

# 41. Brown v. Board of Education (1954)

This case began in Topeka, Kansas (where I was born!), in 1950. At the time, Topeka public schools were segregated by skin color. Each day, eight-year-old Linda Brown and her sister had to walk one mile, crossing several busy railroad tracks, to get to a bus that led them to school across town. An elementary school already existed four blocks from their home, but *this* school was for "white" children only, and Linda Brown and her sister were African American.

Linda's father, Oliver Brown, tried to enroll her in the white-only elementary school, but the school's principal wouldn't allow it. In response, Brown approached the Topeka branch of the National Association for the Advancement of Colored People, or NAACP, and asked them for help. The NAACP, as it turned out, had already been planning on challenging racial segregation in public schools. The organization agreed to help Brown and twelve other African American parents who had attempted to enroll their children in whites-only schools in the Topeka school district. A major goal of the NAACP was to bring down the precedent set up by *Plessy v. Ferguson* (1896), the Supreme Court decision that said segregated public facilities based on skin color was fine, as long as both facilities were the same quality. This became known as the "separate but equal" doctrine.

With the NAACP's help, Brown and the rest of the parents sued the Board of Education of the city of Topeka after the district continued to refuse to let their children enroll in whites-only schools. The parents claimed their children's rights, as protected by the Equal Protection Clause of the Fourteenth Amendment, were violated. The NAACP put Oliver Brown at the head of the roster as a legal strategy, as they believed his case was most compelling since Linda's trip to school was so arduous.

The Board of Education argued that segregation was already a way of life, and segregated schools simply got them ready for the segregation they would encounter as adults. They also claimed that segregated schools were not harmful to Black children.

The US District Court for the District of Kansas heard the case, and ruled in favor of the Board of Education, using the *Plessy* decision as a precedent. Interestingly, though, the three-judge District Court panel argued that segregation *did* hurt African American children. Still, they insisted that whites-only and Blacks-only schools in Topeka were of equal quality in terms of facilities, the qualifications of teachers, transportation, and what they were taught.

Brown and the rest of the parents appealed to the Supreme Court. As it turns out, parents across the country all fiercely fought against school segregation in public schools. In 1952, the Court considered five cases dealing with the issue. Ultimately, it combined all five cases under *Brown v. Board of Education*. The NAACP had been involved in all five cases and appointed Thurgood Marshall to argue the case for Brown.

The Court heard oral arguments in December 1952, but by the spring of 1953, could not reach a decision. They remained divided on the issue of racial segregation and knew whatever they decided would be a big freaking deal. In other words, they didn't want to rush it. Chief Justice Fred Vinson was worried about a close vote that would dramatically change the country, and he decided to postpone the decision. However, he died in September, and President Dwight Eisenhower nominated and the US Senate approved Earl Warren, the former governor of California, as Vinson's replacement. This would prove to be an impactful change. The Court reheard oral arguments in December 1953, with Warren now leading.

For several months, the justices debated and discussed the case. One justice who had thought about voting against Brown, Robert Jackson, suffered a mild heart attack during this time. Warren went to visit him in the hospital, continuing to discuss the case during his recovery. Ultimately, Jackson changed his mind.

## The Big Question in this case:

- Does racial segregation in public schools go against the Equal Protection Clause of the Fourteenth Amendment?

The Court said yes. Warren could do what Vinson could not—he brought all the justices together to agree on a huge decision. On May 17, 1954, the Court announced it had sided with Brown. It was unanimous. This overturned the now infamous *Plessy v. Ferguson* decision, saying segregation of schools based on skin color went against the Equal Protection Clause of the Fourteenth Amendment. The Court also argued that segregated schools made African American children feel inferior and damaged their development. Warren gave the opinion of the Court, saying, "We conclude that in the field of public education, the doctrine of 'separate but equal' has no place. Separate educational facilities are inherently unequal."[112]

112  supreme.justia.com/cases/federal/us/347/483/

Reporters were shocked that it was unanimous. They expected a divided court. They were also shocked to see Robert Jackson there. Jackson had left the hospital and wanted to be there to show the Court was truly united behind the decision.

Now, the Court did *not* announce how their ruling was to be enforced. Instead, it asked the attorney generals of all states enforcing segregation laws for their feedback. The Court heard a bunch more hearings over the next year, and on May 31, 1955, announced a plan for how to proceed with the desegregation of public schools. They said it should occur with "all deliberate speed." Whatever that means, right? That decision became known as *Brown II*, which sounds like a movie sequel.

Predictably, many tried to ignore the ruling, and it would take several years before school systems were fully desegregated. Southern states resisted. In the most famous example of Southern resistance to the *Brown* decision, nine African American students attempted to go to the all-white Little Rock Central High School in Little Rock, Arkansas. Even the state's governor, Orval Faubus, had prevented them from going. The Little Rock Nine, as they became known, were only allowed to attend after President Eisenhower stepped in and sent paratroopers to escort the students every day for an entire school year.

Other than *Marbury v. Madison* (1803), *Brown v. Board of Education* is the most important Supreme Court decision in American history. It was undoubtedly consequential. All of a sudden, seemingly all of American society and even American culture changed after this case. It paved the way for integration and was a huge victory in the Civil Rights Movement. It also proved as a model for using lawsuits to reform society. While many schools are still racially segregated today, it's certainly not because of the law.

# 42. Mapp v. Ohio (1961)

This case began in Cleveland, Ohio, on May 23, 1957. On that day, someone set a bomb off at Don King's house. Don King later became famous as a boxer promoter, but at this time was a controversial bookie with many enemies. One of those enemies was whoever bombed his house that day. The Cleveland police got a tip that another bookie, Virgil Ogletree, might have been involved in the bombing and was hiding out in the house of Dollree Mapp. They also suspected that bomb-making materials might also be at the house.

Three Cleveland police officers arrived at Mapp's house and knocked on the door. Mapp answered. They asked if they could enter the house to look around, but Mapp asked the officers if they had a search warrant. After they said they did *not* have a warrant, she refused to let them in. After this, two officers left, but one decided to hang out across the street to stake out the place. Three hours later, more officers returned and knocked on Mapp's door. This time she didn't answer, and they broke down the door and entered without permission. Mapp angrily approached them, again asking to see a warrant. One of the officers showed her a piece of paper that was supposedly the warrant. She snatched the paper and put it in her blouse. The officer then proceeded to reach inside her clothing to retrieve the paper, but she resisted. He eventually got the piece of paper back, and it was never seen again.

The police handcuffed Mapp to detain her while they continued to search her home. They did find Ogletree, who later was cleared of being connected to the bombing, but while looking for him, they found evidence of illegal gambling, a pistol, and a small collection of sexually explicit books that a previous resident had left behind.

The Cleveland police arrested Mapp for having the gambling stuff, but she was later cleared in court. However, while in custody she didn't cooperate with authorities, and several months later they turned around and charged her with having sexually explicit materials. These sexually explicit materials were also illegal to possess in Ohio at the time. The Cuyahoga County Court of Common Pleas found her guilty and sentenced her to seven years in prison.

With the help of the American Civil Liberties Union, or ACLU, Mapp appealed to the Ohio Court of Appeals for the Eighth District, arguing that the Ohio law banning the possession of obscene materials went against the First Amendment. Surprisingly, the Fourth Amendment wasn't Mapp's focus, but she could have also said the police went against it when they searched through her stuff. Specifically, the police had no probable cause to suspect her of having the sexually explicit books, and they couldn't use the books as evidence in court because the Cleveland police found them without a warrant. In addition, Mapp could have argued that the Fourteenth Amendment made the Fourth Amendment applicable to the state and local levels, not just the federal level.

The Ohio Court of Appeals agreed with the lower court, so Mapp appealed again, this time to the Ohio Supreme Court. It also agreed with the lower courts, so she appealed once more to the *supreme* Supreme Court. By this time, four years had passed since the police had raided Mapp's home. The Court heard oral arguments on March 29, 1961.

It was soon apparent that the Court didn't give a darn about the First Amendment, in this case, at least. Instead, they were focused on the Fourth Amendment. Specifically, they considered the exclusionary rule, which said you couldn't use evidence if the police got it illegally. It had been applied since the ruling for the Supreme Court case *Weeks v. United States* (1914) but only at the federal level. In *Wolf v. Colorado* (1949), the Court declined to extend exclusionary protections to the state level.

## The Big Question in this case:

- Did Cleveland police go against the Fourth Amendment when they confiscated materials from Mapp's home?

The Court said yes. On June 19, 1961, the Court announced that it had sided with Mapp, overturning her conviction, 6–3. They sided with Mapp not because of the First Amendment but because of the Fourth Amendment. The police did not have a valid warrant, and so the Court threw out any evidence the Cleveland police got that day when they raided Mapp's home. They couldn't use *any* of it. In deciding this way, the Court expanded the exclusionary rule to the state level, saying the Fourteenth Amendment gave them the authority to do so.

Justice Tom Clark wrote the majority opinion. "The state, by admitting evidence unlawfully seized, serves to encourage disobedience to the federal constitution, which it is bound to uphold. Nothing can destroy a government more quickly than its failure to observe its own laws, or worse, its disregard of the charter of its own existence."[113] Oh snap, Justice Clark.

*Mapp v. Ohio* was a big win for the Fourth Amendment and privacy. The decision put the Fourth Amendment back on the map. Ha! Get it? Back on the map? And her name was Mapp? Anyway, people later called Dolly Mapp the "Rosa Parks of the Fourth Amendment."

113   www.law.cornell.edu/supremecourt/text/367/643

Unfortunately for Mapp, she still got in trouble after being cleared in this case. In 1971, she was arrested for theft and dealing heroin. During her ten years in prison, however, she became an activist for prisoner rights, especially for reducing sentences for drug offenses. After she was released from prison, she used all of her experience with courts to work for a nonprofit organization that gave legal help to inmates.

# 43. Baker v. Carr (1962)

This case began in Millington, Tennessee, in 1961. Charles Baker, a member of the Millington Board of Aldermen and former mayor of the town, became frustrated with the political structure of Tennessee. For decades, he and his fellow Shelby County residents had felt helpless as they got less government assistance and less representation in government. Shelby County is part of the Memphis metropolitan area, and its population had *dramatically* grown since 1901. Tennessee, and the entire country for that matter, had become more urban during that time.

You might be wondering why I specifically brought up the year 1901. Well, that was the year the Tennessee General Assembly had last redrawn legislative and congressional districts! As it turns out, the Constitution of Tennessee said all districts had to be redrawn every ten years, after the census, to make it so that every district had an equal number of people living in it as possible. However, as previously mentioned, in the fifty years since the Tennessee General Assembly last redrew districts, the population shifted in a way that Shelby County had about ten times as many residents as some of the rural districts of the state. The Memphis, Nashville, and Knoxville metropolitan areas alone had 63 percent of the population of the state but only *thirteen* of the thirty-three state senate seats. That was just 39 percent of state senate representation for them. Simply put, the votes of rural citizens were way overrepresented compared to those of urban citizens of the state.

Baker wasn't the only one mad about this. After the Tennessee government refused to redraw districts again after the 1960 census results, he and a bunch of people sued them. Specifically, they sued Joe Carr, a state official in charge of Tennessee elections. Baker argued that the votes of Tennesseans who lived in urban areas didn't count nearly as much as the votes of Tennesseans who lived in rural areas. In other words, the Tennessee legislature didn't reflect the state's population, and this went against the Equal Protection Clause of the Fourteenth Amendment. They argued every vote should be counted equally.

Carr felt confident in court because he had precedent on his side. The Supreme Court had historically not gotten involved with what state governments did when it came to "political questions." Political questions are ones that involve politics, or how power is distributed, and the Court had consistently tried to stay as apolitical as possible. This meant if a case seemed too political, they often didn't want to go anywhere near it. The Supreme Court had brought up what became known as the "political question doctrine" in several cases before 1961. The most relevant case to the Tennessee government's shenanigans was *Colegrove v. Green* (1946). In that case, the Court ruled that it *couldn't* step in after the Illinois government hadn't redrawn *its* congressional districts since 1901, which led to rural votes counting way more than urban votes.[114]

Now, I call not drawing up new districts "shenanigans" not only since it went against the Constitution of Tennessee but in the context of the Civil Rights Movement. The Tennessee government knew exactly what it was doing. It was giving more power to the rural parts of the state because those parts were more "white," and it was giving less power to the urban parts of the state that had more people of color.

The US District Court for the Middle District of Tennessee dismissed the lawsuit, saying it couldn't do anything because it was a political question. It cited the *Colegrove* case, of course. Baker then appealed directly to the Supreme Court, and boy, were they nervous about taking this case on because they knew that whatever they decided would have a tremendous impact on the future of judicial review. Regardless, they agreed to take on the case anyway, hearing oral arguments in April 1961.

Afterward, the Court had a difficult time coming up with a decision. They argued back and forth, with justices Hugo Black, William Douglas, Earl Warren, and William Brennan all on Baker's side and Felix Frankfurter, John Harlan, and Tom Clark on Carr's side. Justices Potter Stewart and Charles Evan Whittaker were the swing votes. They didn't know what side to choose. However, they *did* know if they sided with Baker, the implications would be huge.

The pressure was too much for Whittaker, so he left Washington, DC, and retreated to a cabin in a remote Michigan forest. However, solitude didn't improve his health, and he eventually suffered a nervous breakdown and became suicidal.

Whittaker did return to the Court when they reconvened in the fall. They heard more oral arguments on October 9. Flash forward to March 1962, and Frankfurter had convinced Whittaker to join Baker's side. However, by that time, Whittaker's mental health was in such poor shape that he checked into Walter Reed Hospital. He would never return to the Court and officially retired from it a few days later.[115]

---

114   supreme.justia.com/cases/federal/us/328/549/
115   Ward, Artemus. *Deciding to Leave: The Politics of Retirement from the United States Supreme Court*. State University of New York Press. 164-167.

## The Big Questions in this case:

- Did Tennessee's legislative districts go against the Equal Protection Clause of the Fourteenth Amendment?
- Should the Supreme Court have the power to step in over questions of legislative apportionment within states?

The Court said yes to both questions. On March 26, 1962, the Court announced it had sided with Baker. As it turns out, they didn't need Whittaker's vote since Potter Stewart and Tom Clark had shifted to Baker's side. It was 6–2 since Whittaker's name was removed from the dissenting opinions. Anyway, the Court ruled that first, they *did* have the authority to rule on questions of legislative reapportionment, and second, Tennessee's legislative districts went against the Equal Protection Clause of the Fourteenth Amendment.

This decision, along with other future decisions, created the basis for the "one person, one vote" doctrine, which said states had to at least try their best to divide their representatives in a way that represented *all* citizens equally so that *no* votes counted any more or less than any other vote. In other words, the Fourteenth Amendment's Equal Protection Clause *did* imply that every vote ought to count equally.[116] Following this decision and other future decisions, most states had to redraw up their districts to make sure that rural votes didn't count more than urban votes. While this *did* lead to more equal representation, one unintended consequence of this decision was it led to more gerrymandering, or the manipulation of legislative boundaries to favor one political party or group. Gerrymandering is something of an infamous American tradition. As much as Americans hate the practice, it's been around since the early days of the republic. It was named after a dude named Elbridge Gerry, who, as governor, signed a bill that approved a weirdly shaped district that benefited his political party in Massachusetts. The district's shape somewhat resembled a salamander. So get it? Gerry, which turned into Gerry plus salamander, equals gerrymander?

Eventually the Court would address racial gerrymandering, or gerrymandering that discriminated against people based on their skin color, in the case *Shaw v. Reno* (1993). Finally, this case made it so that the Court would likely be busier from this point forward. Before this decision, the Court avoided getting involved with political questions. Now, they had to get *much* more involved, although Justice Brennan did identify six situations in which the Court would *not* look at political questions, and here they are:

116  landmarkcases.c-span.org/Case/10/Baker-v.-Carr

1.  "Textually demonstrable constitutional commitment of the issue to a coordinate political department"; as an example of this, Brennan brought up issues of foreign affairs and executive war powers, arguing that cases involving such matters would be "political questions";

2.  "A lack of judicially discoverable and manageable standards for resolving it";

3.  "The impossibility of deciding without an initial policy determination of a kind clearly for nonjudicial discretion";

4.  "The impossibility of a court's undertaking independent resolution without expressing lack of the respect due coordinate branches of government";

5.  "An unusual need for unquestioning adherence to a political decision already made";

6.  "The potentiality of embarrassment from multifarious pronouncements by various departments on one question."[117]

Simply put, from now on the Court would jump in on *some* kinds of politics in *some* cases.

*Baker v. Carr* is one of the most important Supreme Court cases in American history. It opened the floodgates. Although the Court has always been somewhat political, I'd argue this case made it *much* more political. I'd also argue that no Supreme Court case in American history has ever tested our justices more so than this case. I mean, it led to one justice having a nervous breakdown, for crying out loud.

# 44. Engel v. Vitale (1962)

This case began in Albany, New York, in November 1951, when the state's Board of Education said all students could open each day with a nondenominational prayer. Students across New York were to say: "Almighty God, we acknowledge our dependence upon Thee, and we beg Thy blessings upon us, our parents, our teachers and our Country." However, they expected no major pushback since the prayer was *voluntary*. They promoted the prayer as a tool for "character development."[118] If parents did not want their kids saying the prayer, they had to *take action*, and it was an inconvenience.

In July 1958, the Board of Education of Union Free School District Number 9 decided to have its students say the prayer. Students could opt out with their parents' signatures. However, a group of families complained that the prayer went against their religious beliefs. With the help of various organizations, the families decided to fight the prayer in court. Five parents, two Jewish and three who weren't big on organized religion, sued the state school board president, William Vitale, on behalf of their children.[119] They argued that the prayer went against the Establishment Clause of the First Amendment, which should be applied because of the Due Process Clause of the Fourteenth Amendment. It was a separation of church and state issue. Alphabetically, the first parent listed as a plaintiff was Steven Engel, so he got all the attention. Engel later recalled how his kids were bullied at school because of the lawsuit, and the other families received obscene letters and phone calls in the middle of the night.

Vitale and the school board argued that they did not establish one religion with the prayer, nor did they force students to say the prayer. They also brought up that the prayer simply reflected the country's religious heritage.

In the state court system, Engel and his fellow plaintiffs had absolutely no success. In 1959, they lost their case before the Supreme Court of New York. The next year, they lost before the Appellate Division of the Supreme Court of New York. The year after that, they lost before the Court of Appeals of New York, where Chief Judge Charles Desmond wrote, "Not only is this prayer not a violation of the First Amendment (no decision of this or of the United States Supreme Court says or suggests that it is) but a holding that it is

---

118   Underwood, James L. The Proper Role of Religion in the Public Schools: Equal Access instead of Official Indoctrination, 46 Vill. L. Rev. 487 (2001).

119   Gold, Susan Dudley (2006). *Engel V. Vitale: Prayer in the Schools.* Marshall Cavendish. p. 16.

such a violation would be in defiance of all American history, and such a holding would destroy a part of the essential foundation of the American government structure."[120] That was dramatic, Charles.

Vitale and company next, of course, appealed to the Supreme Court, where all of a sudden things began to look a lot better for them. The Court heard oral arguments on April 3, 1962.

- Does the reading of a nondenominational prayer at the beginning of each day in public schools go against the Establishment Clause of the First Amendment?

The Court said yes. On June 25, 1962, the Court announced that it had sided with Engel and company, 6–1. Two of the justices, Felix Frankfurter and Byron White, didn't take part in the decision. The Court said the prayer was unconstitutional. Justice Hugo Black wrote the majority opinion, writing, "It is neither sacrilegious nor antireligious to say that each separate government in this country should stay out of the business of writing or sanctioning official prayers." The Court ruled that the prayer went against the Establishment Clause of the First Amendment.

The one dissenting opinion came from Justice Potter Stewart, who said sometimes religious elements could be added to governments without going against the Establishment Clause. He specifically brought up "In God We Trust" being on currency as an example.[121]

*Engel v. Vitale* reasserted the importance of the separation between church and state. It banned state government officials from trying to make prayer an official part of public schools, and it was the first of several cases in which the Court used the Establishment Clause to ban religious activities in public schools. The decision remains controversial even today.

120   casetext.com/case/matter-of-engel-v-vitale
121   www.mtsu.edu/first-amendment/article/665/engel-v-vitale

# 45. Gideon v. Wainwright (1963)

This case began in Panama City, Florida, on June 3, 1961. On that day, sometime between midnight and eight o'clock in the morning, someone broke into the Bay Harbor Pool Room and stole money from a cash register. One witness later reported that they had seen a man named Clarence Earl Gideon walk out of the poolroom at around five thirty that morning with a wine bottle and his pockets filled with wads of cash. Gideon, a drifter who spent most of his adult life in and out of different prisons for nonviolent crimes, was an easy target. Police arrested him immediately.

As it turns out, Gideon had *no* money. Because he couldn't afford a lawyer to defend himself, he asked a Florida Circuit Court judge to appoint one for him, claiming the Sixth Amendment of the Constitution guarantees everyone a lawyer. The judge denied the request. Florida law only allowed the court to provide a lawyer if the defendant was charged with a capital offense or one so serious that death might be the punishment for it. Gideon faced a felony, but not a capital offense, of course.

Therefore, Gideon had to represent himself, and most say he didn't do that well in court defending himself. In part because of this, on August 4, 1961, the Bay County Circuit Court found him guilty of breaking and entering with the intent to commit a misdemeanor and sentenced him to five years in prison. While serving his sentence in a Florida state prison, Gideon began to teach himself law, which made him even more confident that his rights were violated when the Florida Circuit Court refused to provide a lawyer for him. He decided to sue the Secretary of the Florida Department of Corrections, a dude named Henry Grady Cochran. However, the Florida Supreme Court refused to hear his case. In response, from his prison cell, he mailed a handwritten letter directly to the Supreme Court asking *it* to consider his case. To his surprise, the Supreme Court read his petition and agreed to hear his case.

By this time, Cochran had retired, and in his place was Louie Wainwright. So now Gideon was suing Wainwright. The Court assigned Gideon a well-respected lawyer from the District of Columbia, Abe Fortas, to represent him. Fortas would be a future Supreme Court justice. So why did the Court so easily agree to hear Gideon's case? As it turns out, they had been waiting for this opportunity. As you may recall, in *Powell v. Alabama* (1932), the Court had decided that people accused of crimes should both be notified that they have the right to a lawyer *and* should be provided one if they can't afford one. However, this only applied to capital offenses. In *Betts v. Brady* (1942), the Court said unless there were special circumstances, people didn't have to have a lawyer provided for them by the state. Many on the Court believed the *Powell* decision and *Betts* decision didn't go far enough. They heard oral arguments on March 18, 1963.

**The Big Question in this case:**

- Does the Sixth Amendment's stipulation that citizens have a right to a lawyer in criminal cases extend to all felony cases?

The Court said yes. On March 18, 1963, it announced that it had unanimously sided with Gideon. In doing so, it overturned the *Betts* decision. The Court argued that the Sixth Amendment doesn't point out a difference between capital and noncapital cases. Therefore, *all* felony cases should guarantee the defendant a lawyer if they can't afford one. The Court also argued that the Fourteenth Amendment's Due Process Clause gave the federal government authority to control state laws that denied Sixth Amendment rights.[122]

That said, the decision did *not* free Gideon from prison. Instead, he got a new trial with a new lawyer provided by the government of Florida. The new trial took place on August 5, 1963, five months after the Supreme Court decision. His new lawyer completely discredited the original case against Gideon. The jury found Gideon not guilty after one hour of deliberation. Gideon was free.

*Gideon v. Wainwright* further protected the rights of the accused, which the Warren Court would soon do again with the *Miranda v. Arizona* (1966) decision. The decision also even further expanded the power of the Fourteenth Amendment, protecting individual rights against both federal and state laws that threatened them. The decision created a huge increase in the need for public defenders, and today Americans take it for granted that a lawyer will be provided for them if they can't afford one. However, unfortunately today many states do not provide adequate funding for their public defender systems. As a matter of fact, in recent years the Missouri government got in trouble for not adequately funding its public defender systems.[123]

Speaking of Missouri, that's where Gideon was buried after he died in 1972 after living the rest of his life in relative obscurity. Gideon's grave was unmarked and largely forgotten until 1984, when the American Civil Liberties Union placed a granite headstone

122   www.oyez.org/cases/1962/155
123   www.aclu.org/press-releases/court-rules-missouris-waiting-list-public-defender-violate-
       constitutional-right

on his grave. On the stone is a quote from a letter Gideon had written to Abe Fortas before the Supreme Court saw his case. It says, "I believe that each era finds an improvement in law for the benefit of mankind."

# 46. New York Times Co. v. Sullivan (1964)

This case began in New York City on March 29, 1960. On that day, the *New York Times* published a full-page advertisement called "Heed Their Rising Voices," which brought attention to the persecution of and violence against civil rights protestors throughout the South. It specifically talked trash about the Montgomery, Alabama police force, saying that they had arrested Dr. Martin Luther King seven times and that "truckloads" of them had stormed the Alabama State College Campus. As it turns out, they arrested King *four* times and had only been sent *near* Alabama State College, so the ad had stretched the truth. When Montgomery's police commissioner, L.B. Sullivan, saw the ad, he viewed it as a personal attack on him and his entire police force.

Even though the ad didn't specifically name Sullivan, he decided to write the *New York Times*, asking the newspaper to publish a retraction of the ad. In other words, Sullivan wanted the *New York Times* to take it all back, admitting it published false information. Well, the *New York Times* issued no such retraction. Instead, its lawyers wrote Sullivan a letter that said the newspaper had no good reason to publish a retraction. Specifically, their letter said, "we…are somewhat puzzled as to how you think the statements in any way reflect on you," adding, "you might, if you desire, let us know in what respect you claim that the statements in the advertisement reflect on you."[124]

Sullivan didn't like that so much. He sued the *New York Times*, saying the newspaper broke Alabama's law for libel, written defamation that hurts the reputation of someone or something. He also sued four African American ministers mentioned in the ad. After this, the *New York Times* issued a retraction, but only for the governor of Alabama, John Patterson, not Sullivan. In the Circuit Court of Montgomery County, Sullivan only had to prove that the *New York Times* published mistakes and that they probably hurt his reputation. The court sided with Sullivan, ordering the *New York Times* to award him with $500,000 in damages, nearly five million dollars today. The *New York Times* appealed to the Alabama Supreme Court, but it agreed with the lower court. After this, the newspaper appealed again, this time to the *supreme* Supreme Court, which agreed to hear oral arguments in January 1964. The *New York Times*, of course, argued that the First Amendment protected their right to publish that ad.

124  supreme.justia.com/cases/federal/us/376/254/

- Does Alabama's libel law go against the First Amendment's freedom of speech and freedom of press protections?

The Court said yes. On March 9, 1964, it announced that it had unanimously sided with the *New York Times*. The Court argued that Alabama's libel law was unconstitutional, saying it went against the First Amendment. Justice William Brennan wrote the majority opinion. He stressed that a huge point of the First Amendment was to criticize those working in government. Therefore, the threshold should be high when it comes to restricting such speech.[125]

The Court acknowledged that libel, as well as *all* defamation, should still be taken into serious consideration. To still protect the reputations of public figures, it came up with the "actual malice" test. If a public figure could prove in court that the defamation against them was made "with knowledge that it was false or with reckless disregard of whether it was false or not," then they should win damages. In addition, the Court said a public official seeking damages had to prove the defendant's defamatory message hurt them specifically. In other words, they couldn't win damages if the defamatory message was broadly about government policy. Not only that, the public official had the burden of proof. *The public official* was the one who had to prove the defamatory message was made with "actual malice."[126]

*New York Times v. Sullivan* was a huge victory for freedom of the press and freedom of speech. Prior to this decision, states handled defamation, and laws that handled how public figures could recover damages for having their reputations hurt varied across the country. The *Sullivan* decision effectively standardized defamation, putting the First Amendment at the forefront. In the following years, the Supreme Court would continue to expand media protections from lawsuits not just from government officials but *any* public figures. Because of this case, if you're well-known in society, and someone makes up stuff about you in the media, it's going to be difficult to win damages in court.

125   www.oyez.org/cases/1963/39
126   casetext.com/case/new-york-times-company-v-sullivan-1

# 47. Reynolds v. Sims (1964)

This case began in Birmingham, Alabama, on August 26, 1961. On that day, a group of lawyers from the city, led by M.O. Sims, sued multiple officials in charge of Alabama elections, including a judge known as B.A. Reynolds. The lawyers claimed that state officials had violated the Equal Protection Clause of the Fourteenth Amendment because they had refused to make the state's districts more fair. The votes of Alabama residents who lived in urban areas didn't count nearly as much as the votes of Alabama residents who lived in rural areas. *Wait a second; this sounds familiar.* Why, of course! Just a few months prior, the Supreme Court had heard oral arguments for the case *Baker v. Carr* (1962). In that case, the Court was only considering how *Tennessee* was dividing up its representative districts. However, folks in other states wanted in on the action, too. After all, representative disparities were happening all over the country...like in Connecticut, where one state house district represented just 191 people...or in Utah, where the smallest district represented 165 people and the largest represented 32,380. Holy crap.

Sure enough, there were also big representative disparities in Alabama. The Alabama Constitution established that there had to be only one state senator per county. Well, this led to one county having *forty-one times more voters* than another county. Imagine, if you will, one district has 100,000 people living in it and another district has 4.1 million people, yet both districts both have one senator. This was happening in Alabama. M.O. Sims and the other aforementioned lawyers filed a complaint in the US District Court for the Middle District of Alabama, arguing that, since the population growth of Alabama had been uneven since the last time districts were updated, citizens of urban areas in the state were facing discrimination with respect to legislative representation. The US District Court for the Middle District of Alabama agreed and demanded the Alabama state legislature take action to make the state's representative districts more fair.[127]

Reynolds decided to appeal the case. His lawyers argued that the Constitution said nothing about how states should determine their methods of representation. They argued that the district lines were drawn based on historical precedent and Alabama's unique geography. This didn't worry Sims that much, however, as the Court had decided in *Baker v. Carr* that Tennessee had to redraw *its* districts to make them more representative. While

---

the Supreme Court had five other cases to consider that were similar, it chose *Reynolds v. Sims* as the case it would focus on to settle the equal representation problem once and for all.[128] It heard oral arguments on November 13, 1963. Sims argued that the "one person, one vote" principle should apply to not just federal districts but also *state* legislative districts.

## The Big Question in this case:

- Does the Fourteenth Amendment's Equal Protection Clause require states to have equal representation in their state legislatures?

The Court said yes. On June 15, 1964, it announced it had sided with Sims, 8–1, with Justice John Harlan II being the only one to dissent. The Fourteenth Amendment's Equal Protection Clause *did* require state legislatures to also have equal representation. Chief Justice Earl Warren wrote the majority opinion, saying, "Legislators represent people, not trees or acres. Legislators are elected by voters, not farms or cities or economic interests." This decision now meant that state legislatures had to create their districts based on population to make it so that there were roughly equal numbers of people in each district.[129] In other words, each person's vote had to carry the same weight. All votes ought to be equal. This idea, the "one person, one vote" principle, was not new by this point. As you (hopefully) recall, the Court first brought it up in the *Baker* decision, but it wasn't until Justice William Douglas said the following in a case called *Gray v. Sanders* (1963) that the principle became more widely known:

> How then can one person be given twice or 10 times the voting power of another person in a statewide election merely because he lives in a rural area [in the country]… all who participate in the election are to have an equal vote… This is required by the Equal Protection Clause of the Fourteenth Amendment…political equality…can mean only one thing—one person, one vote.

The Court brought up the principle again in the case *Wesberry v. Sanders* (1964), arguing that Georgia had unequal congressional districts. With *Reynolds v. Sims*, the Court solidified the "one person, one vote" principle. Unlike the *Baker* decision, the *Reynold* decision said *all* states needed to attempt to have as equal representative districts as possible for both state and federal elections. After the *Reynolds* decision, forty-nine state legislatures immediately had to redraw their districts since they weren't fair enough.

128    www.encyclopediaofalabama.org/article/h-2023
129    www.oyez.org/cases/1963/23

*Reynolds v. Sims* ended up becoming another important decision in the Civil Rights Movement, as many of the urban voters who benefited from it were African American. Today, many scholars consider it one of the best Supreme Court decisions in history.[130]

130    time.com/4055934/best-supreme-court-decisions/

# 48. Griswold v. Connecticut (1965)

This case began in New Haven, Connecticut, in November 1961, when Estelle Griswold and Dr. C. Lee Buxton opened a clinic where they gave advice and resources to married couples to help them avoid getting pregnant. They also prescribed contraceptives, or birth control, for married women. This was illegal in Connecticut. Local authorities arrested them for breaking a law that prohibited anyone from using "any drug, medicinal article, or instrument for the purpose of preventing conception." Connecticut had banned using birth control. With the help of P.T. Barnum, the state passed the law in 1879.

Griswold and Buxton, as well as many others, thought the law banning birth control was wrong. After they were found guilty of breaking it and fined a hundred dollars each, they appealed to the Appellate Division of the Circuit Court of Connecticut. Griswold and Buxton argued that banning birth control went against the Fourteenth Amendment of the US Constitution.

The Appellate Division of the Circuit Court disagreed, upholding their conviction, and so Griswold and Buxton appealed again, this time to the Connecticut Supreme Court. They also upheld it, and so Griswold and Buxton appealed once more, this time to the *supreme* Supreme Court. The Court agreed to hear oral arguments in March 1965. Catherine Roraback represented Griswold and Buxton, claiming that the birth control ban violated the right to marital privacy guaranteed by the Bill of Rights. However, the word "privacy" does not appear anywhere in the Constitution. Therefore, Roraback argued that "privacy" was implied by the First, Third, Fourth, and Ninth Amendments.[131] The Ninth Amendment stood out because it says we all had other rights not specifically listed in the Constitution. Throughout American history nobody seemed to give a crap about the Ninth Amendment and rarely brought it up.

## The Big Question in this case:

- Do the First, Third, Fourth, and Ninth Amendments protect the right of marital privacy against state restrictions on birth control?

The Court said yes. On June 7, 1965, the Court announced it had sided with Griswold, 7–2. Sure enough, they referenced the Ninth Amendment to back up their decision. They also brought up that the right to privacy was inherent in the First, Third, Fourth, and even Fifth Amendments, saying that the Due Process Clause of the Fourteenth Amendment should be applied to incorporate Bill of Rights protections to the states. Therefore, the Connecticut law banning birth control was unconstitutional. Again, the word "privacy" is not explicitly listed in the Constitution. However, it's one on which several other rights, including expression, for example, depend. Also, the Court concluded that privacy specifically within marriage was a personal zone that should be off-limits to the government.[132]

Justice William Douglas wrote the opinion. "Would we allow the police to search the sacred precincts of marital bedrooms for telltale signs of the use of contraceptives? The idea is repulsive to the notions of privacy surrounding the marriage relationship."

The two dissenting justices, Hugo Black and Potter Stewart, thought that finding "privacy" in the Constitution was too loose of an interpretation.

Regardless, *Griswold v. Connecticut* is a landmark case that gave Americans the right to privacy. So many cases afterward, including the more famous case *Roe v. Wade* (1973), cited Griswold as justification to expand or defend privacy. The decision is the reason why what happens in the bedroom stays in the bedroom, and it marked a big shift away from more traditional views on birth control. It remains incredibly relevant today, especially since privacy is constantly under threat due to increasingly intrusive technology and mass surveillance.

132   www.oyez.org/cases/1964/496

# 49. Miranda v. Arizona (1966)

This case began in Phoenix, Arizona, on March 13, 1963, when Phoenix police officers arrested Ernesto Miranda, a suspect linked to the kidnapping and rape of an eighteen-year-old woman ten days earlier. In a police lineup, the victim identified Miranda as the attacker. For two hours, officers aggressively interrogated Miranda about the attack. The officers did not tell Miranda that he did not have to answer the questions, nor did they allow him to call a lawyer. So Miranda didn't pay attention when his teacher taught him about the Bill of Rights in government class!

Anyway, the officers broke Miranda down, and he ultimately confessed to the crime, even signing a statement that described the details of the attack. After prosecutors later used this confession in Maricopa County Superior Court, a jury found Miranda guilty of kidnapping and rape, even though Miranda's lawyer had argued that the police *pressured* him to confess. Judge Yale McFate sentenced Miranda to up to thirty years in prison.

Miranda appealed to the Arizona Supreme Court, arguing that his Fifth and Sixth Amendment rights were ignored while the Phoenix police interrogated him. Specifically, the part of the Fifth Amendment that says you cannot be forced to testify against yourself, which is more commonly referred to as "the right to remain silent," and the part of the Sixth Amendment that says you have a right to an attorney. However, the Arizona Supreme Court agreed with the lower court, upholding Miranda's sentence.

Miranda appealed again, this time to the *supreme* Supreme Court, which agreed to hear oral arguments in February and March 1966. This was a tough one. The Court's justices went back and forth on how they would decide. They did decide, however, to focus on the Fifth Amendment, not the Sixth.

## The Big Questions in this case:

- Does the Fifth Amendment's protection against self-incrimination also include the interrogation of a suspect by the police?
- Should the police have to tell a defendant that they have the right to an attorney?

The Court said yes to both questions. However, this was a close one. In a 5–4 decision, the Court announced on June 13, 1966, that it had sided with Miranda, ruling that his confession could not be used as evidence because the officers had denied his right to remain silent when he was interrogated. Chief Justice Earl Warren wrote the majority opinion. Warren said the Phoenix police had messed up by misleading Miranda and not making his rights clear. Warren said, "The person in custody must, prior to interrogation, be clearly informed that he has the right to remain silent, and that anything he says will be used against him in court; he must be clearly informed that he has the right to consult with a lawyer and to have the lawyer with him during interrogation, and that, if he is indigent, a lawyer will be appointed to represent him."[133]

The justices who disagreed with the majority generally argued that the Constitution didn't say anything about making a suspect *aware* of their rights. In other words, they argued it shouldn't be the police's responsibility to teach suspects about their rights. The justices also argued the majority's decision would give too much power to suspects and would make police interrogation work much more difficult. In fact, they were afraid it might lead to it being more difficult to convict criminals.

After the decision, police across the country had to inform suspects of their rights after they arrested them. They became known as the "Miranda rights" or "Miranda warnings." This decision also caused the Supreme Court to more actively attempt to strike a balance between public safety and the rights of the accused. Several later decisions granted exceptions to the Miranda warnings. Some of these exceptions were *big* exceptions. Still, *Miranda v. Arizona* has had a huge impact on law enforcement in the United States by empowering those accused of a crime. According to several studies, the decision has had little effect on detectives' abilities to solve crimes.[134,135]

So whatever happened to Ernesto Miranda? Even though the Supreme Court threw out his original trial, he found himself in Maricopa County Superior Court after prosecutors used different evidence against him. That evidence? A woman who lived with Miranda during the time of the crime testified that he had confessed to her about committing the crime. On March 1, 1967, a different jury found him guilty, and a different judge sentenced him to up to thirty years in prison.[136] However, in 1972, Miranda was released early due to good behavior. He returned to his old neighborhood and made a living autographing

133   www.law.cornell.edu/supremecourt/text/384/436

134   scholarlycommons.law.northwestern.edu/cgi/viewcontent.cgi?article=6874&context=jclc

135   Ryan, Meghan J., Is *Miranda* Good News or Bad News for the Police? The Usefulness of Empirical Evidence (2017). Texas Tech Law Review, Vol. 50, No. 1, 2017, SMU Dedman School of Law Legal Studies Research Paper No. 422

136   www.encyclopedia.com/law/law-magazines/ernesto-miranda-trials-1963-1967

what became known as "Miranda cards," which contained the test of the warning read to suspects. Tragically, he was stabbed to death in a bar fight on January 31, 1976. Soon after, Phoenix police arrested a dude suspected of murdering Miranda. Ironically, that dude, unlike Miranda, exercised his right to remain silent and was later released after there was no evidence to prove that he committed the crime!

# 50. In re Gault (1967)

This case began in Globe, Arizona, on June 8, 1964. On that day, the sheriff of Gila County arrested fifteen-year-old Gerald "Jerry" Gault after his neighbor, Ora Cook, accused him of being obscene to her on the telephone. The sheriff also arrested Jerry's friend, Ronald Lewis, who Cook also accused of saying obscene stuff on the phone to her. At the time of the arrest, Jerry's parents were both at work, and the sheriff had made no effort to let them know about their son's arrest. When Jerry's mom got home from work, she had Jerry's older brother go looking for him. Only after Ronald's family notified the Gaults did they know that Jerry had been arrested. She rushed to the county jail to see him, but the sheriff did not let her take him home.

The next morning, Judge Robert McGhee of the Gila County superior court led Jerry's preliminary hearing. At the hearing, Jerry claimed that Ronald was the one who said all the vulgar stuff. All Jerry admitted to was dialing the number.[137] Regardless, McGhee wouldn't even set him free for a few days, and gave Jerry's family no explanation for keeping him in custody for so long. Jerry got a formal hearing, again led by Judge McGhee, on June 15, 1964, but his parents were not allowed to attend. In fact, Jerry's accuser, Ora Cook, also didn't attend the hearing. Jerry did not get a lawyer to defend him. After Judge McGhee found Jerry guilty of making "lewd phone calls," he ordered him to a juvenile detention center for six years.[138] In other words, he wouldn't be free until he was twenty-one years old. It's worth noting that if an adult had been convicted of the same crime, their maximum punishment only would have been a fifty-dollar fine and two months in jail.

Jerry's parents filed a petition for a writ of habeas corpus, claiming that their son was not given a fair trial. They filed the petition with the Supreme Court of Arizona to try to get Jerry freed. However, the Arizona Supreme Court referred the case back to Judge McGhee, who, you guessed it...denied the petition, claiming that Jerry had committed a misdemeanor by using "vulgar, abusive, or obscene language...while in the presence or hearing of any woman or child."[139] Jerry's parents appealed his conviction to the Arizona Supreme Court, but it agreed with McGhee and upheld the conviction. Jerry's parents appealed again, this time to the *supreme* Supreme Court, and they agreed to hear oral arguments on December 6, 1966. Sure, it was easy for the Court to see how Jerry's Fifth and Sixth Amendment rights were being trampled, but the broader question was whether

137   www.crimefreefuture.com/wp-content/uploads/2016/05/In-re-Gault-387-U.S.-1-1967.pdf
138   www.uscourts.gov/educational-resources/educational-activities/facts-and-case-summary-re-gault
139   supreme.justia.com/cases/federal/us/387/1/#4

the Constitution protected juveniles, or those under eighteen years old, in the same way it protected adults.

## The Big Question in this case:

- Was the way that Gault was committed to a juvenile detention center constitutional under the Due Process Clause of the Fourteenth Amendment?

The Court said no. On May 15, 1967, it announced it had sided with Gault, 8–1. The proceedings of Arizona's Juvenile Court were unconstitutional. Justice Abe Fortas, a known advocate for children's rights, wrote the majority opinion. The Court argued that the Fourteenth Amendment's Due Process Clause had required that juveniles have the same rights as adults in the criminal justice system. More specifically, Jerry Gault, as well as *all* juveniles, had:

1.  The right to remain silent

2.  The right to know the charges against them

3.  The right to a lawyer

4.  The right to have their guilt proven beyond a reasonable doubt

5.  The right to confront and cross-examine witnesses; and

6.  The right to appeal a judge's decision

The Court found that Arizona's Juvenile Court system had failed at protecting all six of these rights. They ordered Gault to be set free.

*In re Gault* was a huge case because it expanded Fourteenth Amendment protections to juvenile defendants. Kids must get the same rights as adults! It dramatically changed the entire juvenile system across the country. After this case, judges could no longer randomly and unfairly give out punishments at juvenile delinquency proceedings. For the first time, the Court clearly said kids deserve constitutional protections, too.

# 51. Loving v. Virginia (1967)

This case began in Central Point, Virginia, in the spring of 1958. It was then that Mildred Jeter, a woman of both African American and Native American ancestry, discovered that she was pregnant, and that Richard Loving, a man of mostly European ancestry, was the father. The two decided to get married. They were, after all, in love, so it made sense.

However, in the state of Virginia, interracial marriages were illegal at the time. Well, this didn't stop Mildred and Richard. They went up to the District of Columbia, where interracial marriages were legal, and tied the knot on June 2, 1958. They then returned home to live with each other back in Virginia. Somehow word must have gotten out about the couple, because shortly thereafter the local sheriff ordered a late-night raid of their home. You read that correctly. In the middle of the night, police not only burst into their home, but also burst into their *bedroom*, hoping to catch them having sex, which was also illegal in Virginia at the time. The Lovings were sleeping at the time and awoke to be arrested for violating Virginia's Racial Integrity Act, the law that said "whites" and "non-whites" could not marry each other.

The Lovings pled guilty, and the judge sentenced them to one year in prison. However, on January 6, 1959, the judge suspended their sentence as long as they moved out of Virginia and never returned as a married couple for twenty-five years. After this, the Lovings moved up to the same city where they had gotten married, Washington, DC. The Lovings did occasionally sneak back down to Virginia, but for five years they lived in DC and hated it. As Mildred and Richard's family grew there, they missed their family back home and a more rural lifestyle.[140] In 1964, tired of living as an exile, Mildred wrote to Attorney General Robert Kennedy. Kennedy got Mildred's letter, referring it to the American Civil Liberties Union, or ACLU, who then reached out to the Lovings.

The ACLU's two volunteer cooperating attorneys, Bernie Cohen and Philip Hirschkop, filed a motion on behalf of the Lovings to the Virginia Caroline County Circuit Court, requesting it to allow the marriage since denying it broke the Fourteenth Amendment's Equal Protection Clause. The County Circuit Court didn't respond, so Cohen and Hirschkop sued the US District Court for the Eastern District of Virginia. After losing that lawsuit, the ACLU helped the Lovings appeal to the Virginia Supreme Court. While the Virginia Supreme

Court also upheld the constitutionality of the interracial marriage ban, it also got rid of the sentence banning the Lovings from the state of Virginia.

It's important to bring up that during all of this, Mildred and Richard Loving got *a lot* of national media attention. They were *not* looking for all of this attention, but it helped raise awareness of their struggle, especially after *Life* magazine took pictures of them.

Meanwhile, the ACLU had expected all the pushback it was getting from the state of Virginia, so they were well prepared to appeal to the Supreme Court, which agreed to take on the case. The Lovings, who were done being in the spotlight, decided to stay home on April 10, 1967, when the Court heard oral arguments. By that time, nine years had passed since they got married.

## The Big Question in this case:

- Did Virginia's law banning interracial marriage go against the Equal Protection Clause of the Fourteenth Amendment?

The Court said yes. On June 12, 1967, it announced that it had unanimously sided with the Lovings, overturning their convictions and ruling Virginia's interracial marriage ban unconstitutional. Chief Justice Earl Warren wrote the majority opinion, stating that Virginia's Racial Integrity Act went against the Equal Protection Clause *and* Due Process Clause of the Fourteenth Amendment. He wrote, "The Fourteenth Amendment requires that the freedom of choice to marry not be restricted by invidious racial discrimination. Under our Constitution, the freedom to marry, or not marry, a person of another race resides with the individual and cannot be infringed by the State."[141] The Court also argued that any laws banning interracial marriage were racist, with the sole purpose to keep white supremacy going.

Despite the Court's unanimous opinion in *Loving v. Virginia*, interracial marriage bans remained on the books in several states, though authorities couldn't enforce them. The last state to get them off the books was Alabama in 2000. After the *Loving* decision, the number of interracial marriages steadily increased across the United States. In 1967, 3 percent of new marriages in the country were considered interracial. By 2015, it was up to 17 percent.[142] Speaking of 2015, that was the year same-sex marriage became legal in the United States due to the Court's decision *Obergefell v. Hodges*. In fact, the *Loving* decision paved the way for the *Obergefell* decision. Today, we get to marry who we want.

---

141  supreme.justia.com/cases/federal/us/388/1/
142  www.pewresearch.org/social-trends/2017/05/18/intermarriage-in-the-u-s-50-years-after-loving-v-virginia/

# 52. Katz v. United States (1967)

This case began in Los Angeles, California, on February 25, 1965. On that day, a dude named Charles Katz made a phone call at a public telephone booth near his apartment on Sunset Boulevard. Katz had made these calls to various states regularly for years. He was a professional gambler, mostly placing bets on college basketball games, and he would conduct his gambling business on these pay phones.

As it turns out, interstate sports gambling was illegal in the country at the time, and the FBI was spying on him. They recorded his conversations after installing hidden listening devices attached to the outside of the phone booth. Shortly after recording these conversations, the FBI arrested Katz at his apartment. They charged him with eight counts of knowingly transmitting wagering information by phone between American states. However, there was one potential problem with the FBI's plan—the agents had not secured a search warrant before spying on Katz. The Fourth Amendment of the US Constitution states that, unless law enforcement officers have probable cause, they need a warrant to spy on a suspect.

Well, perhaps the agents were not that worried since in the case *Olmstead v. United States* (1928), the Supreme Court said the Fourth Amendment didn't apply to wiretapping phones to listen in on conversations. In fact, the Court determined that private phone conversations were no different than conversations overheard in a public area. Unless there was a *physical intrusion* by law enforcement, such spying was okay. This became known as the "trespass doctrine."

Katz may have been out of luck due to the precedent set by *Olmstead v. United States*, but thirty-seven years had passed since that decision. Times had changed. *Technology* had changed. Katz decided to fight back. In the US District Court for the Southern District of California, he tried to prevent the FBI's incriminating phone booth recordings from being used as evidence since they didn't have a warrant. However, the judge denied the request, and he was convicted of transmitting wagering information by telephone based on those recordings.[143]

With the help of young lawyer Harvey Schneider, Katz appealed his conviction to the US Court of Appeals for the Ninth Circuit, but it agreed with the lower court, so Katz appealed once more to the Supreme Court, and it agreed to hear oral arguments on October 17, 1967.

143  www.law.cornell.edu/supremecourt/text/389/347

**The Big Questions in this case:**

- Do people deserve privacy when they step into a phone booth to make calls, regardless of the legality of the conversation they're having on those phones?
- Does the Fourth Amendment's protection against unreasonable searches and seizures make it so that law enforcement has to get a search warrant to wiretap a public pay phone?

The Court answered yes to both questions. On December 18, 1967, it announced it had sided with Katz, 7–1. The Court argued that the recordings could not be used as evidence against Katz because they went against his right to privacy, but, more importantly, went against the Fourth Amendment's protection against unreasonable searches and seizures.[144]

Justice Potter Stewart wrote the majority opinion. "[Katz] has strenuously argued that the booth was a "constitutionally protected area." The government has maintained with equal vigor that it was not. But this effort to decide whether a given "area" viewed in the abstract, is "constitutionally protected" deflects attention from the problem presented by this case. The Fourth Amendment protects people, not places. What a person knowingly exposes to the public, even in his home or office, is not a subject of Fourth Amendment protection. But what he seeks to preserve as private, even in an area accessible to the public, may be constitutionally protected."[145] In other words, the Court ruled that privacy for American citizens had now extended beyond the home, and it expanded privacy into the electronic age. Justice John Marshall Harlan II even described a test to attempt to identify a "reasonable expectation of privacy." With this decision, the Court overturned *Olmstead v. United States*, therefore ditching the trespass doctrine.[146]

*Katz v. United States* might be the most important Supreme Court case to ever look at privacy, and the best example of a case we have in history in which the Court earnestly attempted to clarify what privacy *meant*. Due to rapidly changing communication and surveillance technology, the Court has often been slow to address these privacy concerns. In fact, the next landmark Supreme Court case that dealt with privacy in telecommunications wouldn't happen for another fifty years, with *Carpenter v. United States* (2018).

144   www.oyez.org/cases/1967/35
145   supreme.justia.com/cases/federal/us/389/347/
146   constitutioncenter.org/blog/katz-v-united-states-the-fourth-amendment-adapts-to-new-technology

# 53. Terry v. Ohio (1968)

This case began in downtown Cleveland, Ohio, on October 31, 1963. On that day, Martin McFadden, a Cleveland detective with thirty-nine years of experience, got suspicious when he saw two men pacing in front of a jewelry store.

The two men, John Terry and Richard Chilton, went back and forth, according to various accounts, between twelve and twenty-four times. They took turns starting a block or two away, and then would routinely walk up to the jewelry store window to peek in and return to chat about it. Soon, a third man, Carl Katz, approached Terry and Chilton and talked with them before leaving.

McFadden had seen enough. After the three men rejoined in front of Zucker's, a clothing store, McFadden decided to approach them. McFadden was in street clothes but identified himself as a police officer and asked them for their names. After the men "mumbled something" in response, McFadden frisked them, patting them down to search for hidden weapons or illegal stuff.

After McFadden frisked the men, he found a .38-caliber automatic pistol in Terry's overcoat pocket and a .38-caliber revolver in Chilton's pocket. Later, McFadden would argue he only did a pat-down before reaching into their pockets for the guns. That said, he never reached into the pockets of Katz. McFadden arrested all three men, but since Katz didn't have a weapon on him, the police released him and only charged Terry and Chilton with illegally carrying concealed weapons.[147] Keep in mind that the facts of what Terry, Chilton, and Katz did on that day have been heavily disputed. Regardless, it was McFadden's word against theirs, and McFadden was trusted.[148]

At the trial, Terry and Chilton's lawyer argued that the evidence of the guns couldn't be used in court since McFadden's frisk of them went against the Fourth Amendment. In other words, it was an illegal search and seizure. As you (hopefully) recall from the chapter about *Mapp v. Ohio* (1961), this law, the exclusionary rule, said you couldn't use evidence if the police got it illegally.

The Cuyahoga County Common Pleas Court disagreed, finding Terry and Chilton guilty. They ruled that, due to both the suspicious nature of their behavior and McFadden's concern for his safety, the "stop and frisk," as it's now commonly known, was reasonable. Terry appealed to the Ohio District Court of Appeals, which agreed with the lower court.

147   www.acluohio.org/en/cases/terry-v-ohio-392-us-1-1968
148   olemiss.edu/depts/ncjrl/pdf/katzMSLJO4.pdf

After that, Terry appealed again, this time to the Supreme Court of Ohio, but it dismissed the appeal, saying that it involved "no constitutional question."

By the time Terry had tried to appeal his case to the *supreme* Supreme Court, it was 1967, a time when more and more Americans were losing their trust in the police. African Americans had good reasons not to trust the police, as they faced persecution and discrimination by them across the country. And Terry and Chilton were African American.

Perhaps influenced by the shift in attitude toward the police, the Supreme Court agreed to hear oral arguments on December 12, 1967. By this time, the American Civil Liberties Union, or ACLU, was helping Terry.

## The Big Question in this case:

- Was the stop-and-frisk of Terry and the other men a violation of the Fourth Amendment?

The Court said no. On June 10, 1968, it announced it had sided with Ohio, 8–1. The Court said the police could stop-and-frisk suspects as long as there was a "reasonable suspicion" that the suspect was about to commit a crime. The majority believed the search and seizure of Terry and the others was reasonable since it did seem like it was possible that they would rob that jewelry store. After all, McFadden had thirty-nine years of police experience, so he would know better than most what an armed robbery looked like.

However, this case remains extremely controversial today. Because of that, I will bring up the one dissenting opinion by Justice William Douglas. He *strongly* disagreed with the decision, saying, "We hold today that the police have greater authority to make a 'seizure' and conduct a 'search' than a judge has to authorize such action. We have said precisely the opposite over and over again." He added, "To give the police greater power than a magistrate is to take a long step down the totalitarian path. Perhaps such a step is desirable to cope with modern forms of lawlessness. But if it is taken, it should be the deliberate choice of the people through a constitutional amendment."[149]

*Terry v. Ohio* had huge implications. The case expanded police authority in crime investigations and made it much more difficult to charge police officers with misconduct. It's a controversial case today largely due to its unintended consequences. Today, police departments across the country regularly practice stop-and-frisk, still referred to as "Terry stops." However, many have called for a ban on them, arguing that they have in fact *not* contributed to a decline in the crime rate but instead made systemic racism worse.

New York City probably has the most visible and notorious stop-and-frisk program, but in 2020, the New York City Police Department reassigned its six hundred plainclothes officers in response to the nationwide protests after the killing of George Floyd. The year before they did this, 59 percent of suspects stopped and frisked by New York City Police were African American, even though African Americans made up only 24 percent of New York City's population.[150]

150   www.nyclu.org/en/stop-and-frisk-data

# 54. Tinker v. Des Moines (1969)

This case began in Des Moines, Iowa, on December 16, 1965. On that day, fifteen-year-old John Tinker, his thirteen-year-old sister Mary Beth Tinker, his eleven-year-old sister Hope Tinker, and his eight-year-old brother Paul Tinker, along with his friend, sixteen-year-old Christopher Eckhardt, wore black armbands to school to protest the ongoing Vietnam War. The principals of the schools had all told their students they couldn't wear these armbands or they would be punished. Well, they wore them anyway. The principals suspended John, Mary Beth, and Christopher, saying they couldn't come back to school unless they came not wearing the armbands. The students would not return to school until January, but in protest still wore black clothing every day for the rest of the school year.

Meanwhile, after the suspension of the students made the front page of the *Des Moines Register*, the Iowa Civil Liberties Union approached the Tinkers and told them that the school district shouldn't have been allowed to do that. They suggested that the Tinkers sue the school district and offered to help them. Ultimately, the American Civil Liberties Union, or ACLU, stepped in to help the Tinker family and Eckhardt sue the Des Moines Independent Community School District, arguing that the freedom of speech part of the First Amendment protected the students' right to protest at school.[151] Obviously, the kids couldn't sue, so their parents filed suit.

The US District Court for the Southern District of Iowa upheld the prohibition of armbands. While it acknowledged the students had the right to protest under the First Amendment, their concern was that a school would have a hard time keeping an orderly environment where students could learn stuff if protests like this were going on. The Tinkers and Eckhardts appealed to the US Court of Appeals for the Eighth Circuit, but that court was evenly divided, so they appealed directly to the Supreme Court, which agreed to hear oral arguments on November 12, 1968. By this time, the Vietnam War, and the antiwar movement, had dramatically escalated, so this case got national attention.

While *West Virginia State Board of Education v. Barnette* (1943) had already said students had constitutional protections at school, that case didn't specifically deal with free speech rights as this case did. Dan Johnston, the lawyer for the students, said the district had previously let *other* kinds of political speech occur and that such speech *didn't* disrupt learning at school. Allan Herrick, the lawyer for the school district, said schools should be allowed to limit speech if such speech seems like it could lead to "violence, disorder, and disruption." That didn't seem convincing to most of the Court, however.

## The Big Question in this case:

- Does a public-school ban on symbolic protests by students go against the First Amendment?

The Court said yes. On February 24, 1969, it announced it had sided with Tinker and company, 7–2. The Court argued the armbands symbolized pure speech that was separate from any actions of those wearing them. The Court also argued that being on school property didn't mean the students lost their First Amendment rights.[152] Justice Abe Fortas wrote the majority opinion, saying, "It can hardly be argued that either students or teachers shed their constitutional rights to freedom of speech or expression at the schoolhouse gate."[153]

Justice Hugo Black wrote a dissent, saying that the armbands did, in fact, disrupt school activities. Several future Supreme Court justices agreed with Black, as seen in decisions like *Bethel School District v. Fraser* (1986) and *Morse v. Frederick* (2007), which further limited student speech at public schools.

Regardless, *Tinker v. Des Moines Independent Community School District* has been a hugely influential and frequently cited case regarding First Amendment rights for students. It created the "Tinker Test," or a way to see if student speech is disruptive at school. It weakened the legal idea that the school takes the place of the parent while the student is in attendance. You could even say the *Tinker* decision paved the way for every student protest that has happened ever since. Today, Mary Beth Tinker still goes on speaking tours to schools around the country, teaching students about their rights and promoting youth activism.[154]

152   www.oyez.org/cases/1968/21
153   supreme.justia.com/cases/federal/us/393/503/
154   splc.org/2023/02/student-press-freedom-day-2023/

# 55. Brandenburg v. Ohio (1969)

This case began in rural Ohio, northeast of Cincinnati, on June 28, 1964. On that day, Clarence Brandenburg led a Ku Klux Klan rally. He even invited a Cincinnati television station to cover the event. The television station filmed portions of the rally, showing men in robes and hoods, some carrying guns and others shouting horrible ethnic slurs. The station also filmed KKK members burning a giant cross. Brandenburg concluded the rally with a speech, and portions of it aired on TV. In that speech, Brandenburg said, "If our President, our Congress, our Supreme Court continues to suppress the white, Caucasian race, it's possible that there might have to be some revengeance taken." I don't know what "revengeance" means. I looked it up online, and Urban Dictionary says it's "the act of gaining revenge at a rate of at least 2.54 times greater to that of standard revenge." That doesn't seem too nice to me. It seems threatening.

After the television station aired the KKK rally, local authorities arrested Brandenburg for leading the rally and arranging it to be on the news. They charged him with breaking the Ohio Criminal Syndicalism Act, a law that prohibited promoting violence as a means for social or political change. The Court of Common Pleas in Hamilton County, Ohio, convicted Brandenburg, fined him a thousand dollars, and sentenced him to one to ten years in prison.

Brandenburg argued that his actions were protected under both the First Amendment and Fourteenth Amendment. Even though he personally hated the American Civil Liberties Union, or ACLU, he asked them for help after he ran out of money to pay for a lawyer. In early 1968, Brandenburg appealed to the Ohio First District Court of Appeal, but it agreed with the lower court. He next appealed to the Ohio Supreme Court, who dismissed his appeal without even giving an opinion.[155] To the courts in Ohio, it was clear that this speech was not protected under the First Amendment, and they used the Supreme Court case *Dennis v. United States* (1951) to back this up.[156]

However, Brandenburg and the ACLU weren't done yet. They appealed to the Supreme Court, and the Court agreed to take on the case, hearing oral arguments on February 27, 1969. Brandenburg's lawyer, Allen Brown, convinced Brandenburg to stay

155  brooklynworks.brooklaw.edu/cgi/viewcontent.cgi?article=2220&context=blr
156  www.mtsu.edu/first-amendment/article/189/brandenburg-v-ohio

home, which probably was a wise move. Brown received several threats over the phone for representing a KKK leader. Some even accused him of agreeing with KKK positions. However, Brown later clarified that he was defending free speech.

## The Big Question in this case:

- Did the Ohio Criminal Syndicalism Act go against Brandenburg's right to free speech as protected by both the First and Fourteenth Amendments?

The Court said yes. On June 8, 1969, it announced it had sided unanimously with Brandenburg, thus reversing the decisions of the lower courts. Not one judge authored the decision, showing just how unified the Court was with it. The Court said the Ohio Criminal Syndicalism Act went against Brandenburg's right to free speech, as protected under the First Amendment, and that they had the authority to declare the law unconstitutional thanks to the Fourteenth Amendment.

One case that I didn't cover was *Whitney v. California* (1927), which *upheld* a conviction of someone who had said stuff that threatened society. In that case, the Court had developed the Bad Tendency test, which modified the Clear and Present Danger doctrine first developed by Justice Oliver Wendell Holmes in *Schenck v. United States* (1919). Well, the *Brandenburg* decision ended up throwing out the Bad Tendency test and overruling the *Whitney* decision and *Schenck* decision. While it didn't throw out the Clear and Present Danger doctrine, it modified it by introducing the Brandenburg test, also (more boringly) known as the Imminent Lawless Action Test.

The test had two parts:

1. Speech can be banned if it is "directed at inciting or producing imminent lawless action."

And, more importantly…

2. Speech can be banned if it is "likely to incite or produce action."

Because Brandenburg's rally and speech were somewhat vague and didn't make it seem likely that the KKK was going to carry out a revolt against the government, Jews, and people of color, it passed the Brandenburg test.[157] As disturbing as it was, the KKK's speech was protected by the First Amendment.

*Brandenburg v. Ohio* further protected speech, even extremely offensive and unpopular speech. It provided an answer to the debate between those who wanted more

157   www.oyez.org/cases/1968/492

government control of speech to keep people safe and those who wanted speech to be as free as possible. The Brandenburg test continues to be the standard when Americans want to punish speech meant to get people angry to the point where they get violent. It's the reason why the courts continue to stick up for creators of violent media, even when there is much public outcry.[158]

# 56. Swann v. Charlotte-Mecklenburg Board of Education (1971)

This case began in Charlotte, North Carolina, in 1965. By this time, the Charlotte-Mecklenburg school district had still not desegregated its schools since the decision in *Brown v. Board of Education* (1954), which declared that racially segregated schools were unconstitutional. Vera and Darius Swann were frustrated that their six-year-old son couldn't attend the school closest to their house. With the help of the NAACP, they joined other African American parents to sue the school district. In the US District Court for the Western District of North Carolina, Judge James Craven sided with the Charlotte-Mecklenburg school district, citing that the US Constitution said nothing about governments having to integrate schools.

However, flash forward to 1969, and the Swanns filed the lawsuit again after a new judge was now sitting in the US District Court for the Western District of North Carolina: James Bryan McMillan. In fact, this would be his first important case on the federal bench. McMillan used to be against school integration, but after hearing the arguments, he had a change of heart. He sided with the parents, ordering the Charlotte-Mecklenburg school district to make all its schools as racially mixed as possible. To do this, the district would have to sometimes bus students to go to schools far away from where they lived. Despite the plan ultimately being successful at integrating schools, the school district appealed the case to the US Court of Appeals for the Fourth Circuit, but it agreed with the lower court. So the school district appealed again, this time to the Supreme Court, which heard oral arguments on October 12, 1970. The justices went back and forth regarding where they stood on the issue. The lawyers for the school district argued that the federal government needed to stay out of how local governments implemented racial integration.

## The Big Question in this case:

- Was it okay for federal courts to oversee and mandate plans for implementing racial integration?

The Court said yes. On April 20, 1971, the Court announced it had sided with the Swanns and other parents. It was unanimous. Not only did they say federal courts could step in to enforce racial integration, but they established criteria on how to do that. The now Chief Justice Warren Burger wrote the majority opinion, saying that federal courts had lots of flexible powers to remedy past wrongs to enforce previous federal court decisions.[159] Even though bussing kids all over the district in the name of racial integration may have been a pain in the butt, the Court argued it was still the best way to do it. However, the Court also stressed that this bussing plan was meant to be temporary, and that one day the school district's board could come up with its own plan.

That day came in 2002 after another parent sued the district for not letting his daughter enroll in a magnet school based on her skin color. By then, most Charlotte residents had turned against bussing. Today, most American schools remain highly racially segregated, not because of any law, but because of socioeconomic status. In fact, in some parts of the country, schools are more racially segregated than they were in the 1960s.[160] Why? Well, most American public schools are primarily funded by property taxes.[161] In American urban areas, property taxes are often not enough to cover all the costs of public schools there. Therefore, many of those schools are underfunded and underperforming. While "white" urban families can afford to send their kids to private schools or move out to suburban school districts with more resources, often, Black, Hispanic, and Latino families cannot, and their kids often are stuck at these urban schools. That all said, ironically, racial integration today is most common in suburban school districts, once places where racist families fled Black students in the cities.

Regardless, *Swann v. Charlotte-Mecklenburg Board of Education* caused bussing to become an important tool for achieving racial integration for the rest of the 1970s and 1980s.[162] It also led to the development of new ways for achieving racial integration such as magnet schools and school pairing. Most importantly, the decision highlighted the ongoing struggle for racial equality, a struggle that continues to this day.

159  www.oyez.org/cases/1970/281
160  www.vpm.org/news/2022-06-08/politifact-va-public-schools-are-more-segregated-now-than-in-the-late-1960s
161  www.lincolninst.edu/publications/articles/2022-04-public-schools-property-tax-comparison-education-models
162  www.edweek.org/education/the-busing-debate-charlotte-mecklenburg-county-n-c-and-denver/1984/06

# 57. Lemon v. Kurtzman (1971)

This case began in Harrisburg, Pennsylvania, on June 19, 1968. On that day, the Pennsylvania General Assembly passed a law called the Pennsylvania Non-Public Elementary and Secondary Education Act of 1968. I know, that's an impressive name for a law. The law said the state government could supplement the salaries of teachers of secular subjects in religious schools, and pay for their textbooks and other instructional materials. In other words, religious schools were getting extra government funding, mostly because they were struggling and needed help. Under the law, eligible teachers could only get the funding if they taught courses offered in the public schools, using only materials used in the public schools, and couldn't teach courses in religion. At the time, 25 percent of Pennsylvania's students attended private schools, and about 95 percent of those were Roman Catholic schools.

However, the Pennsylvania Non-Public Elementary and Secondary Education Act was controversial because he was directing taxpayer money to church-affiliated schools. Many argued that it went against the Establishment Clause of the First Amendment, the part that said the government couldn't establish any religion. The Roman Catholic Church seemed to benefit a lot from the new law. Soon after the law passed, a dude named Alton Lemon talked trash about it at a Philadelphia American Civil Liberties Union meeting. After that meeting, a bunch of folks organized and asked him to be the lead plaintiff to fight the law. Lemon was a tax-paying Pennsylvania citizen, after all, with a kid attending public school there. Lemon agreed to be the face of the case, with Philadelphia newspapers calling him a "First Amendment Hero" for volunteering.

Lemon and the others sued David Kurtzman, the Superintendent of Public Instruction of the Commonwealth of Pennsylvania, but the US District Court for the Eastern District of Pennsylvania dismissed the cases. However, Rhode Island had *also* recently passed a similar law, and after *it* passed also had citizens that fought it in court. *Its* US District Court sided with the citizens.[163]

So with these conflicting decisions, the Supreme Court decided to step in to review and consolidate them. It heard oral arguments on March 3, 1971.

- Do laws that provide state funding for non-public, non-secular schools go against the Establishment Clause of the First Amendment?

The Court said yes. On June 28, 1971, the Court announced it had sided with Lemon. It was 8–0 against the Pennsylvania law and 8–1 against the Rhode Island law. As decisive as this decision was, the Court struggled with this one due to the vague language of the Establishment Clause. To solve this, they came up with a three-part test to determine whether a law violated it:

1.  The law must have a secular purpose. In other words, its purpose shouldn't have religion in mind. The Court based this part of the test on the case *Abington School District v. Schempp* (1963), in which the Court ruled that legally sanctioned or officially mandated Bible reading and prayer in public schools was unconstitutional.

2.  The law's primary effect must be one that neither promotes nor restrains religion. The Court based this part of the test on the case *Board of Education v. Allen* (1968), in which the Court ruled that a New York law allowing the loan of secular textbooks to children in religious private schools was fine.

3.  The law must not create "excessive government entanglement with religion." The Court based this part of the test on the case *Walz v. Tax Commission* (1970), in which the Court ruled tax exemptions for religious organizations don't go against the Establishment Clause.

Collectively, this three-part test today is known as the Lemon Test, named after Alton Lemon, of course. According to the Lemon Test, the Court determined both of those state laws were unconstitutional because they broke the *third* part of the test, mostly since the religious school system benefited the mission of the Roman Catholic Church.[164]

While *Lemon v. Kurtzman* established the Lemon Test, afterward the courts unfortunately applied it inconsistently. In *Agostini v. Felton* (1997), the Court modified the Lemon Test, combining the second and third parts of it while also saying that government indoctrination should also be considered. The *Agostini* decision also said it was important to define who exactly were the recipients of government money based on religion.

In 2003, thirty-two years after the *Lemon* decision, Alton Lemon said, "Separation of church and state is gradually losing ground, I regret to say." [165] He was right. Nineteen years later, the Court overturned *Lemon v. Kurtzman* with its decision in *Kennedy v. Bremerton School District* (2022), which I'll examine in a later chapter.

165   www.nytimes.com/2013/05/25/us/alton-t-lemon-civil-rights-activist-dies-at-84.html

# 58. The Pentagon Papers Case (1971)

This case began in Washington, DC, on June 17, 1967. On that day, Secretary of Defense Robert McNamara created the Vietnam Study Task Force at the Pentagon to create a study of the Vietnam War, which, by the way, was raging on at the time with no end in sight. This study was supposed to remain classified but released to the public eventually, as McNamara wanted to leave a written record for historians.

Working on this task force was a dude named Daniel Ellsberg, who became troubled by what he found. The Department of Defense was telling the American public one thing but doing other things. For example, the Pentagon was lying about escalating the war even when victory was hopeless. It had covered up doing some horrible things, like illegal bombings in places like Cambodia and Laos and the use of chemical warfare.

Ellsberg, who had become strongly against the Vietnam War, decided he would fight the power! In October 1969, he and his friend Anthony Russo began secretly photocopying pages from this study, which eventually became known as the Pentagon Papers, named after the headquarters of the Department of Defense. The Pentagon Papers were *thousands of pages long.*

Ellsberg decided to take the photocopies to the press to expose all of the Pentagon's dirty secrets. In March 1971, he gave forty-three volumes of the Pentagon Papers to Neil Sheehan, a reporter for the *New York Times*. On June 13, 1971, the newspaper began publishing a series of articles based on what Ellsberg had leaked. It also included excerpts from the actual Pentagon Papers.[166]

When President Richard Nixon read these articles, he got upset. Nixon worried that the articles made the federal government look bad and put the country's national security at risk. A couple of days later, the Nixon administration got a federal court to force the *New York Times* to stop publishing articles about the Pentagon Papers. Nixon's Attorney General John Mitchell argued that Ellsberg and Russo were guilty of breaking the Espionage Act of 1917, so this "prior restraint," or pre-publication censorship, was justified. In fact, the Nixon administration argued that the *Times* publishing the Pentagon Papers endangered Americans.

---

166  www.mtsu.edu/first-amendment/article/505/new-york-times-co-v-united-states

Meanwhile, the *Washington Post* began publishing articles about the Pentagon Papers. The Assistant US Attorney General William Rehnquist, a future Supreme Court chief justice, also tried to prevent the *Post* from publishing any more Pentagon Papers secrets. Eventually, seventeen other newspapers published parts of the study.

On June 28, 1971 (coincidentally the same day the Supreme Court announced its decision in *Lemon v. Kurtzman*), Ellsberg surrendered to face criminal charges under the Espionage Act. The next day, a young US Senator named Mike Gravel read the Pentagon Papers out loud for three hours, entering them into the Senate record. As you can imagine, by this time the American public was fired up about all the revelations contained in those documents.

Newspapers kept publishing stories about the Pentagon Papers, and the US District Court for the District of Columbia and Court of Appeals for the DC Circuit both let them, so the Supreme Court decided to quickly step in, combining the cases against the *New York Times* and the *Washington Post*. The Court heard oral arguments on June 26, 1971. In case you hadn't figured out by now, this was a First Amendment issue. The federal government argued it was justified in limiting speech to keep the country safe.

## The Big Question in this case:

- Was the Nixon administration justified in preventing the publication of what it called "classified information" in the name of national security?

The Court said no. On June 30, 1971, just four days after it heard oral arguments, the Court announced that it sided with the *New York Times* and the *Washington Post*, 6–3. The Court said prior restraint was *not* justified, and that the press releasing the Pentagon Papers to the public did *not* put the nation's security at risk.[167] It sure made a lot of Americans upset, though, and caused many to lose trust in their government.

Justice Hugo Black wrote the majority opinion, writing, "In the First Amendment the Founding Fathers gave the free press the protection it must have to fulfill its essential role in our democracy. The press was to serve the governed, not the governors. The Government's power to censor the press was abolished so that the press would remain forever free to censure the Government."[168]

167   www.oyez.org/cases/1970/1873
168   www.law.cornell.edu/supremecourt/text/403/713

*New York Times v. United States*, also known as *The Pentagon Papers Case*, was a win for the First Amendment. If the press publishes something that makes the government look bad, the government can't stop it *just because it makes it look bad*. So whatever happened to Daniel Ellsberg and his friend Anthony Russo? They were still charged under the Espionage Act, looking at a maximum sentence of 115 years in prison. However, due to government misconduct and its shady ways of getting evidence, a federal court judge later dismissed all charges against them.

Daniel Ellsberg is still alive at the time of this writing, actively supporting whistleblowers like him who continue to expose government corruption.[169]

# 59. Wisconsin v. Yoder
# (1972)

This case began in Green County, Wisconsin, in September 1968. It was around that time that three Amish students from different families stopped going to school at New Glarus High School. The three students were fifteen-year-old Frieda Yoder, fifteen-year-old Barbara Miller, and fourteen-year-old Vernon Yutzy. However, in Green County, not going to school if you were under the age of sixteen was illegal. After the school district tried to get the students to go to school there, their parents all said the kids were no longer going to school due to their religious beliefs. Green County didn't care if it was their religious beliefs or not and fined the parents five dollars (around forty-four dollars today) for breaking the county's compulsory-attendance law.

The parents argued it was Amish tradition not to enroll their kids in public school after eighth grade. In general, there are two reasons for this. The first reason is practicality— Amish teenagers generally need to begin learning a trade after eighth grade and public high schools usually don't offer adequate training for them. The second reason is that the Amish tend to see high schools and colleges as institutions that might promote ideas that go against their traditional Christian values, and, according to them, are immoral. Jonas Yoder, the father of Frieda, represented the parents in court, but the Amish generally don't like going to court to settle disputes. Therefore, a Lutheran minister named William Lindholm took an interest in their case and decided to help them fight. Lindholm strongly believed the county's compulsory-attendance law went against the Free Exercise Clause of the First Amendment.[170]

They appealed to the Wisconsin circuit court, which agreed with Green County, so they appealed again to the Wisconsin Supreme Court, which agreed with Yoder and the rest, overturning the decision. The Wisconsin Supreme Court said Green County couldn't show that having an educational system for all its citizens was more important than the Amish families' rights to practice their religion freely. The state of Wisconsin decided to appeal the case to the Supreme Court, and the Court agreed to take on the case, hearing oral arguments on December 8, 1971.

---

170   Lindholm, William C., "The National Committee for Amish Religious Freedom," 109–23, in *The Amish and the State*, sec. ed., edited by Donald B. Kraybill (Baltimore: Johns Hopkins University Press, 2003).

At odds with each other were religious freedom and compulsory education. Yoder argued that high school threatened his Amish way of life. Wisconsin argued that some Amish kids may decide to leave the Amish faith after they reach adulthood, and therefore a public education through high school was necessary so that they could more easily adapt to the so-called "real world." If the kids were two or three or four years older, then it wouldn't be an issue, because they'd be considered adults who could choose whatever religion they wanted.

## The Big Question in this case:

- Did Wisconsin's requirement that parents send their children to school at least until age sixteen go against the Free Exercise Clause of the First Amendment?

The Court said yes. On May 15, 1972, the Court announced it sided with Yoder. It was unanimous, although Justice William Douglas gave a partial dissent. First, the Court said the Equal Protection Clause of the Fourteenth Amendment was applicable to the states in the states. Second, it said the Free Exercise Clause of the First Amendment *did* protect the Amish parents' right to take their kids out of school, even though they were under sixteen. That said, the Court said not all belief systems are protected by that clause. If someone had a belief system that severely harmed these children, that's a different story, but the Amish way of life had been around for three centuries. The Court also said there was no evidence that two more years in high school would make these kids any more prepared for the "real world," nor was there any evidence that two more years in high school would prevent them from being a burden on society.[171]

In his partial dissent, Justice Douglas wanted everyone to remember the children. He wrote, "I agree with the Court that the religious scruples of the Amish are opposed to the education of their children beyond the grade schools, yet I disagree with the Court's conclusion that the matter is within the dispensation of parents alone... On this important and vital matter of education, I think the children should be entitled to be heard."[172] The rest of the court responded by saying this case was not about the kids—this was between the parents and the state.

*Wisconsin v. Yoder* further protected the Free Exercise Clause of the First Amendment. It is often *the* case brought up defending a parent's right to homeschool their kids. However,

171   www.oyez.org/cases/1971/70-110
172   www.law.cornell.edu/supremecourt/text/406/205

parents can't take their kids out of school on a whim and teach them some wacky ideology or philosophy. The Court was specific. It was only if it was a well-established religion that was consistent historically about the reasoning for taking the kids out of school in the first place.

# 60. Roe v. Wade (1973)

This case began in Dallas, Texas, in 1969 when a pregnant woman named Norma McCorvey decided to get an abortion. She was twenty-two years old, suffering from various addictions, in poverty, and terrified about her future.[173] However, in Texas, abortions were illegal, except in cases where the mother's life was in danger. McCorvey had planned on having one anyway, at an illegal clinic. Before she could have the abortion, police shut down that clinic. Desperate, Norma soon found out that two lawyers were looking for women seeking abortions to fight the Texas law that banned them. They promised pizza and beer, so Norma came.[174]

The lawyers, Sarah Weddington and Linda Coffee, decided to take Norma's case over several others. The two were not much older than Norma. On March 3, 1970, Coffee officially filed a complaint in the US District Court for the Northern District of Texas, giving Norma a pseudonym, "Jane Roe," to protect her identity. They sued the state, arguing its abortion law was unconstitutional. More specifically, Weddington and Coffee argued that Texas's abortion law went against McCorvey's right to personal privacy, which they said was protected by the First, Fourth, Fifth, Ninth, and Fourteenth Amendments. Defending the state of Texas was Henry Wade, the district attorney of Dallas. By this time, Norma was six months pregnant.

The District Court looked at Norma's case along with two other related cases. On June 17, 1970, the three-judge panel of the Court unanimously called the Texas abortion law unconstitutional, saying it broke the right to privacy assumed under the Ninth Amendment. However, they did not act to stop the enforcement of the law. Wade appealed the ruling, and it eventually went directly to the Supreme Court. Meanwhile, McCorvey had given birth to the baby whose life she had originally thought about ending, putting the baby up for adoption.

The case sat for a year and a half. Finally, the Supreme Court heard oral arguments on December 13, 1971. In his opening argument, defense attorney Jay Floyd was unprofessional, and it probably hurt his case. Going against Weddington and Coffee, he said, "It's an old joke, but when a man argues against two beautiful ladies like this, they are going to have the last word." Well, that "joke" was not well-received. The entire

173  www.washingtonpost.com/national/norma-mccorvey-jane-roe-of-roe-v-wade-decision-legalizing-
     abortion-dies-at-69/2017/02/18/24b83108-396e-11e6-8f7c-d4c723a2becb_story.html
174  newrepublic.com/article/166281/lawyer-argued-roe-v-wade-tragedy-overturn-it

courtroom was silent afterward, and Chief Justice Warren Burger gave Floyd a cold glare.[175] Regardless, by the end of arguments, all of the justices agreed the Texas law was bad, but for different reasons.

The case sat some more, because two justices, Hugo Black and John Harlan, had recently retired and were not yet replaced. In January, justices Lewis Powell and William Rehnquist joined the court, but it wasn't until October 11, 1972, that they heard oral arguments a second time.

## The Big Question in this case:

- Does the Constitution recognize a woman's right to have an abortion?

The Court said yes. On January 22, 1973, it announced it had sided with Roe, 7–2. First, the Court argued that abortion fell under the Fourteenth Amendment's Due Process Clause. It protects against a state's action against the right to privacy, and a woman choosing to have an abortion falls within the right to privacy. Since "privacy" isn't explicitly listed as a right in the Constitution, the Court argued it was implied through the Ninth Amendment, as Weddington and Coffee had originally argued. The Court also ruled that a woman had the right to an abortion until the fetus reached an age of "viability."[176] Viability means that the baby would be able to survive independently, outside of the mother's womb. Back then, doctors believed this to be around the twenty-eighth week of pregnancy. Today, thanks to the wonders of technology, that's around the twenty-second week of pregnancy.

The two justices who disagreed with the decision were Byron White and William Rehnquist, who, if you recall, was one of the new dudes on the bench. White argued the Court made up a new constitutional right and didn't have the authority to do so. Rehnquist argued the other justices expanded the Fourteenth Amendment to mean something more than its original authors had intended.

Regardless, the decision effectively legalized abortion throughout the country and declared many state laws unconstitutional due to this. Before the Roe decision, thirty different states had outlawed abortion, and the other states had restricted it in at least some way.

Roe v. Wade sparked a contentious debate that continues to this day. On one side, supporters of the Roe decision are often called "pro-choice," meaning they believe it should

175   www.scotusblog.com/2017/01/roe-telling-stories-behind-landmark-decision/
176   supreme.justia.com/cases/federal/us/410/113/

be the woman's choice whether she has the abortion. Opponents of the *Roe* decision are often called "pro-life," meaning they believe any abortion should be regarded as murder since life technically begins at conception. Later, in *Planned Parenthood v. Casey* (1992), a more conservative Court upheld and effectively strengthened the *Roe* decision. However, in *Dobbs v. Jackson Women's Health Organization* (2022), the Court overturned the *Roe* decision, arguing that the Constitution does *not* guarantee the right to an abortion. I will cover both these cases in future chapters.

Regardless, the abortion issue has only become even more divisive in recent years. In fact, many people vote for politicians simply based on whether they are pro-life or not.

So whatever happened to Norma McCorvey? Well, in a television interview in 1984, she went public, revealing to the world that she was "Roe." After that, she became a pro-choice advocate, even volunteering at a women's clinic. At first, she told the press that she wanted the abortion because she was raped. However, she later said this was a lie—she had made it up. McCorvey published an autobiography in 1994 called *I Am Roe*. Soon after this, in a surprising turn of events, she quit her job at the abortion clinic and became pro-life. She became a born-again Christian and immediately joined the staff of Operation Rescue, a pro-life organization, at an office next door to the abortion clinic she formerly worked at. She was a pro-life activist for the rest of her life.

However, there's another twist to McCorvey's story. On her deathbed, she admitted that she joined the pro-life movement for the money. In reality, she had never stopped being pro-choice. She had lied again. In an interview featured in the documentary *a.k.a. Jane Doe*, she admitted to it all being an act. "I was the big fish...I took their money and they'd put me out in front of the cameras and tell me what to say."[177]

The baby who started this whole thing is now fifty-two years old at the time of this writing and went public as Shelley Lynn Thornton in 2021. She had several phone conversations with Norma, her biological mother, before she died.[178] While Thornton has insisted that she is neither pro-choice nor pro-life, she did speak out against the *Dobb* decision, the case which overruled *Roe v. Wade*.[179]

177   www.youtube.com/watch?v=gMdEn1ZWGj8
178   www.theatlantic.com/politics/archive/2021/09/jane-roe-v-wade-baby-norma-mccorvey/620009/
179   news.yahoo.com/biological-daughter-jane-roe-slams-014903316.html

# 61. Miller v. California (1973)

This case began in Covina, California, in 1968. That year, publisher Marvin Miller, infamously nicknamed the "King of Smut," began mailing brochures advertising pornography. Specifically, the brochures promoted four books and one film that showed sexual activity between men and women in graphic detail.[180] Miller made the pivotal mistake of sending some of these brochures to people who did not ask for them. One of the people who did not ask for a brochure but was mailed one anyway was a restaurant owner in Newport Beach. After receiving it, the restaurant owner called the police, who promptly arrested Miller and charged him with breaking California's Obscenity law, which said mailing "obscene" material was illegal.

Now, you may be wondering what "obscene" means. Generally speaking, "obscene" means something that is offensive because it goes against someone's morals. However, what's obscene to one person may be totally different to another person. Not only that, but it often was also unclear what was classified as "obscene" *legally*. California lawmakers had written California's Obscenity law under the guidance of two previous Supreme Court cases that dealt with obscenity: *Memoirs v. Massachusetts* (1966) and *Roth v. United States* (1957). In court, Miller argued that his brochures were protected under the First Amendment and had "social value." The jury wasn't convinced and found him guilty in the Superior Court of Orange County.

Miller appealed to the Appellate Division of the Superior Court, arguing that the jury incorrectly used the local community standard of obscenity instead of the national standard. In fact, he used the *Memoirs* decision to back this up. In *that* decision, the Court had ruled that stuff was only obscene if it was "utterly without redeeming social value."[181] The appellate division agreed with the lower court. Miller then appealed again to the California Court of Appeals for the Third District, but it refused to review the case. In response, Miller appealed directly to the Supreme Court, who agreed to hear the case. As it turns out, Chief Justice Warren Burger had been looking for a new obscenity case for the Court to tackle as he hoped to clear up things about it.

---

180  www.mtsu.edu/first-amendment/article/401/miller-v-california
181  supreme.justia.com/cases/federal/us/383/413/

The Court heard oral arguments in January 1972. However, the Court was divided and decided to hold off making a decision. However the Court decided, they knew they would have to establish a test to make it easier to determine if something was obscene. They didn't want a repeat of the somewhat embarrassing rationale in the case *Jacobellis v. Ohio* (1964), a case in which Justice Potter Stewart infamously wrote:

> I shall not today attempt further to define the kinds of material I understand to be embraced within that shorthand description ["hard-core pornography"], and perhaps I could never succeed in intelligibly doing so. But *I know it when I see it*, and the motion picture involved in this case is not that.

"I know it when I see it" wasn't going to cut it anymore. The Court again heard oral arguments on November 7, 1972. Miller's lawyers continued to argue that his brochures were covered under the freedom of speech part of the First Amendment and that the *Memoirs* decision backed up that his brochures had "social value."

### The Big Question in this case:

- Is the sale and distribution of obscene materials by mail protected under the First Amendment?

The Court said no. On June 21, 1973, it announced it had sided with California, although barely, 5–4. First, the Court said obscene material is *not* protected by the First Amendment. Second, the Court had established a test to help judges determine if something was obscene. That test, now known as the Miller Test, had three parts. It said something could be viewed as obscene if:

1.   The average person in that community found it offensive.

2.   It showed, in an obviously offensive way, excretory functions and "sexual conduct specifically defined by the applicable state law."

3.   It lacks "serious literary, artistic, political, or scientific value."

By establishing the Miller Test, the Court rejected the "utterly without redeeming social value" test of the *Memoirs* decision.[182]

In his dissent, Justice William Douglas wrote, "The difficulty is that we do not deal with constitutional terms, since 'obscenity' is not mentioned in the Constitution or Bill of Rights. And the First Amendment makes no such exception from 'the press' which it undertakes to protect nor…is an exception necessarily implied, for there was no recognized exception to the free press at the time the Bill of Rights was adopted which treated 'obscene' publications differently from other types of papers, magazines, and books." He added, "What shocks me may be sustenance for my neighbor. What causes one person to boil up in rage over one pamphlet or movie may reflect only his neurosis, not shared by others."[183] In other words, it was all subjective, and no test could effectively work since every test could theoretically go against the First Amendment.

Despite it being a controversial decision, *Miller v. California* dramatically increased the ability of local communities to determine for themselves whether something was obscene. In the decades since the *Miller* decision, many states, counties, and cities have prosecuted businesses that sell obscene materials. Not only that, but it has also led to more restrictive zoning ordinances for public nudity. Overall, the United States is known for having a free press, but obscenity is one of the few exceptions to this, and it all goes back to Marvin Miller, the "King of Smut."

# 62. United States v. Nixon (1974)

This case began in Washington, DC, on June 17, 1972. On that night, five men broke into the Democratic National Committee headquarters in the Watergate office building. They tried to set up a wiretap and photograph confidential Democratic Party documents. However, the police caught them in the act and arrested them. Little did most know, these men were connected with the Committee for the Re-Election of the President, or CRP (often mocked with the acronym CREEP), the organization directly tied to President Richard Nixon to help him get reelected.

By May 1973 there had been multiple ongoing investigations about the Watergate break-in, and more Americans thought the Nixon administration was directly linked to it. The US Senate Watergate Committee began public hearings, and the Nixon administration appointed Archibald Cox to lead a separate, independent investigation. In July 1973, Americans learned for the first time that there was a new system in the White House that automatically recorded everything in the Oval Office and Cabinet Room. In other words, if Nixon was in on the Watergate break-in, or even if he knew about it and was trying to cover it up, there could be evidence of it in the recordings. Cox, as well as the Senate, immediately subpoenaed the White House recordings, which means Nixon had to submit them to court as evidence. However, Nixon refused to release them, citing his "executive privilege" as president. He even ordered Cox to drop his subpoena, and after Cox refused, Nixon had him fired. It was not a good look for Nixon.

Unfortunately for Nixon, after that the investigations only picked up. In what eventually became known as the Watergate Scandal, a total of sixty-nine people were indicted and forty-eight people convicted for participating in, aiding in, or covering up information about the Watergate break-in. *Many* of these folks were top Nixon administration officials. By early 1974, it was clear President Nixon had at least *known* about the Watergate break-in and had tried to cover it up. However, there was little solid evidence, and Nixon still refused to give up the recordings. On March 1, 1974, a grand jury, or special jury selected to see if an accusation was valid, indicted *seven* former aides of Nixon. They later simply became known as the "Watergate Seven."

Nixon could feel the walls closing in on him. In April, the dude who took Cox's place to investigate the Watergate break-in, Leon Jaworski, had another subpoena, but this one ordered Nixon to release certain tapes and papers. Well, Nixon could feel the heat, but still didn't want to release the recordings. Instead, he turned over *edited* transcripts of *some* of the conversations. After Nixon's lawyer, James St. Clair, asked Judge John Sirica of the US District Court for the District of Columbia to reverse the subpoena, Judge Sirica said, "The President wants me to argue that he is as powerful a monarch as Louis XIV, only four years at a time, and is not subject to the processes of any court in the land except the court of impeachment." Sirica denied the motion and ordered Nixon to turn over the tapes by May 31.

In response, Nixon and Jaworski appealed directly to the Supreme Court, which heard oral arguments on July 8, 1974. Justice William Rehnquist, who had close connections with several of the Watergate conspirators, decided to recuse himself from the case or excuse himself since he might be too biased.

As previously mentioned, Nixon argued he had "executive privilege," meaning that a president can withhold information from the public *if* it's in the public's best interest. Obviously, that could be open to interpretation. Regardless, Nixon said executive privilege gave him the power to withhold the tapes. He also argued that the whole matter shouldn't even be dealt with in the courts since it was a dispute *within* the executive branch. Besides, Nixon argued, even if the judicial branch *were* to chime in, it should respect the need for executive confidentiality.[184]

## The Big Questions in this case:

- Did the Supreme Court have the authority to determine if a president was okay to use executive privilege in certain circumstances?
- Was President Nixon justified in using executive privilege by refusing to release all the White House recordings?

The Court answered yes to the first question and no to the second. On July 24, 1974, it announced it had sided *against* President Nixon. It was unanimous. First, the Court ruled judicial review applied when it came to a president's use of executive privilege. Second, it said a claim of executive privilege by the president in this case was unconstitutional. Therefore, Nixon had to deliver the subpoenaed recordings immediately. While the Court acknowledged that executive privilege was legitimate in certain areas of military or diplomatic affairs, courts could also step in if they thought the executive privilege violated

184　constitutioncenter.org/blog/anniversary-of-united-states-v-nixon the "fundamental demands of due process of law in the fair administration of justice." In other words, if executive privilege was preventing the courts from doing their jobs, the courts could override it.[185]

*United States v. Nixon* was a landmark case that solidified the idea that no one, *not even the president of the United States,* is above the law. It was the first case in which the Supreme Court ruled that executive privilege exists, but it said it is a *qualified* privilege, as opposed to an *absolute* one.[186] In the case of Nixon's secret recordings, it was in the public interest to have them released, and most people ultimately came to realize that Nixon wanted them secret not to protect the country, but only to protect himself.

In fact, just sixteen days after the decision, Nixon became the first and only president in American history to resign.

185   supreme.justia.com/cases/federal/us/418/683/
186   constitutioncenter.org/the-constitution/supreme-court-case-library/united-states-v-nixon-tapes-
      case

# 63. Buckley v. Valeo (1976)

This case began in Washington, DC, on February 7, 1972, when President Richard Nixon signed into law the Federal Election Campaign Act, regulating political campaign spending in the media. In the following four years, the law would be amended multiple times. One amendment created the Federal Election Commission, an independent federal organization whose purpose is to enforce all federal campaign finance laws. Another amendment created public financing for presidential elections. Another limited how much money a political candidate could spend from their personal funds.

However, other amendments were more controversial, such as the amendment limiting contributions political candidates running for federal office could get and the amendment limiting how much those candidates could spend on their campaigns. A diverse coalition of politicians and political organizations argued that those two amendments were unconstitutional because they went against the First Amendment. Led by US Senator James Buckley, they sued the federal government on January 2, 1975. The federal government named Francis Valeo as the defendant. Valeo was a member of the Federal Election Commission.

In the US District Court for the District of Columbia, Buckley and the others that the aforementioned amendments to the Federal Election Campaign Act went against the First Amendment's freedom of speech clause and argued they went against the part of the Fifth Amendment that says no one shall be "deprived of life, liberty, or property without due process of law." The US District Court for the District of Columbia transferred the case to the Court of Appeals for the District of Columbia, who generally sided with Valeo. Buckley and the others appealed to the Supreme Court, which heard oral arguments on November 10, 1975. The Court decided to focus on the implied freedom of expression part of the First Amendment.[187]

## The Big Question in this case:

- Did the limits placed on campaign expenditures by the Federal Election Campaign Act go against the First Amendment?

The Court said yes *and* no. This was a complicated case. In fact, it's the longest opinion ever issued by the Court. Ultimately, the Court unanimously *mostly* sided with Buckley in this case. First, in a 6–2 decision, the Court said it was okay for the federal government to limit contributions to candidates running for public office to protect the "integrity of our system of representative democracy."[188] However, in a 7–1 decision, the Court also said limiting how much those candidates could *spend* on their campaigns was unconstitutional, going against the First Amendment. The Court argued that if a political candidate is spending their own money, that doesn't necessarily lead to corruption and hurt the democratic system. Instead, it argued, it does restrict the quantity of expression, the size of the audience being reached, and the depth at which any given idea or policy could be spread.[189]

*Buckley v. Valeo* was a controversial decision. In fact, those on both sides ended up upset with how the Court decided on it, with many on Valeo's side saying the Court was hurting democracy and many on Buckley's side saying the Court didn't go far enough to free how much money could be spent on political campaigns. The decision greatly changed campaign finance in the country. It was the first major case to look at campaign finance. Ever since, several cases have used it as precedent when attempting to determine whether limitations on campaign spending is "fair" or not.

*Buckley v. Valeo* was later expanded by the decisions in First National Bank of *Boston v. Bellotti* (1978) and *McCutcheon v. Federal Election* (2014) and upheld by the decisions in *Nixon v. Shrink Missouri Government PAC* (2000) and *FEC v. Beaumont* (2003). Most infamously, the Court would later reduce limits on campaign expenditures even further in the case *Citizens United v. FEC* (2010), which we'll look at in a future chapter.

---

188   www.oyez.org/cases/1975/75-436
189   www.fec.gov/legal-resources/court-cases/buckley-v-valeo/

# 64. Gregg v. Georgia (1976)

This case began in Texas and Georgia in the 1960s. Texas had sentenced one man to death and Georgia had sentenced two men to death for crimes involving rape and murder. The Texas defendant, Elmer Branch, who later was found to have low intelligence, had broken into the home of a sixty-five-year-old widow and raped her, holding his arm against her throat. As he left, Branch told the widow if she ever told anyone what had happened, he would come back and kill her. The first Georgia defendant, Peter Jackson, a twenty-one-year-old, broke into a home and held up scissors to a woman's neck, demanding money. After she found no money to give him, he raped her. The second Georgia defendant, Henry Furman, a twenty-six-year-old with multiple mental illnesses, attempted to break into a home and after he couldn't get in, shot through a closed door, killing one person inside. He later claimed his gun accidentally misfired.

All three men awaited the death penalty, meaning the punishment for their crimes was death. However, all of their lawyers argued that they didn't deserve the death penalty for their crimes and appealed their cases.[190] Well, both the Texas Court of Criminal Appeals and the Supreme Court of Georgia disagreed, upholding the death sentences of all three men.

Despite this, the three cases *did* catch the attention of the Supreme Court, which decided to combine them into one case to see if they went against the Eighth Amendment. They wanted to interpret the clause that said there shall be no "cruel and unusual punishments inflicted." Obviously, that could mean *several* things. The Court heard oral arguments for the cases on January 17, 1972. The lawyers of the convicted argued the Fourteenth Amendment said the Eighth Amendment should apply to their punishments.

## The Big Question in this case:

- Did sentencing these three men to death go against the Eighth and Fourteenth Amendments?

The Court said yes. On June 29, 1972, the Court announced it had sided with the three convicted men. It was a close one, though: 5–4. The Court argued that the death penalty was "cruel and unusual punishment" and therefore went against the Constitution. The five justices who said it went against the Constitution couldn't agree on exactly why. Three justices—Potter Stewart, Byron White, and William Douglas—expressed concern with the randomness of how the death sentences were carried out by Texas and Georgia. They called out the likely racial prejudice happening in the courts since the three men convicted were all African Americans and the victims were all of European descent. The other two justices, William Brennan and Thurgood Marshall, believed the death penalty was unconstitutional under *any* circumstances. Marshall wrote, "No matter how careful courts are, the possibility of perjured testimony, mistaken honest testimony and human error remain too real. We have no way of judging how many innocent persons have been executed, but we can be certain that there were some." The four justices who dissented said the federal government ultimately had a difficult time classifying one punishment as "cruel and unusual" while permitting another. It could get too complicated quickly and even become a slippery slope.

Regardless, this case, known as *Furman v. Georgia*, effectively played a temporary ban on all future executions in the country until more guidance came from another court challenge. Suddenly, 630 people on death row were not on death row anymore. Instead, they now faced the rest of their lives in prison. In the meantime, thirty-five states wrote new death penalty laws to attempt to satisfy the Supreme Court's suggestions.[191]

Five of those new death penalty laws are what ultimately got the Supreme Court back in the game on the issue.

On November 21, 1973, a dude named Troy Gregg and his friend, Floyd Allen, were hitchhiking in Florida. Two men, named Fred Simmons and Bob Moore, picked them up and drove them up to Atlanta, Georgia. Despite this good deed, Gregg murdered Simmons and Moore to rob them. Later, Georgia charged him with first-degree murder and armed robbery. Georgia was one of those states that had passed a new law after the *Furman* decision. While Gregg was found guilty of first-degree murder and armed robbery, there was still confusion about his sentencing. He got two trials in Gwinnett County court—one to determine guilt and one for sentencing. At the second trial, the jury found the death penalty acceptable since they didn't think it went against the Eighth Amendment. It was more clear-cut that Gregg deserved it.

Well, Gregg didn't think he deserved it and appealed to the Georgia Supreme Court. It agreed with the lower court, so he appealed again to the *supreme* Supreme Court, who

191     Lain, Corinna Barrett. "Deciding Death." *Duke Law Journal* 57, no. 1 (2007): 1–83. www.jstor.org/
        stable/40040587.

agreed to hear oral arguments in March 1976. The Court decided to combine this case with four other cases since similar laws were passed in Florida, Texas, North Carolina, and Louisiana after the *Furman* decision. Together, these cases became known as "The Death Penalty Cases." The Court heard the same arguments as in the *Furman* decision.

### The Big Question in this case:

- Did the death penalty in these five cases go against the Eighth and Fourteenth Amendments?

This time, the Court said no. On July 2, 1976, almost four years after the *Furman* decision (and almost two hundred years after the United States became a country), it announced it had sided with Georgia and the other states, 7–2. The Court said the death penalty *didn't* go against the Eighth Amendment and Fourteenth Amendment under *all* circumstances. In some extreme criminal cases, like when someone deliberately kills someone else, the death penalty may be fine if there is carefully carried out judgment. It's worth stressing that eight of the nine justices this time were there for the *Furman* decision, yet this time some of the same justices changed their minds to make the decision more definitive. The only two justices who dissented were Brennan and Marshall, the two I mentioned before who believed the death penalty was unconstitutional under *any* circumstances.[192]

The Court established two broad guidelines that state legislatures had to follow to make sure they didn't pass sentencing laws that went against the Eighth Amendment:

1. They had to provide objective criteria to limit how many death sentences were carried out.

2. They had to allow the judge or jury to consider the character and record of an individual defendant.[193]

Regardless, *Gregg v. Georgia* again said the death penalty was legal in the United States. However, the death penalty has remained controversial ever since.[194] Executions resumed in 1977, and since then, more than 1,500 have been executed. Currently, more than 2,500 convicts are on death row.[195]

---

192   law2.umkc.edu/faculty/projects/ftrials/conlaw/gregg.html
193   www.law.cornell.edu/supremecourt/text/428/153
194   www.themarshallproject.org/2016/03/30/it-s-been-40-years-since-the-supreme-court-tried-to-fix-the-death-penalty-here-s-why-it-failed
195   deathpenaltyinfo.org/death-row/overview

Speaking of which, a judge sentenced Tony Gregg to death. However, on July 28, 1980, while on death row, Gregg escaped the Georgia State Prison with three other condemned murderers. It was the first and only death row breakout in Georgia history, and they did it by changing their prison clothing to look like prison guards. However, Gregg was murdered later that night at a biker bar and his body was dumped in a river. No one was ever convicted of his murder.[196]

# 65. Regents of the University of California v. Bakke (1978)

This case began in Los Altos, California, in 1973. That year, Allan Bakke, a thirty-three-year-old man of European origin, applied to various medical schools with hopes of becoming a doctor. Bakke was an accomplished NASA engineer and Marine Corps veteran who served in the Vietnam War. He had always done well in school and scored well on the Medical College Admissions Test, or MCAT. Despite all this, all twelve medical schools he applied to rejected him.

One of those schools that rejected his admission was the University of California at Davis. Bakke applied there in 1973, and the university committee gave him 468 points out of 500 on their rating scale. A 470 automatically got you in. Dr. Theodore West, who interviewed Bakke, said he was "a well-qualified candidate for admission whose main hardship is the unavoidable fact that he is now thirty-three." Dr. West recommended him.

Despite Dr. West's glowing recommendation, Bakke was rejected from the school. After this, Bakke complained to Dr. George Lowrey, the chairman of the admissions committee at the medical school. Lowrey directed him to Assistant Dean Peter Storandt, who probably made the mistake of telling Bakke that he was close to getting in, and if he applied again and got rejected a second time, he might consider suing the college. As it turns out, Storandt later was likely fired due to telling Bakke that.

Regardless, Bakke took his advice and applied again. As you might have guessed, UC Davis rejected him again. In addition, at the time Bakke was rejected, the school had a special admission program, which was an affirmative action quota system. Affirmative action, also known as "positive discrimination," means favoring folks belonging to groups previously discriminated against. It's well-established that the United States has had a long history of discriminating against ethnic minorities. The UC Davis medical school automatically held sixteen spots for each new class of a hundred for "qualified" minorities. This meant that several students with considerably lower academic scores than Bakke were admitted due to being a minority.

On June 20, 1974, Bakke sued the Regents of the University of California, the group that supervised UC Davis. It went through the Superior Court of California in Yolo County.

In court, Bakke argued that the special admission program for minorities at UC Davis went against the Civil Rights Act of 1964. Specifically, Title 6, which said there should not be discrimination based on race, color, or national origin in any program or activity that gets money from the federal government. The legal team for UC Davis argued that Bakke wouldn't have been admitted to the medical school even if the special admission program for minorities didn't exist.

On November 20, 1974, Judge F. Leslie Manker ruled the program unconstitutional, saying that racial quotas in general went against the Equal Protection Clause of the Fourteenth Amendment, and thus Title 6 of the Civil Rights Act. Manker ordered the medical school to stop the special admission program for minorities. Both Bakke and UC Davis appealed. Bakke appealed because he still wasn't admitted to their medical school, and UC Davis appealed because they had to end the special admission program.

It went straight to the California Supreme Court. It surprisingly ruled against the college, upholding the lower court's ruling, 6–1. Justice Stanley Mosk wrote that "no applicant may be rejected because of his race, in favor of another who is less qualified, as measured by standards applied without regard to race." The California Supreme Court said UC Davis had to prove Bakke wouldn't have been accepted into its medical school under a race-neutral program. When UC Davis couldn't do that, they ordered the school to admit Bakke.

The Regents of the University of California then petitioned the Supreme Court to look at the case. The Court agreed, hearing oral arguments on October 12, 1977. This case drew a lot of national attention and was constantly being covered in the media.[197] The Regents hired a high-profile lawyer to represent them, Archibald Cox, a former US Solicitor General. Cox had argued many cases before the Supreme Court and was a Watergate special prosecutor.

### The Big Question in this case:

- Did UC Davis go against the Equal Protection Clause of the Fourteenth Amendment and the Civil Rights Act of 1964 by practicing an affirmative action policy to encourage more minorities in its medical school?

197  www.nytimes.com/1978/06/29/archives/focus-of-historic-battle-in-civil-rights-law-allan-paul-bakke-man.html

The Court said yes. But it also said no. On June 26, 1978, the Court announced its decision, and it was a mess. Officially, the Court ruled 8–1 in Bakke's favor. However, that's misleading. The Court issued six opinions for this case. None of them had the support of a majority of the court. When this happens, we call it a "plurality opinion." I'm not going to go through every opinion. Instead, I'll simplify it for you. Four justices agreed with Bakke that the university's affirmative action quota system went against Title 6 of the Civil Rights Act. Four *other* justices argued that it didn't. Justice Lewis Powell broke the tie by splitting down the middle but still on the side of Bakke. In other words, the Court ruled 5–4 for Bakke based on the argument that affirmative action programs were legal and *could* take ethnic background into account. However, fixed quotas for a certain number of minorities were unconstitutional, as the *methods* of affirmative action went against the Equal Protection Clause of the Fourteenth Amendment.[198]

Therefore, *Regents of the University of California v. Bakke* banned racial quotas for affirmative action but didn't ban affirmative action. It *did* create a lot of confusion regarding how affirmative action could be applied. It became less confusing after the case *Grutter v. Bollinger* (2003), but to this day affirmative action is constantly challenged in court. For now, affirmative action is legal.[199]

Because of this decision, UC Davis admitted Allan Bakke. Bakke, who never liked all the attention he got for this case, quietly graduated from medical school in June 1982, almost ten years after first applying. His first residency was at the Mayo Clinic. He worked as an anesthesiologist in Minnesota after that all the way until his retirement in 2008, then sold medical devices after that. As far as I could tell, he's still alive, but he's a private guy so I'm not 100 percent certain of that.

198   www.oyez.org/cases/1979/76-811
199   www.theatlantic.com/education/archive/2018/10/how-lewis-powell-changed-affirmative-action/572938/

# 66. Sony Corp. of America v. Universal City Studios, Inc. (1984)

This case began in Tokyo, Japan, on May 10, 1975. On that day, Sony developed a new technology called Betamax, the first video tape recording form made widely available to the public. People could use this technology to, for the first time, record from live television, or even from other recordings for future use. Now, eventually Betamax would lose the "videotape format war" of the late 1970s and early 1980s to its archenemy, the dreaded VHS. While Betamax was a formidable opponent, VHS ultimately triumphed, until it eventually was defeated in another video format war to the great DVD.

For the first couple of years, before VHS entered the scene, Betamax was living the dream, with many arguing that it was the next big thing. However, many corporations in the film and television industries did not like this new technology so much. Universal Studios, the Walt Disney Company, and other television and film corporations sued Sony's American-based operations in the US District Court for the Central District of California for copyright infringement. These corporations argued that Sony's customers were using the Betamax recording devices to record copyrighted programs so they could view them later. The nerve of them!

Two years later, the US District Court for the Central District of California ruled in favor of Sony, arguing that recording for noncommercial home use fell under fair use guidelines and that access to free public information was protected under the First Amendment under "fair use." In United States copyright law, "fair use" means you don't have to get the permission of the copyright holder when showing their media, as long as you critique it, report about it, teach using it, or are showing it for research purposes. One major problem with fair use, however, is that it can be interpreted in many ways. You know, like the Bible…or the US Constitution.

Here is what the Copyright Act of 1976 said about fair use:

The fair use of a copyrighted work, including such use by reproduction in copies or phonorecords or by any other means specified by that section, for purposes such as criticism, comment, news reporting, teaching (including multiple copies for classroom use), scholarship, or research, is not an infringement of copyright. In determining whether the use made of a work in any particular case is a fair use the factors to be considered shall include:

- the purpose and character of the use, including whether such use is of a commercial nature or is for nonprofit educational purposes;

- the nature of the copyrighted work;

- the amount and substantiality of the portion used in relation to the copyrighted work as a whole; and

- the effect of the use upon the potential market for or value of the copyrighted work.[200]

Universal Studios and the rest of the corporations weren't satisfied with how the US District Court for the Central District of California interpreted fair use. In 1981, they appealed to the US Court of Appeals for the Ninth Circuit, who reversed the lower court's decision, saying that Sony was contributing to copyright infringement by selling these Betamax machines. It argued the main purpose of Betamax was copying, and even suggested damages to be paid to the TV and film corporations and further legal restrictions on Betamax and similar home recording technologies like VHS. By this time, though, millions of Americans bought Beta and VHS devices.

Sony, of course, appealed to the Supreme Court, which heard oral arguments on January 18, 1983. The Court struggled with this case, not because of any political divide, but because they had a difficult time grasping the implications of this new technology. Justice John Paul Stevens wrote a dissenting opinion expecting the Court to rule against Sony and for Universal and the rest of the media corporations. However, he wrote the opinion as if it was a majority opinion. By sneakily doing this, he may have persuaded two justices, William Brennan and Byron White, to come his way.

## The Big Question in this case:

- Did Sony's sale of Betamax video tape records contribute to copyright infringement?

The Court said no. On January 17, 1984, the Court announced it had sided with Sony, 5–4. To back up their decision, the Court argued that many broadcast copyright holders didn't care if their programming was copied for home use. The most famous example of this involved Fred Rogers of *Mr. Rogers' Neighborhood*. Rogers had testified at the District Court and said he was cool with it, saying it helped his show be seen more. The Court further argued that Universal, Disney, and the other media corporations couldn't prove that they were hurt by Beta and VHS copies of their content for home use.[201]

The dissent argued that taping copyrighted programming was copyright infringement not protected by the First Amendment. Looking back at this case today, however, it's clear that the dissenting minority seems old-fashioned and out of touch. It's almost embarrassing that this case was close, considering how we all generally take for granted how we consume media today.[202]

After the decision, Universal and Disney immediately tried to get Congress to pass a law that would protect them from the effects of home video duplication. However, by that time, it was too late—the political will was not there since VCRs were everywhere and millions of Americans already copied stuff.

*Sony Corporation of America v. University City Studios*, also known simply as *The Betamax Case*, is the most important Supreme Court decision dealing with the development and distribution of home recordings, especially the video cassette recorder. It allowed video, as a format, to become huge in the United States. More importantly, the decision gave more power to the consumer. As it turns out, it also ended up helping the television and film industries anyway, as they ultimately made billions of dollars from the new technology.[203]

It's incredibly difficult to imagine if the Court had argued the other way in this close case. All of us have stuff on our computers that was copied. In fact, YouTube, which you undoubtedly have watched and I make a living off of, wouldn't even *exist* today if not for this case. Goodness, I guess the Supreme Court *does* matter.

201  supreme.justia.com/cases/federal/us/464/417/
202  www.oyez.org/cases/1982/81-1687
203  www.theatlantic.com/technology/archive/2012/01/the-court-case-that-almost-made-it-illegal-to-tape-tv-shows/251107/

# 67. New Jersey v. T.L.O. (1985)

This case began in Piscataway, New Jersey, on March 7, 1980. On that day, a teacher caught two students smoking in a bathroom of Piscataway High School. Since smoking in the bathroom (perhaps obviously) went against school rules, the teacher took the two girls to the principal's office. Assistant Vice Principal Theodore Choplick interrogated the two girls. One of them admitted to smoking. The other girl, a fourteen-year-old freshman later known simply by her initials to protect her privacy, T.L.O., denied that she had been smoking.

Choplick thought T.L.O. was lying. He forced her to come into his office so he could search her purse. Inside the purse, he found a pack of cigarettes. Next to the cigarettes, in plain view, were rolling papers, which he thought might be used for marijuana, so he kept searching the purse. He also found a pipe, empty plastic bags, a bunch of one-dollar bills rolled together, an index card that listed students who owed T.L.O. money, and even two letters seeming to show that T.L.O. was dealing marijuana.

Choplick reported what he found to the local police, giving what he found in the purse to them as evidence. T.L.O. later voluntarily confessed to the police that she had been selling marijuana at the high school.[204] Based on the confession and seized evidence, the state of New Jersey charged T.L.O. with possession of marijuana in the Juvenile and Domestic Relations Court of Middlesex County. However, her lawyer argued that the evidence from the purse shouldn't be allowed in court, as it was obtained illegally since the "exclusionary rule" applied. In other words, T.L.O.'s lawyer argued that the principal taking the purse to search it went against the Fourth Amendment. The Court allowed the evidence to be used anyway and found her guilty, sentencing her to one year of probation. It also fined her a thousand dollars and ordered her expelled from school.

T.L.O. appealed to the Superior Court of New Jersey. However, it agreed with the lower court, saying the exclusionary rule did not apply to school officials and that they could search a student's personal property. So T.L.O. appealed again, this time to the New Jersey Supreme Court, which reversed the lower decision, siding with T.L.O. The New Jersey Supreme Court argued the Fourth Amendment *did* apply to searches and seizures made by school officials in public schools.

So this time New Jersey appealed, and the Supreme Court agreed to hear oral arguments on March 28, 1984, hearing them a second time on October 2, 1984.

## The Big Question in this case:

- Does the exclusionary rule apply to searches conducted by school officials in public schools?

The Court said yes. However, on January 15, 1985, it announced it had sided with New Jersey, not T.L.O. It was 6–3. The Court held that public school officials may conduct searches without a warrant if there is a "reasonable suspicion." According to legal standards, a "reasonable suspicion" is less than probable cause, but it is still more than a hunch. It has to be based on specific facts. In the case of T.L.O., having cigarettes was relevant to whether she was telling the truth, and Mr. Choplick had a reasonable suspicion to think cigarettes were in her purse since the teacher took her straight to his office. In addition, after Mr. Choplick opened the purse, the other stuff was in plain view. *Plain view* is a well-understood exception to the warrant requirement of the Fourth Amendment. Therefore, Mr. Choplick wasn't going against the Fourth Amendment and that evidence could be used in court.[205]

In his dissent, Justice William Brennan argued that Mr. Choplick's search went too far. "When he opened the purse, he discovered the pack of cigarettes. At this point, his search for evidence of the smoking violation was complete." Brennan argued that continuing to rummage through T.L.O.'s purse was a violation of her privacy.[206]

*New Jersey v. T.L.O.* is the decision that makes it clear that if there is a reasonable suspicion, a principal can search a student's backpack at school. Undoubtedly principals across the country have followed through on that ever since.

205   www.oyez.org/cases/1983/83-712
206   law2.umkc.edu/faculty/projects/ftrials/conlaw/tlo.html

# 68. Hazelwood v. Kuhlmeier (1988)

This case began in St. Louis, Missouri, on May 10, 1983. On that day, Robert Reynolds, the principal at Hazelwood East High School, looked over the page proofs that were to be published for *The Spectrum*, the school-sponsored newspaper. *The Spectrum* was a student newspaper published every three weeks as part of a Journalism II class. The class distributed around 4,500 copies to students and sold copies to community members. Hazelwood School District paid for most of the costs to produce the newspaper.

Normally, Principal Reynolds would be excited to reach each new issue. However, this time he found two of the articles in the upcoming issue to be inappropriate. One story was about teen pregnancy and included interviews with students at Hazelwood East who had been pregnant. The story used fake names for the girls. Reynolds thought folks would still figure out who they were, though. Reynolds also thought the article's references to sex and birth control were not appropriate for younger kids at the school to read about. The second article dealt with divorce and brought up personal things that might reveal embarrassing personal family matters involving the students.

Instead of giving the students who reported on and edited the story a chance to respond, Reynolds cut the stories from the issue, and in doing so had to ultimately omit seven articles from it, causing it to go from a six-page issue to a four-page issue. The students only found out that the articles had been left out when the issue was released on May 13.

The three students involved with the two articles were reporters Leslie Smart and Lee Ann Tippett and the editor Cathy Kuhlmeier. They were upset that the articles didn't get published, especially since *The Spectrum*'s advisor, Robert Stergos, had previously approved them. Kuhlmeier, Smart, and Tippett confronted Principal Reynolds, who told the girls that the stories were "inappropriate, personal, sensitive, and unsuitable." Well, the students were not cool with that explanation and made copies of the deleted articles and distributed them to other students on school premises anyway. It's worth noting that they were not punished for doing that.[207]

Later, arguing that the school had violated their First Amendment rights to freedom of the press *and* freedom of speech, Kuhlmeier, Smart, and Tippett sued Hazelwood School

207   www.mtsu.edu/first-amendment/article/657/hazelwood-school-district-v-kuhlmeier

District and got their case to the US District Court for the Eastern District of Missouri. However, the US District Court for the Eastern District of Missouri agreed with Hazelwood, saying that because the school district mostly paid for the newspaper, they could control what was in it. Kuhlmeier and the others appealed to the US Court of Appeals for the Eighth Circuit, which reversed the lower court's decision, saying the newspaper was a "public forum" that went beyond the walls of the school, so therefore, the articles couldn't be censored.

After this reversal, Hazelwood School District appealed to the Supreme Court, which heard oral arguments on October 13, 1987. By this time, the girls had long graduated from Hazelwood East High School. It was impressive that they kept fighting in this case.

### The Big Question in this case:

- Did Principal Reynolds go against the students' First Amendment freedom of the press and freedom of speech rights?

The Court said no. On January 13, 1988, the Court announced it sided with Hazelwood, saying that school administrators could censor school-sponsored expressions like student newspapers, assembly speeches, and similar speech *if* the censorship is "reasonably related to legitimate pedagogical concerns." In other words, if it could potentially disrupt learning at school, the principal can prevent the expression. This idea is called prior restraint, a legal concept I first mentioned in the *Near v. Minnesota* (1931) chapter. Since school administrators represent the state, they can jump in to limit students from saying controversial stuff. Off-campus speech by students was still protected, so Kuhlmeier, Smart, and Tippett making photocopies and distributing the articles themselves was still fine.[208]

If you want to remember one thing about *Hazelwood School District v. Kuhlmeier*, it ought to be that schools *can* censor students *if* it's school-sponsored stuff. Later, in *Hosty v. Carter* (2005), the Supreme Court even applied it to the university level.[209] Still, today the case remains controversial, and several states have passed laws that protect the First Amendment rights of students.

208   supreme.justia.com/cases/federal/us/484/260/
209   casetext.com/case/hosty-v-carter

# 69. Hustler Magazine v. Falwell (1988)

This case began in Cincinnati, Ohio, in November 1983. That month, *Hustler*, a pornographic magazine also known for crude humor and political satire, published a parody ad that targeted popular Christian fundamentalist televangelist and conservative political commentator Jerry Falwell. It was right inside the front cover of the issue. It mimicked the advertisements of Campari, an Italian alcoholic beverage that featured interviews with celebrities that always started with a question about their "first time." In this parody ad, Jerry Falwell was portrayed sharing details about having sexual relations with his mother. Now, the ad *did* carry a small disclaimer at the bottom of the page that said, "ad parody—not to be taken seriously," and the magazine's contents also listed the ad as "Fiction; Ad and Personality Parody."

Regardless, after Falwell found out about it, he sued Larry Flynt, the publisher of the magazine, and Flynt's distribution company, for libel, invasion of privacy, and "intentional infliction of emotional distress." Remember, libel is a written form of defamation and defamation means ruining someone's good reputation. Falwell seemed worried that people might think this parody ad *was true*. Suing in the US District Court for the Western District of Virginia, he asked for $45 million in damages, around $100 million today.

The jury ruled against Falwell on the libel claim, saying the ad clearly wasn't referring to something that *really* happened. Still, the jury ruled in favor of Falwell on the claim of intentional infliction of emotional distress, awarding him $150,000 in damages.

Well, Flynt didn't like this, so he appealed to the US Court of Appeals for the Fourth Circuit, but it agreed with the lower court. By this time, Flynt and his lawyers had brought up the landmark Supreme Court ruling in *New York Times v. Sullivan* (1964). As you hopefully recall, in that case the Court ruled that if a public figure sues someone for defamation, they must prove there was "actual malice" involved. In other words, they have to prove the defendant either knew they were spreading lies or were recklessly disregarding whether they were spreading lies. It made it hard for public figures to win defamation lawsuits. Anyway, Flynt was frustrated the federal courts seemed to be misrepresenting the *Sullivan* ruling by saying that Falwell deserved defamation compensation (also known as "damages") due to "intentional infliction of emotional distress." Couldn't *any* public figure say this about *any* kind of parody or criticism of them? Falwell and his lawyers argued that *his family* had been defamed, and they were not public figures.[210] Regardless, Flynt appealed again, this time to the Supreme Court, and it agreed to hear oral arguments on December 2, 1987.

**The Big Question in this case:**

- Does the First Amendment's freedom of speech protection extend to the making of offensive statements about public figures that could result in suffering from emotional distress?

The Court said yes. On February 24, 1988, it announced it had unanimously sided with Larry Flynt and *Hustler*. The Court said the parody ad was protected speech under the First Amendment. It also said public figures like Jerry Falwell can't get money for suing for suffering from emotional distress without showing that the offending publication had a false statement of fact that was made with "actual malice." The Court leaned on *New York Times v. Sullivan* for this case, adding that protecting free speech was more important than protecting public figures from offensive speech.[211]

*Hustler Magazine v. Falwell* made it easier to make fun of celebrities. It represented two wildly different perspectives. On one end was Flynt, who in several ways represented the counterculture movement of the 1960s and 1970s that pushed the boundaries of free speech. On the other end was Falwell, who represented a culturally conservative and religious backlash to that. Their feud was later dramatized in the film *The People vs. Larry Flynt*, but interestingly, right after this case ended Flynt and Falwell put aside their differences and regularly met up to talk philosophy, later becoming good friends. In fact, they appeared on television together on multiple occasions. Falwell died in 2007 and Flynt died in 2021.

Since the *Hustler* magazine decision, hundreds of courts have cited the case, and today it remains one of the most important First Amendment Supreme Court cases in American history.

---

210   www.mtsu.edu/first-amendment/article/559/hustler-magazine-v-falwell
211   www.oyez.org/cases/1987/86-1278

# 70. Graham v. Connor (1989)

This case began in Charlotte, North Carolina, on November 12, 1984, when Dethorne Graham, who suffered from diabetes, had an insulin reaction. He had his friend, William Berry, drive him to a nearby convenience store to get some orange juice to counteract the reaction. Once he got inside, he saw a long line, making the store not so "convenient" anymore. He rushed back out to the car, directing his friend to drive him somewhere else to get the sugar he needed.

Meanwhile, someone across the street was watching them. That someone was M.S. Connor, a police officer who was uneasy about what he had just witnessed. To him, it looked like Graham was robbing the convenience store because he entered and exited the store so quickly in what seemed to be a getaway car.

Officer Connor immediately followed Graham and Berry's car, flashing the patrol lights to pull them over about half a mile away from the store. As Connor approached the car, Berry frantically told him that Graham had diabetes and needed sugar immediately. Not believing him, Connor told the two to wait while he tried to figure out what happened back at the store. As Connor called for backup in his patrol car, Graham got out of the car, ran around it twice, and collapsed on the curb.

After that, Connor handcuffed Graham. By the time the backup of four other cops arrived, Graham had regained consciousness. The cops assumed Graham was drunk. Some didn't believe Graham had diabetes. When Graham pleaded with them to check his wallet for a diabetic identification card, one of the officers told him to "shut up" and slammed him down on the hood of the car. The officers roughed up Graham badly, throwing him headfirst into a patrol car. Later Graham claimed the police officers gave him a bunch of cuts and bruises, injured his shoulder, and broke his foot.

As Graham waited in the back of the patrol car, a friend came by with some orange juice for him. However, the officers didn't let him have it! Eventually, Officer Connor got a report that Graham had done nothing wrong at the convenience store, and the officers drove him home and released him.[212] *No hard feelings, man. So we're cool, right?*

Well, Graham was *not* cool with how those police officers treated him. He later sued the five involved, as well as the city of Charlotte. Graham argued that his constitutional right to be free from excessive force had been violated. The US District Court for the Western District of North Carolina used a due process test from a circuit court case known as *Johnson v. Glick* (1973) to determine if the officers acted out of "good faith" or "maliciously or sadistically." In other words, were the cops trying to keep order or were they abusing their power? The US District Court for the Western District of North Carolina agreed with the city of Charlotte, justifying the actions of the police officers. Graham then appealed to the Court of Appeals for the Fourth Circuit, but it agreed with the lower court.

Graham then appealed once more, this time to the Supreme Court, which agreed to hear oral arguments on February 21, 1989, more than four years after the incident. Because Graham claimed the Charlotte police violated his Fourth Amendment rights, the Court had to decide based on how reasonable it was for the cops to do what they did strictly based on that part of the Constitution. Because "objective reasonableness" could be interpreted in many ways, the Court concluded such a case would be better judged from the perspective of the officers on the scene.

## The Big Questions in this case:

- Did Graham have to show that the police acted "maliciously and sadistically for the very purpose of causing harm" to establish a claim that they used excessive force?
- Must Graham's claim that the police used excessive force be examined under the Fourth Amendment's "objective reasonableness" standard?

The Court answered no to the first question and yes to the second question. On May 15, 1989, it announced that it had unanimously sided with Connor. The Court told the Fourth Circuit to look at the case again through the lens of the Fourth Amendment. They argued that doing that would make subjective concepts like malicious intent not applicable. While the Court said the burden of proof was not on Graham to prove that the police used excessive force, their actions were still reasonable. Connor was reasonably justified in assuming that Graham had broken laws. Because Connor believed a crime probably happened given the circumstances from his perspective, he was not held liable.[213]

*Graham v. Connor* set the precedent that an "objective reasonable" standard should always apply when somebody claims a cop used excessive force. The case has made it seem okay for cops to assume the worst or they are dealing with a criminal. Ultimately, this led to stuff like the "reasonably scared cop rule." This means that now police officers can easily justify the use of force when their lives might be in danger. It can be a slippery slope, especially because "objective reasonableness" can easily turn into "*subjective reasonableness.*" Police officers have difficult jobs, often making life-or-death decisions in a split second. This is likely why the Court determined that reasonable assumptions are fine for cops to effectively do their jobs.

Unfortunately, cops "doing their jobs" has sometimes led to horrible unintended consequences. Many Americans have been abused or died because of the use of excessive force by police officers. Because of the *Graham* decision, excessive force is often justified in court. After the Black Lives Matter movement raised awareness about police brutality, this case received renewed scrutiny.[214] It remains probably more relevant today than ever before.

214    www.salon.com/2014/09/06/shoot_first_ask_later_why_the_concept_of_reasonable_fear_is_
anything_but_reasonable/

# 71. Texas v. Johnson
# (1989)

This case began in Dallas, Texas, on August 22, 1984. On that day, protestors marched through the streets, destroyed property, spray-painted walls, broke windows, and threw dirty diapers and beer cans outside of the Republican National Convention. Someone stole an American flag from a downtown building. Eventually, that flag ended up in the hands of Revolutionary Communist Youth Brigade member Gregory Lee Johnson. At the height of the protests, Johnson poured kerosene on the flag and set it on fire. While the flag burned, he chanted stuff like, "Red, white, and blue, we spit on you; you stand for plunder, you will go under," and "Reagan, Mondale, which will it be? Either one means World War III." Although no one got physically hurt because of it, some people who saw Johnson do this were offended.

Soon after, police arrested Johnson and charged him with violating a Texas law that said you couldn't vandalize respected objects if such an action was likely to get people angry. A jury in the Dallas County Criminal District Court convicted Johnson and a judge fined him two thousand dollars (around six thousand in today's money) and sentenced him to one year in prison. He appealed his case to the Fifth Court of Appeals of Texas, arguing that burning the American flag was protected under the First Amendment, but he lost the appeal. After that, he appealed again to the Texas Court of Criminal Appeals, and it overturned his conviction, saying the First Amendment protects American flag burning as symbolic speech. It also argued that Johnson did not hurt or threaten anyone by burning the flag.

Texas decided to appeal the case as the decision by the Texas Court of Criminal Appeals undermined its law. The Supreme Court agreed to take it on, and it heard oral arguments on March 21, 1989. At first, the Court considered whether the First Amendment protected *non-speech* acts, since this wasn't about Johnson's verbal communication. They wondered if the act of burning the American flag should be considered expressive conduct.[215]

## The Big Question in this case:

- Is destroying the American flag a form of speech protected under the First Amendment?

The Court said yes. In a highly controversial decision, the Court announced on June 21, 1989, that it had sided with Johnson, 5–4. The Court said that Texas could not ban flag burning. It also argued that the Texas law that said you couldn't vandalize respected objects didn't prevent disturbing the peace. Another Texas law already existed to prevent disturbing the peace without targeting flag burning.

Justice William Brennan delivered the opinion, but I'd rather quote Justice Anthony Kennedy, as he summed up the decision well. Kennedy wrote, "The hard fact is that sometimes we must make decisions we do not like. We make them because they are right, right in the sense that the law and the Constitution, as we see them, compel the result. And so great is our commitment to the process that, except in the rare case, we do not pause to express distaste for the result, perhaps for fear of undermining a valued principle that dictates the decision. This is one of those rare cases."[216]

The Court had two major dissents. The first, by the justices William Rehnquist, Byron White, and Sandra Day O'Connor, argued that the American flag had a "unique status" that should be protected from desecration. Rehnquist wrote, "The Flag is not simply another 'idea' or 'point of view' competing for recognition in the marketplace of ideas. Millions and millions of Americans regard it with an almost mystical reverence regardless of what sort of social, political, or philosophical beliefs they may have."[217]

Justice John Paul Stevens had a slightly different dissent, arguing it was more than about the flag being an important symbol. He argued that Johnson was only punished for *how* he expressed his opinion, not the opinion itself.[218]

The decision automatically made laws in forty-eight of the fifty states invalid. However, two weeks later, Congress passed the Flag Protection Act, making it a federal crime to desecrate the American flag. This move was kind of like a middle finger to the Supreme Court's decision. However, the Court had the last laugh. The next year, the same five-person majority of justices struck down that law in *United States v. Eichman* (1990). Since then, many in Congress have tried to pass a constitutional amendment outlawing flag burning, but each time they have come up short.

*Texas v. Johnson*, in many ways, started the American flag-burning debate, which continues to this day. It has remained important to those who value true freedom of speech, even if that speech is offensive to the majority of the country's citizens.

---

216   www.law.cornell.edu/supremecourt/text/491/397
217   Ibid.
218   Ibid.

# 72. Shaw v. Reno (1993)

This case began in Raleigh, North Carolina, in 1990. That year, none of North Carolina's eleven representatives in the United States Congress were African American, even though 20 percent of the state's population was. As a matter of fact, since the American Civil War, only a total of four African Americans had been elected to the US House of Representatives in the state. After the 1990 census, North Carolina gained a district, so they got a new US Representative. The state legislature had realized the state needed an African American representative, and they intentionally created a district made of mostly African Americans under the assumption that they would vote one in. After the legislature submitted their plans to the US Department of Justice, Attorney General Janet Reno rejected them, saying there still needed to be more districts where African Americans had a better chance to represent constituents to comply with the Voting Rights Act.

After that, North Carolina's state legislature went back to the drawing board (quite literally), this time drawing up another district to help get an *additional* African American to represent North Carolina in the US House of Representatives. Now, one could easily argue that this district was *oddly* shaped. It looked like a deformed snake, running along Interstate 85 for 160 miles, breaking up counties and towns and grouping places typically *not* grouped together. In some places, the district was only as wide *as the highway itself.* The gerrymandered districts accomplished the goal they aimed for. After the congressional elections of 1992, residents of both of those redrawn districts elected African Americans to represent them. Incredibly, both were North Carolina's first African Americans to get into Congress in the twentieth century.

However, this made some North Carolina folks upset. Again, gerrymandering, or the manipulation of legislative boundaries to favor one political party or group, was a controversial issue that folks out of the state were concerned about. Specifically, North Carolina residents were concerned that those districts were racially gerrymandered to get African Americans elected there, probably because they were. Five North Carolina residents, led by Ruth Shaw, sued both the state and federal governments, arguing that District 12 was gerrymandered so much that it went against the Fourteenth Amendment's tubular Equal Protection Clause. Again, they argued it was racial gerrymandering, not partisan gerrymandering, and the drawn district didn't go against the "one person, one vote" principle established in *Reynolds v. Sims* (1964).

Shaw and the rest took their case to the US District Court for the Eastern District of North Carolina. The District Court simply dismissed the lawsuit, saying their hands were tied due to a previous case, *United Jewish Organizations of Williamsburgh v. Carey* (1977), in which the Supreme Court ruled that splitting a Hasidic Jewish community with redistricting did *not* go against the Equal Protection Clause.

Shaw and the others appealed their decision directly to the Supreme Court, who agreed to take on the case, hearing oral arguments on April 20, 1993. Arguments kept returning to whether North Carolina's redistricting plan went against the Equal Protection Clause. Janet Reno's defense team argued that the Voting Rights Act of 1965 encouraged creating districts where minorities were the majority, and that this was a justifiable form of affirmative action to help those groups historically discriminated against.[219]

## The Big Question in this case:

- Did North Carolina's racially gerrymandered district go against the Equal Protection Clause of the Fourteenth Amendment?

The Court said yes. On April 20, 1993, the Court announced that it had sided with Shaw, 5–4. The Court sent the case back to the lower court to see if the district could be justified in terms other than by the skin color of the residents who lived there. The Court said that creating a district like District 12 based solely on the color of skin set a dangerous precedent. In addition, the majority argued that racial gerrymandering, even if it had noble intentions like preventing groups from being marginalized, might cause representatives to only focus on the needs of certain constituents, not the entire group.

Four justices wrote separate dissents for this case. Overall, they all argued that they sided with Reno because they believed gerrymandering helped a group historically underrepresented in North Carolina. They said people of the same skin color often share the same interests and often vote in the same way. Also, in their minds, racial gerrymandering only went against the Equal Protection Clause of the Fourteenth Amendment if the purpose of making those boundaries was to further give power to the group who already *had* the power. However, it was clear African Americans from North Carolina didn't currently have much power in Congress and hadn't ever had it.[220]

*Shaw v. Reno* made gerrymandering on racial and ethnic grounds unconstitutional. While it is one of the most important Supreme Court cases when it comes to

219    www.oyez.org/cases/1992/92-357
220    www.law.cornell.edu/supct/html/92-357.ZS.html

gerrymandering, today partisan gerrymandering, or manipulating districts to favor one political party, continues to be a huge problem that most Americans are against. Unless a constitutional amendment bans partisan gerrymandering, however, it shall remain a problem because the Court has since decided it doesn't have the authority to strike it down. In *Rucho v. Common Cause* (2019), the Court said that partisan gerrymandering is not something they can rule on since it involved a political question since political power was at stake. Regardless, gerrymandering will continue to be a hot-button issue.

# 73. United States v. Lopez (1995)

This case began in San Antonio, Texas, on March 10, 1992. On that day, Alfonso Lopez, Jr., a senior at Edison High School, brought a concealed .38-caliber revolver into the school. Although the gun was not loaded, he also brought bullets for it. After receiving an anonymous tip about the gun and bullets, school authorities confronted Lopez about it. Lopez admitted to having the gun and bullets but claimed that he brought them to school to sell to someone. Well, that didn't matter. It was illegal and terrifying to know a student brought such a dangerous weapon to school. He was charged with breaking a Texas law that banned guns on school property.

However, the next day there was good news and bad news for Lopez. The good news was that the charges against him were dropped. The bad news was that the only reason why the charges were dropped was that now he was charged for breaking a *federal* law, the Gun-Free School Zones Act, making it a federal offense for anyone to bring a gun into a school zone.[221]

In the US District Court for the Western District of Texas, Lopez's lawyers argued that the Gun-Free School Zones Act was unconstitutional. According to them, there was nothing in the Constitution about controlling what happened at public schools. Therefore, the Tenth Amendment applied. However, the US District Court disagreed, ruling that the Gun-Free School Zones Act was a "constitutional exercise of Congress' well defined power to regulate activities in and affecting commerce, and the 'business' of elementary, middle and high schools...affects interstate commerce."[222] In other words, the US District Court argued that the commerce clause of the Constitution gave Congress the power to regulate guns in public schools, and their rationale was that, since guns in schools led to gun violence, people might be reluctant to travel through these areas from other states. The District Court added that the disruptions in schools caused by weapons being there resulted in a less-educated population, which could negatively affect commerce in the future.

Well, Lopez and his lawyers thought this was quite a reach, to say the least. After Lopez was found guilty and sentenced to six months in prison, followed by two years of probation, he appealed the case to the Fifth Circuit Court of Appeals, arguing that the

221   billofrightsinstitute.org/e-lessons/united-states-v-lopez-1995
222   www.law.cornell.edu/supct/html/93-1260.ZO.html

Commerce Clause didn't apply to guns in schools.[223] The Fifth Circuit Court of Appeals agreed with Lopez and reversed his conviction. After, the federal government got the Supreme Court to weigh in, and it heard oral arguments on November 8, 1994. The lawyers who argued on behalf of the federal government had another unique argument. They argued that, because violent crime causes physical harm and creates monetary expenses, this could directly lead to higher insurance costs, which are spread throughout the entire economy of the country. Therefore, the Commerce Clause applied.

### The Big Question in this case:

- Was the Gun-Free School Zones Act unconstitutional because it went against the Commerce Clause?

The Court said yes. On April 26, 1995, it announced that it had sided with Lopez, but this was another close one, 5–4. The Court generally thought the arguments by the lawyers representing the federal government were a stretch, too. It said that bringing a gun to a public school zone was not an economic activity and had little effect on interstate commerce. It declared the Gun-Free School Zones Act unconstitutional, stating that the Commerce Clause did *not* authorize it.[224]

Chief Justice William Rehnquist wrote the majority opinion, identifying three categories of economic activity that could regulate under the Commerce Clause:

1. Any economic activity on channels (roads, waterways, and airways)

2. Any economic activity on instrumentalities (any kind of network that moves goods and/or persons)

3. Any economic activity "substantially" affected by or related to interstate commerce.[225]

Obviously, much of this was still up to much interpretation, and the dissenting justices interpreted this case quite differently. In his dissent, Justice John Paul Stevens argued that not only did the Commerce Clause allow Congress to prohibit guns in school zones, but it could prohibit them *anywhere*.[226]

Regardless, *United States v. Lopez* dramatically reduced the power of Congress with a narrower interpretation of the Commerce Clause while simultaneously increasing the strength of the Tenth Amendment, and thus state legislatures. The Court would further

223   billofrightsinstitute.org/e-lessons/united-states-v-lopez-1995
224   www.oyez.org/cases/1994/93-1260
225   www.law.cornell.edu/supct/html/93-1260.ZO.html
226   Ibid.

limit congressional powers regarding the Commerce Clause in the case *United States v. Morrison* (2000). Ever since *United States v. Lopez*, the Supreme Court has often made federalism great again by generally reducing the power of the federal government and strengthening the power of state governments.

# 74. US Term Limits, Inc. v. Thornton (1995)

This case began in Arkansas on November 3, 1992. On that day, citizens from across the state voted to approve Amendment 73 to the Arkansas Constitution, saying any federal congressional candidate who has already served three terms in the US House of Representatives or two terms in the US Senate couldn't be on the ballot in elections. Now, representatives could still run for a *fourth* term and senators could still run for a *third* term. However, this amendment would require that their names would have to be written in on the ballot. For people who can't spell, though, I suppose that might have been a problem.

Regardless, Amendment 73 passed. However, many Arkansans were not happy about it passing. One such Arkansan was Bobbie Hill, a member representing the League of Women Voters. She sued the state, arguing that the amendment went against the *United States* Constitution, Article 1, Section 2, which stated:

> No Person shall be a Representative who shall not have attained to the Age of twenty five Years, and been seven Years a Citizen of the United States, and who shall not, when elected, be an Inhabitant of that State in which he shall be chosen But wait, there's more. It's Article 1, Section III: No Person shall be a Senator who shall not have attained to the Age of thirty Years, and been nine Years a Citizen of the United States, and who shall not, when elected, be an Inhabitant of that State for which he shall be chosen.

Hill also brought up that the amendment went against the Seventeenth Amendment.

Ray Thornton, a US Representative representing the Second District of Arkansas, was one of the folks who would not have his name on the ballot in the next election. He joined forces with Hill and the League of Women Voters for another lawsuit. Representing Arkansas in the lawsuit by Hill was Attorney General Winston Bryant. Representing Arkansas in the lawsuit by Thornton was US Term Limits, the organization that helped get Amendment 73 to pass.[227]

The Arkansas circuit court sided with Thornton and Hill. On appeal, the Arkansas Supreme Court also ruled in favor of both Thornton and Hill. US Term Limits and Bryant appealed yet again, this time to the *supreme* Supreme Court, which agreed to hear both cases, hearing oral arguments on November 29, 1994.

227  encyclopediaofarkansas.net/entries/u-s-term-limits-inc-v-thornton-4166/

US Term Limits argued that Amendment 73 didn't prevent anyone from running for an additional term—she or he could run as a write-in candidate. However, Thornton and Hill argued this additional obstacle was enough to go against both Sections Two and Three of Article One of the Constitution.

## The Big Question in this case:

- Could states slightly alter the qualifications to run for US Congress that are specifically listed in the Constitution?

The Court said no. On May 22, 1995, it announced it had sided with both Thornton and Hill. It was another close one, 5–4, and another decision seemingly split on political ideology. The more conservative justices sided with US Term Limits.

Justice John Paul Stevens wrote the majority opinion, using the Seventeenth Amendment specifically to back it up. He wrote, "The Congress of the United States...is not a confederation of nations in which separate sovereigns are represented by appointed delegates, but is instead a body composed of representatives of the people."

Writing for the dissent, Justice Clarence Thomas wrote, "Nothing in the Constitution deprives the people of each State of the power to prescribe eligibility requirements for the candidates who seek to represent them in Congress."[228] In other words, this was another signal by the more conservative justices on the bench that they preferred the state to have more power over the federal government.

Regardless, *US Term Limits, Inc. v. Thornton* made it clear that if people wanted there to be term limits for members of the United States Congress, there would have to be a constitutional amendment. This means this likely isn't going to happen anytime soon, even though one recent poll showed that 82 percent of Americans said that they thought members of Congress should have term limits.[229]

What's fascinating is that the issue seems to be bipartisan—both Democrats and Republicans have supported congressional term limits. In 2019, Ted Cruz, a US Senator from Texas, and Francis Rooney, a US Representative from Florida, introduced an amendment to the Constitution to restrict US Senators to two six-year terms and US Representatives to three two-year terms.[230] It never gained any traction.

228   supreme.justia.com/cases/federal/us/514/779/
229   mclaughlinonline.com/2018/02/08/ma-poll-voters-overwhelmingly-support-term-limits-for-
       congress/
230   www.cnn.com/2019/01/04/politics/term-limits-ted-cruz-proposal/index.html

# 75. Bush v. Gore (2000)

This case began in Florida on November 8, 2000. On that day, in one of the closest presidential elections in American history, George Walker Bush held a narrow lead over Al Gore. Out of nearly six million ballots in the state, only 1,784 votes separated the two. Under Florida law, and since the United States has a winner-takes-all system, the candidate with the most votes in the state got all of its electoral votes. Because it was so close, state law said there had to be a machine vote recount. However, after the recount, it was even closer! Now, Bush's lead was just *327*.

But no worries. Florida law also allowed Gore the option of a manual vote recount, meaning counting them by hand, in whatever counties Gore wanted. Gore gladly accepted that offer, picking four counties for such a recount: Broward, Miami-Dade, Volusia, and Palm Beach. The problem was, though, that Gore was running out of time. Florida law also said (Florida law says a lot) that the state's election results have to be certified within seven days of the election. Since Election Day was on November 7 that year, that meant the deadline was November 14. Well, three of those four counties didn't get their manual recounts done before that deadline. Despite those counties trying to get an extension, the Florida Secretary of State, Katherine Harris, announced that she would be certifying the votes, ending all the recounts.

Al Gore was not happy to hear this news. He and Palm Beach County tried to get an injunction against Secretary Harris to prevent her from certifying the votes until those three counties got their recounts done. The Florida Supreme Court said that was fine and granted the injunction on November 17. On November 21, it ruled that Secretary Harris had to let those counties finish recounting with a new deadline of November 26. However, Miami-Dade County argued that was not enough time, and, believe it or not, it gave up counting! Gore told Miami-Dade County that it *had* to count those votes. He tried to get another court order to force them, but that one failed. On November 26, Harris certified the election in Florida, giving Bush what was now just a 537-vote victory.[231]

Gore then sued Harris, arguing the certified results were invalid because the recount process wasn't finished yet. The Leon County Circuit dismissed his lawsuit, so Gore appealed to the Florida Supreme Court. On December 8, it ruled in favor of Gore and demanded that all votes not counted by voting machines had to be manually recounted if they hadn't been already.

231  law2.umkc.edu/faculty/projects/ftrials/conlaw/bushvgorell.html

Now, George W. Bush stepped in, saying the Florida Supreme Court was wrong and appealing its decision to the *supreme* Supreme Court. And, wouldn't you know it, *the next day* the Supreme Court reviewed the case. Why did the Supreme Court respond more quickly than it ever had before? Well, this was obviously important. Soon, the deadline for electors to formally submit their choice would be there, and soon after that the new president would have to be sworn in. Things needed to move along. The Court heard oral arguments on December 11.

During all of this, protestors lined the streets outside. Rarely was there a time in American history when the country had seemed so divided. Things were tense, to say the least.

The Court considered whether the Florida Supreme Court violated Article 2, Section 1, Clause 2 of the Constitution, specifically the part that says: "Each State shall appoint, in such Manner as the Legislature thereof may direct, a Number of Electors…"

The Court also considered whether the recounts were constitutional to begin with. Bush had argued that the recounts went against both the Equal Protection Clause and Due Process Clause of the Fourteenth Amendment since Florida didn't have a statewide standard for recounting votes. Each county did it their way. In response, Gore argued the "intent of the voter" standard applied here. The "intent of the voter" standard lets you know who a voter *meant* to vote for in case there were anomalies on the ballot, and Gore argued the Equal Protection Clause *required* it. In addition, if Florida's standard wasn't good enough, certainly other states' standards would *also* go against the Equal Protection Clause.

### The Big Questions in this case:

- Did the Florida Supreme Court go against Article 2, Section 1, Cause 2 of the Constitution?
- Can manual recounts go against the Equal Protection Clause and Due Process Clause of the Fourteenth Amendment?

The Court said yes to both questions. On December 12, 2000, it announced it had sided with Bush, which means Bush got Florida's electors, sealing his presidential victory. It was another close decision along political ideological lines, which of course outraged Gore supporters. In a 5–4 decision, with the five more conservative justices siding with Bush, the Court argued that different standards being applied from ballot to ballot with recounts in Florida went against the Equal Protection Clause of the Fourteenth Amendment. The

Court argued that the recount gave special treatment to some ballots over others. It ordered the recount stopped.

However, most people don't realize that the Court also decided in this case *not* along ideological lines. In a 7–2 decision, the Court also decided that the Florida Supreme Court recounting plan *did* go against the Constitution.[232]

Therefore, Bush, not Gore, would serve the next eight years as the country's forty-third president. Because of the unpopularity of Bush as president in later years, *Bush v. Gore* ultimately became one of the most controversial Supreme Court cases in history. More than ever before, critics accused the Court of "judicial activism" after this case. Judicial activism generally means that judges and justices let their political views influence how they decide, rather than a precedent or an objective view of the law.

Critics often pointed out how the justices in the Court who normally had supported federalism and states' rights suddenly ignored that for this case. One of the two people on the Court who dissented in both decisions in this case was Justice John Paul Stevens. In his dissent, he wrote, "Although we may never know with complete certainty the identity of the winner of this year's presidential election, the identity of the loser is perfectly clear. It is the Nation's confidence in the judge as an impartial guardian of the rule of law."[233] Justice Stevens had a point. The *Bush v. Gore* decision, at the least, had damaged the reputation of the Supreme Court, and that reputation hasn't recovered.[234]

232   www.oyez.org/cases/2000/00-949
233   www.law.cornell.edu/supct/html/00-949.ZPC.html
234   news.gallup.com/poll/4732/supreme-court.aspx

# 76. Lawrence v. Texas (2003)

This case began in Harris County on September 17, 1998. On that night, John Lawrence, a gay man, hosted two other gay men at his apartment. One of those men, Robert Eubanks, had been John's friend for at least twenty years. The other man, Tyron Garner, was the boyfriend of Eubanks. Eubanks and Garner had a tumultuous relationship. While the two were often intimate with each other, they also often didn't get along.

On the night of September 17, Garner and Eubanks had planned on staying over as they had no safe way to get home. Eubanks had been drinking a lot, anyway. After Lawrence flirted with Garner, he angrily left Lawrence's apartment. Eubanks then called the local police to report that there was a "Black male going crazy with a gun" at Lawrence's apartment. Four Harris County sheriff's deputies were there within minutes and met up with Eubanks, who pointed them to the apartment. Because the officers had probable cause and didn't know Eubanks was lying, they prepared to enter the apartment with their weapons drawn. The door was unlocked, and they walked in and saw Lawrence and Garner having consensual sex. It's worth noting that only two of the officers later reported that they saw Lawrence and Garner having sex. While Garner was an African American, the deputies found no gun on him.

However, the deputies still arrested both men, charging them with breaking a Texas law that made "deviant sexual intercourse" between people of the same sex illegal. At their hearing the next day, Lawrence and Garner both claimed they were innocent of the crime. Eubanks did get in trouble for filing a false police report but didn't bother defending himself and served some time in jail.

Lambda Legal, an organization that focuses on protecting the civil rights of the LGBT+ community, offered to help defend Lawrence and Garner, as it had been fighting laws restricting sodomy for years. In the modern sense, "sodomy" means sexual intercourse involving anal sex or, more broadly, any sexual activity that does not result in reproduction. This may sound strange, but Lambda Legal was excited to take this case on. After all, people often weren't arrested for having sex...for perhaps obvious reasons. "It was their arrest that gave us the opportunity to challenge the [law]," Mitchell Katine, the lawyer who represented Lawrence and Gardner, later said.[235]

Anyway, Lawrence and Garner gladly accepted Lambda Legal's help. However, Lambda Legal suggested that the two not defend themselves in a trial as the organization ultimately wanted to appeal their case to higher courts. After Lawrence and Garner pleaded "no contest" and waived their right to a trial, the Justice of the Peace, Mike Parrott, found them guilty and fined them $100 plus court costs, or about $183 in today's money. As it turns out, this backfired for Lambda Legal, as the fine was below the minimum required to let them appeal their convictions. After Mitchell Katine realized this, he asked the judge to give Lawrence and Garner a higher penalty. Long story short, Katine worked out a deal with the prosecution in Harris County Criminal Court and ultimately the penalty was high enough so that Lawrence and Garner could appeal to the Texas Fourteenth Court of Appeals, which heard the case on November 3, 1999. Katine argued that the Texas law forbidding sodomy went against the Equal Protection Clause of the Fourteenth Amendment. However, the odds were stacked against Lawrence and Garner, as the Supreme Court had already ruled on this issue in *Bowers v. Hardwick* (1986). In that decision, the Court upheld a Georgia law banning sodomy since the Constitution didn't say anything about the right to engage in homosexual sex.

Regardless, on June 8, 2000, in a 2–1 decision, the Texas Fourteenth Court of Appeals sided with Lawrence and Garner, declaring the Texas law banning sodomy unconstitutional, meaning it went against the Texas Constitution. Specifically, they argued it went against the 1972 Equal Rights Amendment to the Texas Constitution, which, among other things, prohibits discrimination based on sex. However, after more judges from the Texas Court of Appeals looked at the case, they reversed the three-judge panel's decision and upheld the law's constitutionality. Katine then attempted to appeal to the Texas Court of Criminal Appeals, but it denied the request.[236]

But Katine stayed determined. On July 16, 2002, almost four years after the arrest of Lawrence and Garner, he directly asked the Supreme Court to consider the case, and it did.[237] The Court heard oral arguments on March 26, 2003. In oral arguments, Katine argued that consensual sex between heterosexual couples in the privacy of their homes was allowed, so consensual sex between homosexual couples should be allowed, too.

235   www.khou.com/video/entertainment/television/programs/great-day-houston/a-look-back-at-landmark-civil-rights-case-lawrence-v-texas/285-a1468197-a25d-4a23-9bfe-d10683de6b38
236   www.law.cornell.edu/wex/lawrence_v._texas
237   www.chron.com/news/houston-texas/article/Gay-group-takes-Houston-case-to-high-court-2103134.php

**The Big Questions in this case:**

- Does the law restricting sodomy in Texas go against the Equal Protection Clause of the Fourteenth Amendment?

- Is consensual sexual intimacy between two adults protected under the Equal Protection Clause of the Fourteenth Amendment?

The Court said yes to both questions. On June 26, 2003, it announced that it had sided with Lawrence and Garner, 6–3. The Court said any law that restricted consensual sexual activity between two adults, in the privacy of their homes, went against the Equal Protection Clause of the Fourteenth Amendment. In deciding this way, the Court also overturned *Bowers v. Hardwick*.[238] Justice Anthony Kennedy wrote the majority opinion, writing Lawrence and Garner "are entitled to respect for their private lives. The State cannot demean their existence or control their destiny by making their private sexual conduct a crime."[239] Kennedy considered previous decisions like *Griswold v. Connecticut* (1965), *Roe v. Wade* (1973), and *Planned Parenthood v. Casey* (1992) with this decision and argued that the *Bowers* decision went *against* the precedent.

It's worth noting that none of the dissents *agreed* with the Texas law restricting sodomy. They generally thought the Constitution didn't say anything about privacy and thought the Court didn't have the authority to weigh in on this case.

*Lawrence v. Texas* was seen as a huge victory for gay rights advocates, and it paved the way for future decisions like *United States v. Windsor* (2013), which said the federal government couldn't make a law defining marriage as a union between one man and one woman, and *Obergefell v. Hodges* (2015), which effectively legalized same-sex marriage. At the time of the *Lawrence* decision, thirteen states had laws outlawing sodomy. After this, all those laws were gone.

While both had generally done their best to avoid the spotlight during the process, John Lawrence and Tyron Garner were undeniably proud to be a part of this historically significant case. "I don't really want to be a hero," Garner said, "but I want to tell other gay people, 'Be who you are, and don't be afraid.' "[240] Garner died in 2006, and Lawrence died in 2011.

238   www.oyez.org/cases/2002/02-102
239   supreme.justia.com/cases/federal/us/539/558/
240   www.nytimes.com/2006/09/14/obituaries/14garner.html

# 77. Crawford v. Washington (2004)

This case began in Olympia, Washington, on August 5, 1999. On that day, Sylvia Crawford told her husband, Michael Crawford, that a man named Kenneth Lee had attempted to rape her. Michael Crawford, who had been heavily drinking, didn't go to the police. Instead, the angry and drunk Crawford went to Kenneth Lee's apartment. Crawford and Lee got into a fight, and the next thing you know, Crawford stabbed Lee in the stomach. During the stabbing, Crawford's hand also got cut.

After the Olympia police department got involved, they arrested Michael and Sylvia Crawford and interrogated them separately. While Michael and Sylvia gave similar accounts of what happened, there was one important difference. Michael claimed that he had stabbed Kenneth out of self-defense, but Sylvia said Kenneth did *not* have a weapon. This would cause the police to question Michael's story. After all, how could it be "self-defense" if Kenneth didn't have a weapon?[241]

In District Court, the State of Washington charged Michael Crawford with assault and attempted murder. State law said married people didn't have to testify against each other in court, so at Michael's trial, Sylvia didn't take the stand. However, the police had recorded her interrogation, and the judge allowed the deputy prosecutor, Robert Lund, to use that tape as evidence backing up that Michael was attempting murder, not acting in self-defense.

Crawford's lawyers protested Lund using the tape as evidence in court. They argued that Sylvia's recorded statements couldn't be used as evidence in court unless they were able to cross-examine her, which, as I mentioned earlier, they couldn't do under state law. Regardless, Crawford's lawyers argued that this went against the Confrontation Clause of the Sixth Amendment. They said Crawford had a right to confront his accuser in court, and you can't cross-examine a recording of a voice, as it turns out.

Nevertheless, the judge allowed the tape recording to be used as evidence. It ended up being *extremely influential* evidence. Michael Crawford was convicted of attempted murder and assault. The judge sentenced him to fifteen years in prison.

---

241   Thomas J. Reed, *Crawford v. Washington* and the Irretrievable Breakdown of a Union: Separating the Confrontation Clause from the Hearsay Rule, 56 S. C. L. Rev. 185 (2004).

Crawford appealed his case to the Washington Court of Appeals, who reversed the lower court's decision and overturned his sentence. It argued that, due to the precedent set by the Supreme Court case *Ohio v. Roberts* (1980), Sylvia Crawford's recorded testimony was not reliable enough. *Ohio v. Roberts* also dealt with the Confrontation Clause of the Sixth Amendment and set up this reliability standard. The state appealed to the Washington Supreme Court, and it sided with the state, overturning the Washington Court of Appeals decision, saying that Sylvia's recorded testimony was reliable because it complemented Michael's testimony well. Therefore, the state reinstated his conviction.

Because there were all these different interpretations of the exact same evidence, the Supreme Court decided it wanted in on the action, and it requested to review the case on June 9, 2003. On November 10, it heard oral arguments.

## The Big Question in this case:

- Does using testimony from out of the court, with no chance for cross-examination, go against the Confrontation Clause of the Sixth Amendment?

The Court said yes. On March 8, 2004, it announced it had sided with Crawford. Surprisingly, it was unanimous. The Court said Sylvia Crawford's recorded statement from the police interrogation went against Michael Crawford's Sixth Amendment right to confront her about it in court. Justice Antonin Scalia gave the majority opinion. He argued that any out-of-court statement that is "testimonial" should not be allowed as evidence, *unless* this statement came from a person who had no way of testifying in court *and* this person could be cross-examined by the defendant ahead of time.[242] This decision overturned *Ohio v. Roberts*.

*Crawford v. Washington* was a big victory for the Sixth Amendment. It made it much more difficult to allow "hearsay" evidence to be used in court. In other words, if a statement was made by someone involved in a criminal case but *outside* of court, that statement likely won't be used as evidence.

# 78. Gonzales v. Raich (2005)

This case began in California on November 5, 1996, when the majority of citizens voted to make medical marijuana legal. This may not seem like a big deal today, but at the time, it was a *big* freaking deal, as marijuana was illegal across the country, thanks to the Controlled Substances Act.

In the following months and years, many Californians began to produce marijuana to sell for medicinal purposes. Some grew marijuana at home for personal use. One such person was Diane Monson, an accountant from Oroville. In 1998, she began taking medicinal marijuana after her doctor prescribed it to her for pain. However, on August 15, 2002, police officers from the Butte County Sheriff's Department and agents from the Drug Enforcement Administration raided her home, confiscating or destroying all of her marijuana plants, despite Monson showing a doctor's note.[243] The plants were still considered illegal at the federal level, under the aforementioned Controlled Substances Act.

After Angel Raich, an Oakland resident, read about what Monson went through, she reached out to her. Raich had been using medical marijuana since 1997 for what she described as chronic pain and had since become somewhat of an activist for medical marijuana use.[244] Together with two anonymous caregivers, Raich and Monson sued the federal government on October 9, 2002. In the US District Court for the North District of California, Raich argued that the Controlled Substances Act went against the commerce clause of the Constitution, the Due Process Clause of the Fifth Amendment, the Ninth Amendment, and the Tenth Amendment. Raich argued that Congress didn't have the power to regulate drugs—it was a state power. Raich even got her doctor to testify under oath that her life was at stake if she couldn't use marijuana anymore. The federal government argued that the Supremacy Clause of the Constitution gave them authority to make drugs illegal, and warned if *any* exceptions were made to the Controlled Substances Act, it would make the entire law nearly impossible to enforce.[245]

The US District Court for the North District of California sided with the federal government. However, the Ninth Circuit Court of Appeals sided with Raich and Monson,

---

243  www.washingtonpost.com/archive/politics/2005/01/01/i-really-consider-cannabis-my-miracle/8885ac94-bec1-4e28-aba4-699fe46e390e/

244  angeljustice.org/angel/Who_is_Angel_Raich.html

245  www.law.cornell.edu/supct/html/03-1454.ZS.html

ordering the federal government not to interfere with marijuana patients in the state. It ruled that medical marijuana didn't "substantially affect" interstate commerce. Therefore, Congress shouldn't regulate it.[246]

The federal government appealed to the Supreme Court, which agreed to hear oral arguments on November 29, 2004. By this time, the case had attracted considerable national attention. Several prominent organizations filed amicus briefs, or information that's in support or against one side from third-party sources not directly involved with the case. While organizations like the Partnership for a Drug-Free America filed an amicus brief against Raich, several libertarian organizations, like the influential Cato Institute, filed amicus briefs *supporting* her. By the time the Court had made up their minds, Attorney General Alberto Gonzales was representing the federal government.

## The Big Question in this case:

- Does the Controlled Substances Act go against the commerce clause of the Constitution?

The Court said no. On June 6, 2005, it announced that it had sided with Gonzales, 6–3. The Court said that the Commerce Clause gave Congress the authority to regulate and restrict marijuana production. Justice John Paul Stevens wrote the majority opinion, saying, "Regulation is squarely within Congress' commerce power because production of the commodity meant for home consumption, be it wheat or marijuana, has a substantial effect on supply and demand in the national market for that commodity."[247]

This case seemed to add credibility to the Supreme Court, as the justices who presumably were against marijuana being banned still decided to uphold it, and the three more conservative justices who presumably were fine with marijuana being banned decided *against* it. In his dissent, Justice Clarence Thomas wrote, "If Congress can regulate this under the Commerce Clause, then it can regulate virtually anything—and the federal government is no longer one of limited and enumerated powers."[248]

Regardless, *Gonzales v. Raich* returned more power to the federal government, yet it did so in an incredibly controversial way. It arguably reenergized the debate about whether marijuana, a plant that no one has ever overdosed on, should be legal or not. In the years since the decision, many states have legalized medical and *recreational* marijuana. In fact, according to Gallup, 68 percent of Americans now favor legalizing recreational

246   www.oyez.org/cases/2004/03-1454
247   www.law.cornell.edu/supct/html/03-1454.ZS.html
248   Ibid.

marijuana.[249] Yet, even though it's likely to be legal in all fifty states, that doesn't change the fact that the Commerce Clause gives Congress more power than ever before, and the Drug Enforcement Agency continues to raid private residences for marijuana possession.[250]

249   news.gallup.com/poll/405086/marijuana-views-linked-ideology-religiosity-age.aspx
250   norml.org/blog/2022/06/16/dea-reports-significant-uptick-in-marijuana-related-seizures-arrests/

# 79. Kelo v. City of New London (2005)

This case began in New London, Connecticut, in 1997. At one point that year, Susette Kelo had driven by a run-down house along the Thames River that had been for sale for a while. Even though the house was run-down, she fell in love with it and bought it. She spent months renovating the 107-year-old Victorian-style cottage, painting it pink. The house had a great view of the water and was in a working-class neighborhood called Fort Trumbull. Unfortunately, the neighborhood had been in decline for years, as there were few decent-paying jobs in the area. However, Susette didn't care. She loved her little pink house and its view of the harbor. She soon met a dude named Tim LeBlanc, who helped her do exterior work on the house. Eventually the two got married and lived there together.

In January 1998, real estate agents began knocking on her door, offering lots of money to buy her house on behalf of "an unnamed buyer." Kelo was suspicious and turned down all offers. However, agents began to tell her if she didn't sell her house, she would be forced out of her home by the city due to eminent domain. As you hopefully recall, eminent domain is the right for the government to take private property for public use. In other words, if the government thinks it is in the best interest of all its citizens, it can kick you out of your house. The Takings Clause of the Fifth Amendment and the Fourteenth Amendment of the Constitution say the government can use eminent domain as long as the folks who lose their private property get "just compensation."

Anyway, Susette Kelo didn't care how much money New London was offering her. She loved her little pink house and wasn't planning on going anywhere. Neither were fourteen other Fort Trumbull residents. They teamed up and decided to fight.

So why was New London trying to kick them out? Well, a multinational pharmaceutical corporation named Pfizer was opening a new facility in New London, right next to the Fort Trumbull neighborhood. Part of the deal were plans to "fix up" Fort Trumbull, including building a new hotel, conference center, and fancy housing for the scientists working at Pfizer. This would require major government help. Specifically, the state of Connecticut would pitch in $73 million ($135 million today) to kick out the Fort Trumbull residents, demolish their homes, and update the area with new roads and utilities.

Once Kelo and the other Fort Trumbull residents who didn't want to leave their homes found out about this, they sued the city. Meanwhile, the New London Development Corporation, or NLDC, was already demolishing homes. By the time of the trial, which went to the New London Superior Court in July 2001, the NLDC had already acquired around eighty buildings and destroyed most of them. Pfizer had also already built their facility.

The Institute for Justice, a libertarian-leaning nonprofit law firm, agreed to represent Kelo and the others who were going to lose their homes. Scott Bullock, their lead lawyer, later said, "We got involved because what was going on was an outrageous abuse of power. There was so little respect shown for these people. The city wanted to take an entire neighborhood and make it anew. They were not willing to compromise."[251]

In court, Bullock argued that eminent domain didn't apply in this case, since ultimately the purpose was profits for private developers. In other words, New London taking over Fort Trumbull didn't qualify as something that would benefit the entire community—just one company. In March 2002, the New London Superior Court said that some could stay but others had to go. Both sides were not happy, so both sides appealed.

In late 2002, Kelo's husband, Tim LeBlanc, was in a horrible car accident and went into a coma for two weeks. Now there were two fights for Kelo. While he was still in the hospital, the Connecticut Supreme Court began hearing the appeal. While things were looking up for LeBlanc as he slowly recovered, things were looking bad for staying in the little pink house. In March 2004, the Connecticut Supreme Court said New London's use of eminent domain was fine.

Kelo and the others appealed again to the *supreme* Supreme Court, which agreed to take on the case on September 28, 2004. It was rare for the Court to take on an eminent domain case. Kelo and LeBlanc, and many other neighbors, were present at oral arguments on February 22, 2005. By this time, more than seven years had passed since real estate agents began knocking on Kelo's door. Also by this time, Kelo was well-known in the country and a symbol of the fight against unjust eminent domain. At this moment, it seemed like most Americans were on her side. However, the Court was split. This would be another close decision.

## The Big Question in this case:

- Did New London go against the Takings Clause of the Fifth Amendment?

251   newengland.com/living/a-house-divided/

The Court said no. On June 23, 2005, the Court announced that it had sided with the city of New London, 5–4. Justice John Paul Stevens argued that eminent domain in this case had a "public purpose" because it meant creating jobs in a city that had high unemployment.[252] He wrote, "Promoting economic development is a traditional and long-accepted function of government."

The dissent argued that this use of eminent domain was Robin Hood in reverse—taking from the poor to give to the rich. In her dissent, Justice Sandra Day O'Connor argued that the decision got rid of "any distinction between private and public use of property—and thereby effectively delete[d] the words 'for public use' from the Takings Clause of the Fifth Amendment."[253]

This was a controversial decision. In fact, it made people mad on both sides—everyone was united in their disgust with the Court in this decision. In one poll, 95 percent of respondents disagreed with it.[254] On the one-year anniversary of the decision, President George W. Bush issued an Executive Order that told the federal government to limit its use of eminent domain.

Although Kelo and the other homeowners kept fighting for a while, eventually they all settled with New London for reportedly lots of money.[255] Kelo's house wasn't demolished after all. In fact, you can visit it today. In 2008, Kelo sold the house for one dollar to a dude named Avner Gregory, who moved the house across town. Today it's a museum that honors the battle over eminent domain.[256] Kelo moved to a different town. Around that time, the economy was crappy since it was at the height of the Great Recession, and Pfizer had shut down its New London facility.

Ironically, by the time New London had finally cleared the Fort Trumbull neighborhood, it no longer had plans to redevelop it. While the city is finally talking about redevelopment there today, for the past fourteen years the former neighborhood has been abandoned, home to mostly just feral cats. Tragically, it seems they were kicked out of their homes for nothing.[257]

However, *Kelo v. New London* had a big impact. It led to a huge nationwide backlash against eminent domain. It caused forty-five of the fifty states to change their eminent

252   www.oyez.org/cases/2004/04-108
253   billofrightsinstitute.org/e-lessons/kelo-v-new-london-2005
254   www.theday.com/local-news/20150622/could-the-supreme-court-overturn-the-kelo-decision/
255   www.courant.com/2018/04/04/film-little-pink-house-tells-eminent-domain-story-from-new-london/
256   historicbuildingsct.com/the-kelo-house-1890/
257   www.bostonglobe.com/opinion/2014/03/12/the-devastation-caused-eminent-domain-abuse/yWsyOMNEZ91TM94PYQlhOL/story.html

domain laws, and today the fight continues. In 2017, a film, *Little Pink House*, further raised awareness of the case.

I'd argue that Susette Kelo may have lost the battle, but she certainly didn't lose the war. She remains a hero to many Americans in the fight against unjust eminent domain.

# 80. Castle Rock v. Gonzales (2005)

This case began in Castle Rock, Colorado, on June 4, 1999, when Jessica Lenahan-Gonzales got a restraining order against her husband, Simon. Though the two had long been separated, she got the restraining order because he had been stalking her. The order said Simon could not go within a hundred yards of Jessica or her four children except during a specific visitation time.

On June 22, Simon violated the order and abducted three of the children, the three who were his biological daughters aged seven, nine, and ten. Jessica called the Castle Rock police four times and visited the police station in person, desperately trying to get them to look for and arrest Simon. However, the police refused, telling her to wait to see if he would return the children. They justified not looking for Simon by saying he had told Jessica he was taking them to an amusement park. He was allowed to take the children for small amounts of visiting time.[258]

Well, it's safe to say the Castle Rock police messed up with their judgment in this instance. In the early hours of June 23, Simon showed up at the Castle Rock police station with a gun he had purchased a few hours before. He burst in and started shooting. The police returned fire and killed him. They then searched his vehicle, where they sadly found all three daughters dead. Simon had murdered them before he got to the police station.

Gonzales sued the city of Castle Rock, its police department, and the three police officers who didn't attempt to find her estranged husband after she pleaded with them to do so. She argued their inaction directly not only led to the deaths of her three daughters but specifically went against the Due Process Clause of the Fourteenth Amendment of the Constitution. However, the US District Court for the District of Colorado dismissed the case, saying the Castle Rock police had qualified immunity, meaning those working on behalf of the government are not liable for bad things happening *unless* those working on behalf of the government *clearly* went against a constitutional right.

Gonzales then appealed to the Tenth Circuit Court of Appeals. It agreed with the lower court regarding the inaction of Castle Rock police with regard to the Due Process Clause. However, it *did* say Gonzales had a "protected property interest in the enforcement of the terms of her restraining order." In other words, there could be a good argument that you could sue the local government for failing to actively enforce your protection of the property you own.

There was still hope for Gonzales, but Castle Rock appealed to the Supreme Court, which agreed to take on the case, hearing oral arguments on March 21, 2005.

### The Big Question in this case:

- Can someone who has a restraining order sue a local government if that local government doesn't actively enforce the order?

The Court said no. On June 27, 2005, the Court announced that it sided with Castle Rock, 7–2. The Court said the Constitution didn't protect the property interest of Gonzales in the enforcement of the restraining order. The police were not obligated to act. *They didn't have to help her.* Justice Antonin Scalia wrote the majority opinion, stating that for Gonzales to have "property interest" with something as abstract as a restraining order, she would have needed a "legitimate claim of entitlement." Because enforcement of her restraining order was *not* mandatory under Colorado state law, that legitimate claim of entitlement simply was not there.[259] The Court said, "Look, our hands are tied."

Mostly because of the horrific nature of the case, *Castle Rock v. Gonzales* remains one of the most controversial Supreme Court decisions in recent decades. In 2011, the Inter-American Commission on Human Rights condemned the decision. Critics have argued that it says it's okay for the police to ignore restraining orders.

Decided on a technicality, it's easy to understand why this decision is so unsettling to so many when it began with police refusing to enforce a restraining order and learning that enforcing that restraining order could have saved the lives of three innocent children.

# 81. Morse v. Frederick
# (2007)

This case began in Juneau, Alaska, on January 23, 2002, when Joseph Frederick, a student at Juneau-Douglas High School, excitedly waited with his friends for the Olympic Torch Relay runner to come. Despite the cold, the school had decided to have a small field trip to let its students see the Olympic relay pass through on its way to the games in Salt Lake City. Frederick and the other students gathered across the street from the school. They were surrounded by the media, also there to capture the moment.

As the Olympic Relay approached, Joseph and his friends revealed a fourteen-foot banner that read, "Bong Hits 4 Jesus." The media captured the whole thing. As soon as she noticed it, the principal of Juneau-Douglas High School, Deborah Morse, immediately came over and told the students to take it down. After Joseph refused, she snatched the banner away and later suspended Joseph for ten days. Morse cited the school's anti-drug policy, as the banner referenced marijuana. Joseph later recalled that the original suspension was five days, but Morse doubled it after he referenced a Thomas Jefferson quote about why free speech was so important. Morse also argued that the banner was never about promoting drug use. He wanted to attract the media's attention.[260]

Well, I'd argue he succeeded. Helped by the American Civil Liberties Union, or ACLU, Joseph Frederick sued the principal and the Juneau school district, arguing that he was denied his freedom of speech protection as guaranteed by the First Amendment to the Constitution. Frederick also wanted to clear his name and sought monetary awards for the trouble of going through the process.

The US District Court for the District of Alaska dismissed Frederick's case based on the legal precedent set by *Bethel School District v. Fraser* (1986), where the Court ruled that vulgar or offensive speech could be banned in schools.

However, Frederick argued that the speech was technically off school grounds, and he appealed to the US Court of Appeals for the Ninth Circuit. It unanimously agreed with Frederick, arguing that Frederick and his friends absolutely had the right to hold the banner, even if it *was* on school grounds. It claimed that the *Fraser* decision didn't apply here. It said *Tinker v. Des Moines* (1969), the Supreme Court that protected student

260   www.aclu.org/press-releases/student-supreme-court-free-speech-case-speaks-about-suspension-over-bong-hits-4-jesus

political speech, applied here instead. It went on to argue that what Joseph did wasn't as offensive and more political in nature than the vulgar speech examined in the *Fraser* case. Frederick's speech didn't cause a disturbance at the school.

Morse and the Juneau School Board appealed to the Supreme Court, and it heard oral arguments on March 19, 2007. Ken Starr, the famous lawyer who heavily investigated the administration of President Bill Clinton during the 1990s, represented the school district. He said, "To promote drugs is utterly inconsistent with the educational mission of the school. The Court has spoken more broadly with respect to the need to defer to school officials in identifying the educational mission."[261]

Joseph Frederick's lawyer, Douglas Mertz, argued that the case was about free speech, and he emphasized that the torch relay was not school-sponsored, nor was the banner on school property. In fact, Frederick had not been to school the entire day.

**The Big Questions in this case:**

- Does the First Amendment allow public schools to prevent students from displaying messages promoting illegal drugs at school-supervised events?
- Does a school official have qualified immunity from a lawsuit for disciplining a student for displaying messages promoting illegal drugs at a school-supervised event?

The Court said yes to the first question but said it wasn't allowed to decide on the second question. It was another close decision. It ruled 5–4 in favor of Morse and the Juneau School Board. First, the majority viewed the event as a "school event." Second, the Court argued that the First Amendment does not prevent schools from limiting speech at a school event, especially when it promotes illegal drug use.

Chief Justice John Roberts classified the banner as "school speech," which protects student speech due to the First Amendment. However, it also protected the school's right to limit student speech if it was disruptive. He cited *Bethel School District v. Fraser* and *Hazelwood School District v. Kuhlmeier* (1988), where the Supreme Court decided that school officials could censor school-sponsored speech, to back up this legal precedent. In other words, this wasn't about protecting political protest—this was about protecting students from the dangers of drug abuse.

261  laulima.hawaii.edu/access/content/user/jjudd/edef290/edef_assignments/standard_HTSB_10_learning_
community/assignment_HTSB_10_case_study/learning_resources_case_study/bong_hits_for_Jesus_
decision.htm

Justice Clarence Thomas not only agreed but added that student speech should be limited even further, arguing that the *Tinker v. Des Moines* decision should also be overturned.

Four justices on the Court strongly disagreed. Justice John Paul Stevens wrote the dissenting opinion, saying, "The Court does serious violence to the First Amendment in upholding…a school's decision to punish Frederick for expressing a view with which it disagreed." He added, "The school's interest in protecting its students from exposure to speech 'reasonably regarded as promoting illegal drug use'…cannot justify disciplining Frederick for his attempt to make an ambiguous statement to a television audience simply because it contained an oblique reference to drugs. The First Amendment demands more, indeed, much more."[262]

The Court did not resolve the damages Joseph Frederick claimed. The school district paid Joseph $45,000 ($64,000 today) to settle all remaining claims and paid a constitutional law expert to lead a forum on student speech at Juneau-Douglas High School.

While *Morse v. Frederick* further restricted student speech, it didn't completely resolve the student speech debate. Many continue to demand more protection for speech in schools and not just for students. The original "Bong Hits 4 Jesus" banner hung for many years in the First Amendment gallery of the Newseum in Washington, DC. After the Newseum shut down in 2020, the First Amendment Museum in Augusta, Maine, acquired it, and that's where you can see it today.[263]

262   supreme.justia.com/cases/federal/us/551/393/
263   firstamendmentmuseum.org/exhibits/on-site-exhibits/bong-hits-4-jesus-exhibit/

# 82. DC v. Heller (2008)

This case began in the District of Columbia in 2002, when Robert Levy of the libertarian organization the Cato Institute sought to challenge a DC law that made it illegal to possess handguns, automatic guns, or high-capacity semi-automatic guns. In fact, the law, which has been in effect since 1976, said DC residents couldn't keep them in their homes.

Levy went on a mission to find DC residents to sue the city, based on his argument that the gun ban went against the Second Amendment of the Constitution. Levy would fund the whole thing. He ultimately found six residents with various backgrounds who agreed to sue. Among them was Shelly Parker, a software designer who wanted a gun to defend herself against violent drug dealers in her neighborhood. Levy chose her to be the leading plaintiff. Also among the plaintiffs was a dude named Dick Heller. Heller was a licensed police officer who got to carry a gun for his security job guarding federal buildings, yet it was illegal for him to have a gun in his home. Heller was passionately against the gun ban and spent years fighting it, even previously going to the NRA to sue the city. The NRA had declined.[264]

In the US District Court for the District of Columbia, Levy and his plaintiffs had no success. In fact, District Court Judge Ricardo Urbina dismissed the lawsuit. However, the US Court of Appeals for the District of Columbia Circuit reversed that dismissal, saying DC's gun ban was unconstitutional. The Court of Appeals argued that the Second Amendment "protects an individual right to keep and bear arms."[265] It also argued that the right existed before the Constitution and the idea of owning a gun was that it could be used for things like hunting and self-defense. Not only self-defense from intruders to the home but even tyrannical governments. These were controversial statements and caught the attention of national media outlets. The Court of Appeals also said the only plaintiff who could claim damages was Dick Heller because he was the only one who had applied for a handgun permit but was rejected.

The District of Columbia appealed to the Supreme Court, and Levy and Heller were both happy to see them do so since the highest court in the country had kept silent on the Second Amendment throughout American history. In fact, the Supreme Court hadn't considered the true meaning of the Second Amendment for about seventy years, so when it agreed to hear the case on November 20, 2007, it was a historic moment. The Court heard oral arguments on March 18, 2008.

264   reason.com/2008/11/18/how-the-second-amendment-was-r/
265   www.cga.ct.gov/2008/rpt/2008-r-0578.htm

The Big Question in this case:

- Did the DC law restricting access to guns in the home go against the Second Amendment?

The Court said yes. On June 26, 2008, it announced it had sided with Heller, 5–4, another close and controversial decision. The Court argued that the Second Amendment wasn't just about having a well-regulated militia, and "militia" wasn't just those serving in the military. It said the Second Amendment was also about individuals having the right to have weapons to defend themselves.[266] In other words, the "well-regulated militia" part of the Second Amendment was independent of the "the right of the people to keep and bear arms" part of it.

With this decision, any laws that entirely banned guns commonly used for protection went against the Second Amendment. However, the Court added that the Second Amendment is not unlimited. Not everyone should be able to get a weapon. It also wasn't a right to have a weapon whenever you wanted or for whatever purpose you wanted. The *type* of weapon also mattered. Extremely dangerous weapons, not commonly used for hunting or self-defense, could still be banned. After all, most of the arguments in this case revolved around the self-defense argument.

Writing for the dissent, Justice John Paul Stevens argued that the Second Amendment *doesn't* protect an unlimited right to have guns for self-defense purposes and that it was about the right for Americans to have weapons for *military* purposes.[267] The dissenting justices read the Second Amendment more as a whole.

Critics accused Justice Antonin Scalia, who wrote the majority opinion in this decision, and the rest of the majority justices, of judicial activism, meaning judges and justices let their political views influence how they decide, rather than a precedent or an objective view of the law.

Regardless, *DC v. Heller* is the Supreme Court decision that made it crystal clear that the Second Amendment was about an *individual's* right to own guns. It was a rare time when the Court explicitly said what the Second Amendment means, although it still left some gray area, and today the gun-control debate is far from being settled. With the unfortunate regular occurrence of mass shootings in the United States, this decision remains controversial. However, those who want to further limit guns in the United States will likely have more success passing new laws or even amendments to the Constitution, not more lawsuits.

266   www.oyez.org/cases/2007/07-290
267   supreme.justia.com/cases/federal/us/554/570/

# 83. Citizens United v. FEC (2010)

This case began in the District of Columbia in 2007 when a self-described conservative nonprofit corporation called Citizens United attempted to release a documentary film called *Hillary: The Movie*. The film talked a bunch of trash about Hillary Clinton, who was running in the upcoming presidential election of 2008. Citizens United wanted to distribute and advertise the film within a month before the Democratic primary elections began in January 2008.

However, this would be a direct violation of the Bipartisan Campaign Reform Act, or BCRA, which is more well-known today as the McCain-Feingold Act, named after John McCain and Russ Feingold, the two lead sponsors of it. BCRA was the latest law that limited how political campaigns were paid for, saying corporations or labor unions couldn't spend money from their general treasury to broadcast anything through the mass media that specifically brought up a candidate running for federal office within thirty days of a primary.

Anticipating the Federal Election Commission, or FEC, might attempt to stop the release of its documentary, Citizens United took the FEC to the US District Court for the District of Columbia, arguing that the FEC was wrong to enforce BCRA. Specifically, Citizens United claimed BCRA didn't apply to *Hillary: The Movie* because that film wasn't for or against a candidate. It also claimed that the Supreme Court decision in the case *FEC v. Wisconsin Right to Life* (2007) justified releasing the film within thirty days of the Democratic primaries. Not only that, but Citizens United argued that portions of BCRA violated the First Amendment to the Constitution.

On January 15, 2008, the three-judge panel in the US District Court for the District of Columbia announced it had sided with the FEC. It denied Citizen United's request for an injunction and said the FEC could still fully enforce BCRA. The District Court said the film was meant to get people not to vote for Hillary Clinton. I mean, it was called *Hillary: The Movie*, after all. It also said the film was meant to be strategically shown right before the primaries for this purpose, and it cited another Supreme Court decision, in the case *McConnell v. FEC* (2003), as justification that the FEC could prevent the showing of this film.

Citizens United appealed to the Supreme Court, but as you probably have recognized by this point in the book, this can be a long process. What ended up happening was

Hillary Clinton did *not* get the Democratic nomination. Barack Obama did and was elected president later that year. However, that ended up being irrelevant other than the fact that Obama had nominated and the US Senate had approved a new justice to the Supreme Court, Sonia Sotomayor, replacing Justice David Souter. As it turns out, it was still irrelevant after all, as Sotomayor and Souter had similar views on the role of the FEC and BCRA. Two separate times during 2009, the Court heard oral arguments about the case. Like other major cases over the previous decade, the Court had remained divided on the issue. However, their disagreements were more philosophical than political.

## The Big Question in this case:

- Did the Bipartisan Campaign Reform Act of 2002 go against the First Amendment?

The Court said yes. On January 21, 2010, it announced that it had sided with Citizens United in another 5–4 landmark decision. The Court said that the First Amendment's freedom of speech protections prohibited the government from limiting money spent by corporations, labor unions, and other associations on political campaigns. Specifically, it was referencing independent political expenditures, or political campaign contributions not directly affiliated with the candidate. Justice Anthony Kennedy wrote the majority opinion, saying, "If the First Amendment has any force, it prohibits Congress from fining or jailing citizens, or associations of citizens, for simply engaging in political speech."[268] With this decision, the Court partially overturned both *McConnell v. FEC* and BCRA.

The Court's ruling ultimately was broader than most people predicted. It freed corporations and unions to spend as much money as they wanted to elect or defeat candidates, as long as they didn't contribute *directly* to candidates or political parties. The Court also argued that the First Amendment protects *associations* of individuals, not just individual speakers, so you can't prohibit speech based on the identity of the speaker. In other words, corporations have free speech rights like you and me.

*Citizens United v. FEC* strengthened the idea of Corporate personhood, or the legal notion that corporations share some of the same legal rights and responsibilities held by individuals. Corporate personhood as a concept has been around for thousands of years, but the Supreme Court first applied it to United States law in *Santa Clara County v. Southern Pacific Railroad Co.* (1886). In the *Citizens United* decision, the Court made it clear that corporations are people.

268   www.law.cornell.edu/supct/html/08-205.ZS.html

Justice John Paul Stevens wrote the dissenting opinion. Stevens was upset about how this one turned out. His dissent was ninety pages long, and he passionately summarized it for twenty minutes from the bench. Stevens was so frustrated by this decision that it motivated him to later write a book explaining that a constitutional amendment should be passed to make sure money doesn't influence politics.

Today, *Citizens United v. FEC* continues to be an extremely controversial decision. Protestors have passionately called for its reversal, and organizations like Wolf PAC were created in response to the decision.[269] This is another decision that likely will be discussed and debated for many years.

# 84. McDonald v. Chicago (2010)

This case began in Chicago, Illinois, in 2008. That year, Otis McDonald had become increasingly frustrated with the rise of crime in his neighborhood in the South Side. Gangs and drug dealers had been terrorizing him and his neighbors. McDonald, an elderly man who had lived in his house since 1971, owned several shotguns, but they weren't enough to help him prevent robbers from invading his home and taking what they wanted. Therefore, he wanted to purchase a handgun for self-defense.

However, Chicago had generally banned the new registration of handguns since 1982, so McDonald couldn't purchase one. After he heard about the Supreme Court ruling in *DC v. Heller* (2008), where the Court said the Second Amendment was about individuals having the right to have weapons to defend themselves, McDonald joined forces with three other Chicago residents to sue the city in the US District Court for the Northern District of Illinois.[270] However, the US District Court for the Northern District of Illinois dismissed the lawsuits.

After this, McDonald appealed to the Court of Appeals for the Seventh Circuit, but it also dismissed the lawsuits, arguing that the decision in *DC v. Heller* dealt with a federal law, but *these* lawsuits dealt with local laws.[271] McDonald appealed again, this time to the Supreme Court, which actively accepted the case, hearing oral arguments on March 2, 2010.

During oral arguments, McDonald's lawyers claimed the Chicago law effectively banning handguns was unconstitutional because it was too broad and created too many hoops Chicago residents had to jump through if they wanted *any* kind of gun. The Supreme Court considered the *DC v. Heller* decision, but it still wasn't clear whether the Second Amendment applied to states, counties, and cities. McDonald's lawyers argued that the *Slaughterhouse Cases* (1873) needed to be overturned. As you hopefully recall, the Supreme Court decided in those cases that the Privileges or Immunities Clause of the Fourteenth Amendment only applied *in areas controlled by the federal government* and did not apply to the Bill of Rights. McDonald's lawyers thought that the Privileges or Immunities Clause was meant to give the federal government power to enforce the Bill of Rights against states,

270   www.nbcchicago.com/news/local/the-man-behind-the-gun-suit/2091294/
271   www.law.cornell.edu/supct/cert/08-1521

including the Second Amendment. Because of this, both right-leaning and left-leaning activists united to support McDonald in their quest to overturn the *Slaughterhouse* decision. The Due Process Clause of the Fourteenth Amendment, however, could also make the Bill of Rights apply to the states.

## The Big Question in this case:

- Does the Privileges or Immunities Clause or Due Process Clause of the Fourteenth Amendment allow the Second Amendment to be applied to the states?

The Court said yes. On June 28, 2010, it announced it had sided with McDonald, 5–4, with the more right-leaning justices giving the majority opinion. The Court said the Fourteenth Amendment makes the Second Amendment's right to have guns for the purpose of self-defense applicable to state and local laws as well. Justice Samuel Alito wrote the majority opinion, saying that the right to self-defense was a "fundamental" right that was "deeply rooted in this Nation's history and tradition."[272]

The Court did not overturn the *Slaughterhouse* decision because it ultimately did not rely on the Privileges or Immunities Clause of the Fourteenth Amendment to decide in this case—it used the *Due Process Clause* of the Fourteenth Amendment. There were lots of concurring opinions in this case, but the only one I will focus on is the concurrence by justices Stephen Breyer, Ruth Bader Ginsburg, and Sonia Sotomayor, who all argued that the Second Amendment does *not* say that owning a gun is a "fundamental right" worth protecting through the Fourteenth Amendment.[273]

*McDonald v. Chicago* opened a flood of lawsuits, many by the National Rifle Association, against local and state governments across the country. It has not won all those lawsuits, and since the decision lower courts have upheld that bans on certain guns are still constitutional, as well as additional restrictions on how people can get and carry guns.[274] Today, around 45 percent of American households own at least one gun,[275] and the United States, by far, has the highest gun ownership rate in the world.[276]

272   www.oyez.org/cases/2009/08-1521
273   supreme.justia.com/cases/federal/us/561/742/
274   giffords.org/lawcenter/gun-laws/second-amendment/the-supreme-court-the-second-amendment/
275   www.statista.com/statistics/249740/percentage-of-households-in-the-united-states-owning-a-firearm/
276   worldpopulationreview.com/country-rankings/gun-ownership-by-country

# 85. Snyder v. Phelps (2011)

This case began in Westminster, Maryland, on March 10, 2006, when family and friends attended the funeral of Matthew Snyder at St. John's Catholic Church. Snyder, a soldier for the United States Marine Corps, had died in the Iraq War a week earlier. Snyder's father, Albert Snyder, had announced the funeral to the public in local newspapers the day before.

As Snyder's family and friends arrived for the funeral, Fred Phelps, the leader of the Westboro Baptist Church, and six of his relatives and fellow church members protested the funeral approximately a thousand feet from the church. They were on public land but held up signs that said horrible and hateful things, like, "Thank God for Dead Soldiers," "God Hates Fags," "You're Going to Hell," and "God Hates You." As the family and friends of Matthew Snyder arrived at the funeral, some of them understandably were offended by these protests.

If you already know about the Westboro Baptist Church, these hateful protests shouldn't be surprising. Unfortunately, I am familiar with the group as they are headquartered close to where I live, in the city I was born in: Topeka, Kansas. I have come across their protests at least a dozen times throughout my life. If you don't know who the Westboro Baptist Church is, it's a small, unaffiliated Primitive Baptist church founded in 1955 by the late Fred Phelps. Today, there are likely less than seventy church members, but they get a lot of media attention despite their small numbers by provocatively protesting events, mostly to bring attention to their Antisemitic, Islamophobic, and anti-LGBT+ views.[277] During the Iraq War, they routinely protested the funerals of dead American soldiers with the simple purpose of spreading their hateful views. On the day of Matthew Snyder's funeral, Phelps and his relatives protested at two other locations with the same signs.

Albert Snyder was understandably upset that the Westboro Baptist Church had protested his son's funeral. After seeing them get more media coverage for the protest, he became angry. After seeing the Westboro Baptist Church's website specifically talking trash about Albert and Matthew's mother, Julie Snyder, for raising their son Catholic, saying that they "taught Matthew to defy his Creator" and "raised him for the devil," he became even angrier at them. In the US District Court for the District of Maryland, Albert decided to sue Fred Phelps and two of his daughters, Rebekah Phelps-Davis and Shirley Phelps-Roper, for civil conspiracy, defamation, intentional infliction of emotional distress, intrusion upon seclusion, and publicity given to private life.[278]

The US District Court for the District of Maryland dismissed the defamation charge since it was based on the Westboro Baptist Church posting stuff on their website, and it also dismissed the publicity given to the private life charge since the funeral was already made public by Albert Snyder, as he had announced it in local newspapers. However, the District Court considered the rest of the charges. In the trial, Albert Snyder testified, "[The Westboro Baptist Church] turned this funeral into a media circus and they wanted to hurt my family. They Wanted their message heard and they didn't care who they stepped over. My son should have been buried with dignity, not with a bunch of clowns outside."[279] Snyder also argued that the protests of the Phelps family had caused his health to decline. Shirley Phelps-Roper, a trained lawyer who had been working for the Phelps family's law firm for years, represented them in Court. She argued that they had complied with local ordinances and obeyed the instructions of the local police. Not only that, Phelps-Roper argued that they had been peaceful and did not shout at the funeral attendees. Therefore, their protests were protected under the First Amendment of the Constitution.

Regardless, on October 31, 2007, the jury announced it had sided with Snyder and ultimately awarded him $10.9 million in damages ($15.8 million today). The judge, Richard Bennett, later reduced those damages to $5 million ($7.3 million today) and said if the Phelps couldn't afford to pay those damages, the government would seize their church buildings in Topeka.

Not only did the Phelps' appeal to the US Court of Appeals for the Fourth Circuit, but they also announced that they would continue to protest military funerals.[280] The US Court of Appeals for the Fourth Circuit sided with the Phelps, reversing the lower court's jury decision. It argued that the First Amendment protected their protests, and even ordered Albert Snyder to pay the court costs of the Phelps. The national media heavily covered this verdict, and it caused Americans across the country to become outraged. Bill O'Reilly, a prominent political pundit on Fox News, even pledged to cover all current and future court costs of Snyder.[281]

278   www.mtsu.edu/first-amendment/article/1474/snyder-v-phelps
279   Marso, Andy (2011-03-02). "Supreme Court Upholds Anti-Gay Church's Protest Rights in Md. Case." *Capital News Service*.
280   Dominguez, Alex (2007-11-01). "Jury Awards Father $11M in Funeral Case." *USA Today*.
281   thedailyrecord.com/2011/03/08/snyder-will-fight-westboro-on-court-costs-lawyer-says/

Snyder appealed to the Supreme Court, which agreed to hear the case on March 8, 2010. Multiple media and civil rights organizations joined forces to support the Phelps family, including the American Civil Liberties Union and National Public Radio. Multiple veterans' groups and forty-two members of the United States Senate joined forces to support Snyder. This case got more national media attention than most Supreme Court cases, likely due to the notoriety of the Westboro Baptist Church, which Americans almost unilaterally despised and continue to despise. The Court heard oral arguments on October 6, 2010.

## The Big Question in this case:

- Does the First Amendment protect protestors at a funeral from liability for creating emotional distress for the family of the deceased?

The Court said yes. On March 2, 2011, it announced it had sided with Phelps. It was surprisingly a lopsided decision: 8–1. Only Justice Samuel Alito sided with Snyder. Chief Justice John Roberts wrote the majority opinion, saying, "What Westboro said, in the whole context of how and where it chose to say it, is entitled to 'special protection' under the First Amendment and that protection cannot be overcome by a jury finding that the picketing (protesting) was outrageous."[282] Roberts said that the First Amendment protects the Westboro Baptist Church from being sued for protesting because it didn't disrupt the funeral, was on public land, and was dealt with "matters of public concern."[283] "Public concern" means it's highly relevant to the community's values or interest.

*Snyder v. Phelps* reaffirmed the principle that, even if speech is ridiculously offensive and unpopular, it's still protected by the First Amendment. In other words, the government can't restrict speech simply because it's extremely distasteful or causes emotional harm. As long as you protest peacefully on public land, you can say the most outrageous things imaginable. The Phelpses still regularly do this.

282  law2.umkc.edu/faculty/projects/ftrials/conlaw/SnydervPhelps.html
283  www.uscourts.gov/educational-resources/educational-activities/facts-and-case-summary-snyder-v-phelps

# 86. Brown v. Entertainment Merchants Association (2011)

This case began in Sacramento, California, on September 9, 2005. On that day, the California State Legislature passed a law that prohibited the sale of violent video games to anyone under the age of eighteen, saying anyone guilty of doing so would be fined up to $1,000 (around $1,600 today) each time they did it. The California law also required that all violent video games be labeled with a giant sticker.[284] Now, what made a video game "violent"? Fortunately, the California State Legislature covered this, too. It used a version of the Miller Test, the three-part test to tell if something was obscene, as decided in the Supreme Court case *Miller v. California* (1973).

After California Governor Arnold Schwarzenegger signed the law, what's now known as the Entertainment Merchants Association, a nonprofit international trade association, sued the California government, saying the new law would greatly hurt the video game industry. In the US District Court for the Northern District of California, Judge Ronald Whyte ruled with the video game industry, saying the new law went against the First Amendment. Whyte argued that there was not sufficient evidence to prove that violent video games caused violent behavior.

Governor Schwarzenegger appealed the ruling to the US Court of Appeals for the Ninth Circuit, even publicly stating he would "vigorously defend this law."[285] However, the US Court of Appeals for the Ninth Circuit agreed with the lower court, saying the California law was unconstitutional. California had cited the Supreme Court case *Ginsberg v. New York* (1968) to back up its arguments. This backfired, though, as the circuit court said the *Ginsberg* decision only dealt with speech dealing with sex, not violence. It argued that violent video games were not considered "obscene," at least according to the First Amendment. It argued that California didn't have a "compelling interest" in preventing harm to kids allegedly caused by video games. In other words, these video games weren't proven by the state to be necessary.

Governor Schwarzenegger appealed again, this time to the Supreme Court, but they didn't hear oral arguments until November 2, 2010. By that time, Schwarzenegger was on

284  www.gamespot.com/articles/violent-games-bill-passes-california-legislature/1100-6132907/
285  Dobson, James (August 10, 2007). "Schwarzenegger To Appeal California Game Law Ruling."

his way out of office and Jerry Brown was about to take over as governor of the state again. Therefore, Brown would soon be named as the defendant.

The oral arguments for this case were interesting. Much of the discussion centered on the controversial video game *Postal 2*, where a player can urinate on and set fire to non-player characters. However, the Court seemed concerned about the slippery slope that may be created if they sided with the California law. After all, Justice Antonin Scalia wondered out loud, couldn't the vague definition of "violence" also be applied to children's books like *Grimms' Fairy Tales*?[286]

## The Big Question in this case:

- Can a state restrict the sale of violent video games to minors?

The Court said no. On June 27, 2011, it announced it had sided with the Entertainment Merchants Association, 7–2. Justice Scalia wrote the majority opinion, saying the California law restricting violent video games to those under eighteen years old went against the First Amendment. He wrote, "Like the protected books, plays, and movies that preceded them, video games communicate ideas—and even social messages—through many familiar literary devices (such as characters, dialogue, plot, and music) and through features distinctive to the medium (such as the player's interaction with the virtual world). That suffices to confer First Amendment protection."[287] Scalia added that speech about violence is not "obscene."

Despite the two dissenting justices, Justice Clarence Thomas and Justice Stephen Breyer, often representing two wildly different political ideologies, agreed in this case that states could limit speech in this way.[288]

*Brown v. Entertainment Merchants Association* was not only a big victory for the video game industry but also another big victory for the First Amendment. California could not convincingly prove that violent video games cause children to behave violently. In fact, in the years since this decision, studies have continued to find little, if any, connection between the two.[289]

286   Kendall, Brent (November 2, 2010). "Court Voices Doubts on Violent Videogame Law." *The Wall Street Journal*.
287   www.oyez.org/cases/2010/08-1448
288   www.law.cornell.edu/supct/html/08-1448.ZS.html
289   www.apa.org/about/policy/resolution-violent-video-games.pdf

# 87. Maryland v. King (2013)

This case began in Salisbury, Maryland, on April 10, 2009, when local police arrested Alonzo King, Jr. for waving a gun at a group of people. Officers later found a twelve-gauge shotgun in King's car and charged him with assault. Back at the police station, officers got a sample of King's DNA by swabbing the inside of his cheek. They then sent it to be analyzed and uploaded to a criminal database. If this sounds creepy, keep in mind that this was and still is legal due to Maryland's DNA Collection Act.

On August 4, 2009, the results came back and showed King's DNA matched the DNA in an unsolved rape case from 2003. A Wicomico County grand jury decided this was probable cause to indict him, so instead of facing a trial for assault, he faced trial for raping a fifty-three-year-old woman in her Salisbury home six years prior. King's lawyer argued that this indictment was unconstitutional since it was unrelated to the original purpose of King's arrest. King filed a motion to block the DNA evidence from being used in the circuit court for Wicomico County, arguing that his Fourth Amendment rights were broken because the DNA swab fell under "unreasonable searches and seizures." The judge denied his motion, and King pleaded not guilty to the rape charge. The DNA sample was the only real evidence linking King to the rape. The circuit court for Wicomico County found him guilty, and he was sentenced to life in prison.

However, King appealed to the Maryland Court of Appeals, and it reversed his conviction. It argued that the DNA sampling went against the Fourth Amendment, as King and his lawyer had argued. The Maryland Court of Appeals added that King's right to privacy was more important than Maryland's desire to use his DNA to identify him. It still said the DNA Collection Act was constitutional.[290]

Maryland appealed the ruling, asking the Supreme Court to look at the case, and it agreed to hear oral arguments on February 26, 2013. King's lawyers said it wasn't arguing that the police could never collect and analyze DNA. Instead, it specifically was concerned about folks arrested but not convicted of serious crimes having their DNA collected.

290   www.baltimoresun.com/latest/bs-md-court-ruling-dna-20120424-story.html

The Big Question in this case:

- Does the Fourth Amendment let states collect and analyze DNA from people arrested but not convicted of serious crimes?

The Court said yes. On June 3, 2013, it announced it had sided with Maryland, 5–4, but it wasn't your typical "left-leaning" versus "right-leaning" divided court. After all, you had the often–right-leaning Justice Antonin Scalia siding with the left-leaning justices of Elana Kagan, Sonia Sotomayor, and Ruth Bader Ginsburg.

Justice Anthony Kennedy gave the majority opinion, arguing the DNA swab test did *not* violate the Fourth Amendment because it served the safety of the state of Maryland, yet wasn't too invasive where a warrant would be needed. The Court also argued that the DNA records were an extension of other ways the police already kept databases of people they arrested to help solve future crimes, comparing it to things like fingerprinting.

Justice Scalia wrote a passionate dissent, arguing that the Fourth Amendment prohibits the police from searching a person for evidence of a crime if it's a different crime than what the person was arrested for. Scalia added that, while the DNA of arrested people could help the police solve more crimes, they could also solve more crimes if they collected DNA any time someone enrolled in public school or got a driver's license, which most people would agree is an absurd thing to consider.[291]

*Maryland v. King* has big implications for those living in one of the thirty-one states where they can arrest you, force you to give a DNA sample, and then later charge you with a different crime based on the results of the DNA sample.[292] It's a Supreme Court decision that hardly any Americans even know about, but it's another example of how the Fourth Amendment is consistently threatened as more advanced technology becomes more and more invasive.

291   www.law.cornell.edu/supremecourt/text/12-207
292   www.ishinews.com/dna-collection-practices-for-arrests-by-state/

# 88. Salinas v. Texas (2013)

This case began in Houston, Texas, on December 18, 1992, when someone shot and killed brothers Juan and Hector Garza. Houston police arrived at the murder scene shortly after to find shotgun shell cases but not much else. Soon after, officers invited Genovevo Salinas to a Houston police station for questioning. Salinas had been at a party at the Garza residence the night before the murder.

Salinas voluntarily went down to the station, and the police did not arrest him nor read him the Miranda warning since he was free to leave at any time. They questioned Salinas for approximately one hour, and he even agreed to let the police have his shotgun for testing. However, according to the police report, Salinas stopped answering questions once the cops asked him if the gun would match the shells from the crime scene. The police also reported that after he was asked the question, he acted much more nervously and seemed deceptive. Salinas left shortly after this.

Soon after Salinas left, police found out that Salina's gun *did* match the casings at the murder scene. They also heard from a witness who said Salinas had admitted to killing the victims. The Houston police got a warrant for his arrest. However, they couldn't find him. They later found out that he had fled to Mexico.

Fifteen years later, Houston police arrested a dude under a different name for drug charges. The fingerprints matched those of someone already in their system. That person? Genovevo Salinas. Salinas was surprised after he realized he was now arrested for the murder of the Garza brothers.[293]

However, Salinas wasn't going down without a fight. At his trial in the 230th District Court in Harris County, the prosecutor brought up how Salinas was silent after the police asked him if the gun casings matched his shotgun, which was evidence that he was guilty. Salinas and his lawyer argued that the Fifth Amendment of the Constitution protected his right to remain silent to avoid self-incrimination. However, the 230th District Court in Harris County ultimately found Salinas guilty of the murders. Interestingly, his sentence was twenty years in prison and a five thousand dollar fine.

Salinas appealed to the Fourteenth Court of Appeals of Texas, but it agreed with the lower court. Salinas appealed again to the Court of Criminal Appeals of Texas, but it *also* agreed with the lower courts. By the time Salinas had appealed once more to the Supreme Court, six years had passed since he was first arrested for the murder of the Garza brothers and more than twenty years had passed since they were murdered. The Court agreed to take on the case, hearing oral arguments on April 17, 2013.

The lawyers for Salinas argued that the Supreme Court decision in *Miranda v. Arizona* (1966) and its decision in *Griffin v. California* (1965) set the precedent that the Fifth Amendment's Self-Incrimination Clause protects a defendant's refusal to answer questions by police officers before being arrested. The *Griffin v. California* decision specifically established that prosecutors couldn't use a suspect's silence as evidence against a person to the jury. As you hopefully recall, the *Miranda v. Arizona* decision established that the Fifth Amendment's Self-Incrimination Clause requires that the police must tell a suspect they are interrogating about their due process rights before they charge them. However, the prosecution for Texas argued that the Fifth Amendment protected citizens from being *forced* into incriminating themselves. Salinas was not *forced* to be there. He volunteered.

**The Big Question in this case:**

- Does the Fifth Amendment's Self-Incrimination Clause protect a defendant's refusal to answer questions to the cops before the person is read the Miranda warning or is arrested?

The Court said no. On June 17, 2013, it announced it had sided with Texas, 5–4. Those five justices all voting against Salinas had different reasons. Chief Justice John Roberts and Justices Samuel Alito and Anthony Kennedy said Salinas had to say he was using his Fifth Amendment right to not incriminate himself to benefit from it. Justices Antonin Scalia and Clarence Thomas said even if Salinas clearly said he was using his Fifth Amendment right to not incriminate himself, he still wouldn't have the privilege. It seemed Scalia and Thomas didn't like the *Miranda* and *Griffin* decisions either.

Justice Stephen Breyer wrote the dissenting opinion. He argued that Salinas' silence was all that he needed to get his Fifth Amendment protections and warned that this decision could further hurt all those in custody of the police who don't know their rights.[294]

*Salinas v. Texas* weakened the Self-Incrimination Clause of the Fifth Amendment. Now, even people who are not arrested have to watch what they say around law enforcement. They also have to be more proactive when letting law enforcement know about their right to remain silent since they don't have to hear the Miranda warning if they're not officially arrested. While Americans have had to be even more careful when being questioned by the police ever since, it also has arguably made the jobs of both police officers and prosecutors easier to get the information they need to conduct a case.

# 89. Shelby County v. Holder (2013)

This case began in Shelby County, Alabama, on April 27, 2010. On that day, the county sued the United States Attorney General Eric Holder. Shelby County sued Holder because it argued that parts of the Voting Rights Act of 1965 were unconstitutional. In case you do not remember American history class, the Voting Rights Act is the same law that Martin Luther King, Jr. and many other civil rights activists fought hard to get passed to end voter discrimination that often targeted African Americans in the South. Shelby County had an issue with Section 5 of the Voting Rights Act, which required certain state and local governments to get clearance from the attorney general if they wanted to change their election laws. It also had a problem with Section 4b of the Voting Rights Act, which described a formula used to determine which governments would be subject to that preclearance requirement in Section 5.

Shelby County argued that it wasn't discriminating against voters anymore, so the federal government shouldn't discriminate against *it*. It argued that Sections 5 and 4b of the Voting Rights Act were unconstitutional, and the times had changed, so they were outdated anyway. In the US District Court for the District of Columbia, Judge John Bates sided with Holder, saying such requirements were still needed to fight discrimination.

Shelby County appealed to the US Court of Appeals for the DC Circuit, but on May 18, 2012, it announced that it agreed with the lower court. Shelby County appealed again, this time to the Supreme Court, and it agreed to hear oral arguments on February 27, 2013.

The Court had a lot to consider in this case. Obviously, it considered the Voting Rights Act, but it also considered the Fourteenth Amendment, which protects everyone's right to due process under the law, the Fifteenth Amendment, which protects everyone from having their right to vote taken away based on "race, color, or previous condition of servitude," and finally the Tenth Amendment, which reserves all rights not granted to the federal government to the states.

## The Big Question in this case:

- Did state and local governments still have to follow Sections 4b and 5 of the Voting Rights Act?

The Court said no. On June 25, 2013, it announced it sided with Shelby County by a vote of 5–4. It was another close landmark decision. Chief Justice John Roberts wrote the majority opinion, arguing that federal protection was no longer needed. He added that Section 4b of the Voting Rights Act was unconstitutional because the coverage formula was based on information that was more than forty years old. While the Court did *not* strike down Section 5, without Section 4b, no jurisdiction could be subject to preclearance, at least until Congress established a new coverage formula. To this day, Congress has not done that. The Court added that Congress couldn't subject a state to preclearance simply based on past discrimination.

Justice Ruth Bader Ginsburg wrote the dissenting opinion, acknowledging that, while voting discrimination had decreased since the Voting Rights Act passed, this was only because of *the law existing in the first place*. She wrote, "Throwing out preclearance when it has worked and is continuing to work to stop discriminatory changes is like throwing away your umbrella in a rainstorm because you are not getting wet." Ginsburg added that the Fourteenth, Fifteenth, Nineteenth, Twenty-fourth, and Twenty-sixth Amendments all provided enough evidence that Congress had the authority to control how state and local governments conducted elections to ensure every vote was equal.[295]

Today, *Shelby County v. Holder* remains a controversial decision. Critics have argued that the ruling has made it easier for state officials to make it more difficult for people of color to vote. In fact, since the ruling, several states that used to have to get preclearance under the Voting Rights Act have passed laws that have made it more difficult to vote by getting rid of things like early voting and same-day voter registration.[296]

Five years after the ruling, around a thousand polling places had already been closed around the country. As it turns out, most of those closed polling places were in counties with African American majority populations.[297] One study also found that jurisdictions that used to have to get preclearance under the Voting Rights Act have dramatically kicked more citizens off voter registration lists.[298] Many of those taken off voter registration lists don't know that they've been kicked off.

295   www.law.cornell.edu/supct/cert/12-96
296   www.aclu.org/news/civil-liberties/block-the-vote-voter-suppression-in-2020
297   www.nytimes.com/2018/11/03/us/politics/voting-suppression-elections.html
298   Feder, C., & Miller, M. G. (2020). Voter Purges After Shelby: Part of Special Symposium on Election Sciences. *American Politics Research*, 48(6), 687–692. doi.org/10.1177/1532673X20916426

# 90. Burwell v. Hobby Lobby (2014)

This case began in Oklahoma City, Oklahoma, on September 12, 2012. On that day, the Green family, who owns and operates Hobby Lobby Stores, Inc., sued Kathleen Sebelius, the United States Secretary of the Department of Health and Human Services. They were challenging the Patient Protection and Affordable Care Act, also known as Obamacare, because part of that law went against their religious beliefs. The Green family was Evangelical Christians and had long publicly said that they ran Hobby Lobby, their popular arts and crafts store, according to the principles of their faith. Under Obamacare, employment-provided health insurance had to provide certain preventive care, including some contraceptive (birth control) methods. Well, the Greens thought contraception was immoral and went against their religion. They argued that the contraception requirement of Obamacare went against the Free Exercise Clause of the First Amendment. They also said it went against the Religious Freedom Restoration Act of 1993, or RFRA, a law that strengthened religious freedom in the country. The Supreme Court had weakened RFRA in *City of Boerne v. Flores* (1997).

In the US District Court for the Western District of Oklahoma, District Judge Joe Heaton denied the Green family's request to have the federal government not carry out the requirement of Obamacare that employment-provided health insurance had to cover contraception. Heaton said, while there are exemptions available for religious employers and nonprofit religious organizations, there were no exemptions for for-profit retailers like Hobby Lobby.[299]

The Greens appealed to the US Court of Appeals for the Tenth Circuit, which said Hobby Lobby is legally a "person" and therefore has religious freedom. Therefore, Hobby Lobby should be exempt from the contraception requirement. Neil Gorsuch, a future Supreme Court justice, ruled with Hobby Lobby in the US Court of Appeals for the Tenth Circuit decision.

As it turns out, the Greens weren't the only ones suing Kathleen Sebelius over the contraception requirement going against their religious beliefs. Mardel, a Christian book and educational supplies store, as well as Conestoga Wood Specialties, a Christian manufacturer of cabinets and furniture, also fought back against it. The Supreme Court decided to combine all their fights into one case and heard oral arguments on June 30, 2014. These oral arguments lasted an hour and a half, thirty minutes longer than most. By the time the Court had finished considering this case, Kathleen Sebelius had resigned as the US Secretary of Health and Human Services and Sylvia Burwell had taken her place.

**The Big Question in this case:**

- Can a for-profit religious employer be exempt from the requirement of Obamacare that employment-provided health insurance had to cover contraception, based on the Free Exercise Clause of the First Amendment?

The Court said yes. On June 30, 2014, it announced it had sided with Hobby Lobby, Mardel, and Conestoga Wood Specialties. It was 5–4, with the five politically right-leaning justices with the majority opinion and the four politically left-leaning justices with the dissenting opinion. The Court argued that, because the contraception requirement of Obamacare forces religious corporations to pay for what goes against their religious beliefs or face fines, it goes against the Free Exercise Clause of the First Amendment. The Court said that the contraceptive mandate was specifically the only part of Obamacare that was unconstitutional. Finally, the Court stated the RFRA was constitutional and applied to corporations, thus reinforcing the legal idea of corporate personhood. In his concurring opinion, Justice Anthony Kennedy wrote the federal government hadn't proven that there was a meaningful difference between "nonprofit" and "for-profit" religious organizations.

Justice Ruth Bader Ginsburg wrote the dissenting opinion, arguing that this decision could lead to a slippery slope. She wrote, "In a decision of startling breadth, the Court holds that commercial enterprises, including corporations, along with partnerships and sole proprietorships, can opt out of any law (saving only tax laws) they judge incompatible with their sincerely held religious beliefs…the Court suggests, there always will be whenever, in lieu of tolling an enterprise claiming a religion-based exemption, the government, i.e., the general public, can pick up the tab."[300] She was concerned this decision might lead to more corporations trying to get out of laws.

*Burwell v. Hobby Lobby* is another recent controversial Supreme Court decision. Critics said it was a step back for reproductive rights and gender equality, as the decision arguably disproportionately hurts women who rely on employer-provided health insurance for contraceptive coverage. Others criticized the decision to expand the

300   www.law.cornell.edu/supremecourt/text/13-354

definition of religious freedom to include corporations, which technically are legal entities, not individuals. Finally, even others have argued that *Burwell v. Hobby Lobby* potentially opened the door to other types of discrimination under the guise of "religious belief." While several other court cases challenged other parts of Obamacare in recent years, the law remains popular with most Americans.[301]

301   www.kff.org/interactive/kff-health-tracking-poll-the-publics-views-on-the-aca/#?response=Favorable--Unfavorable&aRange=twoYear

# 91. Obergefell v. Hodges (2015)

This case began in Cincinnati, Ohio, on June 26, 2013, when Jim Obergefell read a news story online about the Supreme Court decision *United States v. Windsor* (2013). In that case, the Court had decided that part of the Defense of Marriage Act was unconstitutional. This meant that same-sex married couples could have federal benefits as long as they were married in states where same-sex marriages were legal.

Jim turned to his boyfriend of more than twenty years, John Arthur, who was lying in bed. Arthur could no longer walk due to amyotrophic lateral sclerosis, more commonly known as Lou Gehrig's disease. The disease was quickly destroying his body. Obergefell kissed Arthur on the forehead and said, "Let's get married." "Okay," Arthur replied.[302]

They chose Maryland as the state to get married in, as same-sex marriage was illegal in their home state of Ohio. Turning to friends and family on Facebook, the couple raised $13,000 to have an ambulance take them to the airport, where they then boarded a medically equipped plane to the Baltimore-Washington International Thurgood Marshall Airport. On that day, July 11, 2013, they were married inside the plane on the tarmac.

Unfortunately, once they returned to Ohio, they learned Jim would not be listed on John's death certificate as his surviving spouse since Ohio didn't recognize their marriage for any purpose. In response to this, Jim and John sued John Kasich, the governor of Ohio. Jim would be the only one moving forward with the lawsuit, though, as John was too weak to act. In the US District Court for the Southern District of Ohio, Jim argued that Ohio discriminated against same-sex couples who had married legally outside of the state. On July 22, Timothy Black, the district judge, recognized the marriage and prevented Ohio from leaving John's name off the death certificate after he died. Just three months later, John Arthur passed away.

While Jim's name did appear as John's surviving spouse on the death certificate, Ohio had appealed this to the US Court of Appeals for the Sixth Circuit. Several others were also suing their states for the same reason. The US Court of Appeals for the Sixth Circuit combined six different decisions from four different states. Jim Obergefell's case was one of the six. On November 6, 2014, by a vote of 2–1, the US Court of Appeals for the Sixth

---

302  www.washingtonpost.com/local/how-jim-obergefell-became-the-face-of-the-supreme-court-gay-marriage-case/2015/04/06/3740433c-d958-11e4-b3f2-607bd612aeac_story.html

Circuit ruled in favor of the states with the laws banning same-sex marriage. It cited the case *Baker v. Nelson* (1971), a Supreme Court decision in which the Court said states could limit marriage to persons of the opposite sex, as justification for its ruling. Writing the majority opinion, Judge Jeffrey Sutton said, "Not one of the plaintiffs' theories...makes the case for constitutionalizing the definition of marriage and for removing the issue from the place it has been since the founding: in the hands of state voters."[303]

Jim and all the others challenging the state same-sex marriage bans appealed to the Supreme Court. The Court agreed to hear four of the cases that directly challenged state laws banning same-sex marriage. One of these cases was *Obergefell v. Hodges*. If you're confused about who Hodges is, he was the new dude appointed by Governor Kasich to be Ohio's health director back in August 2014. Sometimes names randomly go down in history. *Obergefell v. Hodges* became the lead case.

All of those challenging the same-sex marriage bans argued that such bans went against the Equal Protection Clause and Due Process Clause of the Fourteenth Amendment. One group even brought claims under the Civil Rights Act. The Court heard oral arguments on April 28, 2015. During arguments, it was clear this would be another close one divided along ideological lines. Chief Justice John Roberts and Justice Anthony Kennedy seemed to be on the fence, however.

### The Big Questions in this case:

- Does the Fourteenth Amendment mandate that a state give a marriage license to two people of the same sex?
- Does the Fourteenth Amendment mandate that a state recognize the marriage of two people of the same sex who were legally married in another state?

The Court said yes to both questions. On June 26, 2015, exactly two years after Jim Obergefell asked John Arthur to marry him, the Court announced a 5–4 decision in their favor. As it turns out, Justice Kennedy had proved to be the crucial fifth vote. The Court argued that the Fourteenth Amendment required all states to recognize same-sex marriages in other states and recognize *all* same-sex marriages. Just like that, it legalized same-sex marriage in the United States and overturned *Baker v. Nelson*. The Court held that marriage is a fundamental right to same-sex couples, as protected by the Equal Protection Clause and Due Process Clause of the Fourteenth Amendment.

---

303   www.scotusblog.com/2014/11/sixth-circuit-the-split-on-same-sex-marriage/

Writing for the majority opinion and putting his reputation on the line as he had traditionally been one of the more socially conservative justices on the Court, Justice Kennedy said: "It would misunderstand these men and women to say they disrespect the idea of marriage. Their plea is that they do respect it, respect it so deeply that they seek to find its fulfillment for themselves. Their hope is not to be condemned to live in loneliness, excluded from one of civilization's oldest institutions. They ask for equal dignity in the eyes of the law. The Constitution grants them that right."[304]

It's important to note that the four justices who dissented weren't necessarily against gay marriage. They generally thought it wasn't the Court's job to decide on this matter. In their view, the Constitution didn't grant them such power, and so therefore it should be left to the states.[305]

*Obergefell v. Hodges* is one of the most impactful Supreme Court cases in American history. Hundreds of thousands of same-sex couples have got married since, which has had the added benefit of adding billions of dollars to the economy and creating tens of thousands of jobs.[306] There was initially some pushback in certain states, and in some counties they still don't even issue marriage licenses at all to get around it, but overall this decision is not as controversial as you might think.[307] One recent Gallup poll showed that 71 percent of Americans support gay marriage. When Gallup polled the issue in 1996, just 27 percent of Americans supported gay marriage.[308]

Today, Jim Obergefell remains a public figure. He still tours the country, giving speeches, and honoring the legacy of his late husband, John.

304   www.law.cornell.edu/supremecourt/text/14-556
305   www.oyez.org/cases/2014/14-556
306   www.nbcnews.com/feature/nbc-out/gay-marriage-generated-3-8b-over-5-years-study-
      finds-n1221211
307   www.al.com/news/birmingham/2018/06/three_years_after_supreme_cour.html
308   news.gallup.com/poll/393197/same-sex-marriage-support-inches-new-high.aspx

# 92. Murphy v. NCAA (2018)

This case began in New Jersey on November 8, 2011, when New Jersey citizens voted to make sports betting legal in the state. This was a big deal, because, at the time, 97 percent of all sports bets placed in the country were illegal.[309] The New Jersey state legislature then passed and New Jersey Governor Chris Christie signed into law the Sports Wagering Act of 2012, letting citizens place sports bets at casinos and racetracks. Well, the National Collegiate Athletic Association (NCAA), National Basketball Association (NBA), National Football League (NFL), National Hockey League (NHL), and Major League Baseball (MLB) didn't like this new law so much. All five of those sports organizations sued Governor Christie, arguing that New Jersey legalizing sports betting went against the Professional and Amateur Sports Protection Act, or PASPA, passed by Congress in 1992. This law banned betting on sports except for a few special places around the country that were exempt. New Jersey was not special enough to be exempt.

Governor Christie didn't seem to be worried about the lawsuit or PAPSA. In his opinion, the Tenth Amendment of the Constitution was on New Jersey's side.[310] As a reminder, the Tenth Amendment states that all powers not delegated to the federal government by the Constitution are reserved to the states or the people. Christie had a Supreme Court precedent to back up his opinion. The Court had previously established the Anti-Commandeering Doctrine in two separate cases, *New York v. United States* (1992) and *Printz v. United States* (1997). The doctrine says the federal government can't force states or state officials to adopt or enforce federal laws.

Soon, the US Department of Justice joined forces with the sports leagues, and when they went to trial in the US District Court for the District of New Jersey in February 2013, *its* main argument was that sports gambling hurt not only their leagues but also the integrity of the sports. The judge agreed and ruled with the sports leagues and US Department of Justice.

Governor Christie and New Jersey appealed to the US Court of Appeals for the Third Circuit, but it upheld the ruling. After the Supreme Court refused to hear another appeal in the spring of 2014, the New Jersey legislature went back to the drawing board. Since the

309   via.library.depaul.edu/cgi/viewcontent.cgi?article=4004&context=law-review
310   www.cato.org/blog/while-you-fill-out-bracket-chris-christie-busts-ncaas-racket

Sports Wagering Act was unconstitutional, they repealed parts of existing New Jersey laws from 1977 that banned sports gambling. It was a sneaky way to legalize sports gambling. However, Governor Christie vetoed these repeals, arguing that the state couldn't bypass the Third Circuit's ruling. In another plot twist, though, Christie changed his mind and signed it into law a few months later.

In November 2014, the NCAA, NBA, NFL, NHL, and MLB sued New Jersey again, and again the US District Court for the District of New Jersey and the US Court of Appeals for the Third Circuit ruled in favor of the sports organizations. Christie and New Jersey begged the Supreme Court to consider an appeal again, specifically bringing up *New York v. United States* (1992), a decision that strengthened the Tenth Amendment, as more evidence that precedent was on their side. That got the Court's attention. They agreed to hear the case on June 27, 2017, but didn't hear oral arguments until December 7, 2017. By this time, New Jersey had elected a new governor, Phil Murphy. During oral arguments, the Court considered whether the Commerce Clause gave the federal government the authority to say a state couldn't repeal old laws.

## The Big Question in this case:

- Does a federal statute that prohibits the modification or repeal of state laws on private conduct go against the commerce clause of the Constitution?

The Court said yes. On May 14, 2018, it finally announced it had sided with New Jersey. It was 7–2, although Justice Stephen Breyer only partially sided with the majority, so you could argue it was also 6–3. Regardless, the Court ruled that PASPA went against the Anti-Commandeering Doctrine because it specifically said what a state could and could not do.[311]

One month later, New Jersey made sports gambling legal again. Almost immediately, Atlantic City, New Jersey's economy, which had been stagnant for years, began to prosper. Other states soon followed New Jersey's lead in legalizing sports betting. This case opened the floodgates. Today, sports betting is legal in most states in the country.[312]

*Murphy v. NCAA* was a win for states' rights and the Tenth Amendment. It strengthened the Anti-Commandeering Doctrine, and states have been bolder in passing and upholding laws that went against federal laws ever since. A great example of this is

311   www.oyez.org/cases/2017/16-476
312   www.actionnetwork.com/news/legal-sports-betting-united-states-projections

state policies on cannabis. The decision has made it clear that the federal government can't prevent states from legalizing cannabis.[313] While there have still been ways for the federal government to regulate cannabis and prevent its legalization *indirectly*, it has generally been more difficult for it to stop the dramatic rise in cannabis legalization at the state level. At the time of writing this book, most states have decriminalized cannabis.[314]

313   thehill.com/opinion/judiciary/387653-murphy-v-ncaa-its-about-much-more-than-gambling-on-sports/
314   www.cnn.com/2023/03/07/us/20230306-oklahoma-marijuana-vote-five-charts-dg/index.html

# 93. Masterpiece Cakeshop v. Colorado Civil Rights Commission (2018)

This case began in Lakewood, Colorado, on July 19, 2012, when Charlie Craig and David Mullins entered Masterpiece Cakeshop hoping to buy a cake for their upcoming wedding reception. However, the owner of the shop, Jack Phillips, denied their request, saying he didn't make cakes for same-sex weddings due to his Christian beliefs. Craig and Mullins left the bakery in frustration. When Craig's mom called to speak with Phillips the next day, he also told her that he didn't make wedding cakes for gay couples also since same-sex marriage was still illegal in Colorado at the time.

While another bakery eventually did make a wedding cake for the couple, Craig and Mullins filed a complaint about Masterpiece Cakeshop to the Colorado Civil Rights Commission. In the complaint, Craig and Mullins claimed the Masterpiece Cakeshop broke Colorado's public accommodations law, the Colorado Anti-Discrimination Act, which said businesses couldn't discriminate against their customers based on skin color, religion, gender, or sexual orientation. With the assistance of both the Colorado Civil Rights Commission and the American Civil Liberties Union, Craig and Mullins sued Masterpiece Cakeshop. By the time the lawsuit went to trial, Craig and Mullins had married in Massachusetts. In Colorado Administrative Court, Judge Robert Spencer sided with Craig and Mullins, ordering Phillips to no longer refuse the business of gay couples in the future. Phillips responded by saying he'd rather close his business than bake cakes for same-sex marriages.[315] Ultimately, though, he kept his business open and refused to follow the judge's orders.

Meanwhile, with the help of the Christian legal advocacy organization Alliance Defending Freedom, or ADF, Phillips appealed the decision to the Colorado Court of Appeals, but it agreed with the lower court. Phillips then appealed again, this time to the Supreme Court of Colorado, but it refused to hear the case. On July 22, 2016, over four years after Craig and Mullins first attempted to buy a cake from Masterpiece Cakeshop, Phillips requested the Supreme Court look at the case. Almost another full year after that, the Court agreed to take it on and ultimately heard oral arguments on December 5, 2017. The ADF argued that Phillips

315   www.csmonitor.com/USA/Justice/2013/1207/Colo.-judge-orders-Christian-baker-to-bake-gay-wedding-cake.-Will-he-say-no

creating a wedding cake for a same-sex wedding went against his religious freedom and his artistic expression. It said both are protected under the First Amendment of the Constitution.

## The Big Questions in this case:

- Does the Colorado Anti-Discrimination Act require that a baker has to make a cake, even if it goes against their religious beliefs?
- Does the Free Exercise Clause of the First Amendment give a baker the freedom to not make a cake for customers based on their religious beliefs?

The Court said no to the first question and yes to the second question. On June 4, 2018, it announced it had sided with Phillips and Masterpiece Cakeshop, 7–2. The Court said Phillips was protected from having to bake a cake for a same-sex wedding based on the Free Exercise Clause of the First Amendment. While the Court said gay couples still should have civil rights protections under the laws and the Constitution, religious and even philosophical objections to same-sex marriage are protected forms of "expression."[316] This decision was narrow. The Court did not address the broader question of whether businesses had a constitutional right to discriminate against same-sex couples. [317] Still, critics said this decision could lead to further discrimination against marginalized groups under the guise of religious freedom.

*Masterpiece Cakeshop v. Colorado Civil Rights Commission* highlighted the tensions between religious freedom and anti-discrimination laws. More accurately, it highlighted the tensions between Christians and the LGBTQ+ community. Despite all the progress the LGBTQ+ community has made in recent decades, it's a community that millions of Americans still refuse to accept.

While Charlie Craig and David Mullins never liked the spotlight and have kept a low profile ever since this decision, Jack Phillips has become somewhat of an activist. He later got in trouble for breaking the Colorado Anti-Discrimination Act again for refusing to bake a cake for a transgender person. On January 26, 2023, Phillips lost that case in the Colorado Court of Appeals.[318]

316   www.oyez.org/cases/2017/16-111
317   www.supremecourt.gov/opinions/17pdf/16-111_j4el.pdf
318   www.usatoday.com/story/news/nation/2023/01/27/colorado-masterpiece-baker-court-appeal-rejected/11134975002/

# 94. Carpenter v. United States (2018)

This case began in Detroit, Michigan, in April 2011. That month, Detroit police officers arrested four men suspected of robbing a series of Radio Shacks and T-Mobile stores in the area. One of the four men confessed to robbing nine stores in Michigan and Ohio over the previous four months, and he identified fifteen accomplices. He soon gave the FBI cell phone numbers of some of the accomplices. After this, the FBI reviewed his phone records to get more phone numbers of possible suspects in the robberies. Based on those records, the FBI used the Stored Communications Act to get permission from judges to get more records the phone numbers could reveal, like where the phone calls were made. The Stored Communications Act lets the federal government get access to telecommunication records when "there are reasonable grounds to believe that the contents of a wire or electronic communication, or the records or other information sought, are relevant and material to an ongoing criminal investigation."[319]

Anyway, the judges gave them permission, and, based on those new records, FBI agents confirmed Timothy Carpenter, a man who wasn't originally arrested by the Detroit police, almost certainly was involved with the string of robberies in Michigan and Ohio. Keep in mind that the judge *didn't give the FBI a warrant*. The FBI was able to get 12,898 different location points to track Carpenter's movements. Based on this new evidence, FBI agents arrested Carpenter and he was charged with six counts of robbery and six counts of carrying a firearm during a federal crime of violence.[320]

In the US District Court for the Eastern District of Michigan, Carpenter and his lawyers argued that the warrantless collection of his location data went against his Fourth Amendment rights against unreasonable searches and seizures. The federal government, on the other hand, argued that this data was *not* protected by the Fourth Amendment because Carpenter had *voluntarily* shared it with his cell phone provider. The US District Court for the Eastern District of Michigan found Carpenter guilty and sentenced him to an incredible *116 years* in prison.[321]

Carpenter appealed his conviction to the US Court of Appeals for the Sixth Circuit, but it was upheld. The US Court of Appeals for the Sixth Circuit cited the Supreme Court

319   www.supremecourt.gov/opinions/17pdf/16-402_h315.pdf
320   Ibid.
321   law.justia.com/cases/federal/appellate-courts/ca6/14-1572/14-1572-2019-06-11.html

case *Smith v. Maryland* (1979) as a precedent to back up its decision. Carpenter appealed his case again; the Supreme Court agreed to hear it. By the time it heard oral arguments on November 29, 2017, nearly seven years had passed since the robberies.

### The Big Question in this case:

- Does the warrantless search and seizure of cell phone records, which include the location and movements of cell phone users, go against the Fourth Amendment?

The Court said yes. On June 22, 2018, it announced it had sided with Carpenter, 5–4, with Chief Justice John Roberts being the swing vote by siding with the more left-leaning justices on the bench. The Court said the federal government had to have a warrant before it acquired Carpenter's cell phone records that revealed his movements. Simply put, the Fourth Amendment applied in this case. In deciding this way, the Court ruled that the Fourth Amendment protected not just "property interests" but also expectations of privacy. Roberts wrote, "Unlike the nosy neighbor who keeps an eye on comings and goings, [new technologies] are ever alert, and their memory is nearly infallible. There is a world of difference between the limited types of personal information addressed in [*Smith v. Maryland*] and the exhaustive chronicle of location information casually collected by wireless carriers today."[322]

The justices who dissented in this case had different reasons for disagreeing with the majority. Justice Neil Gorsuch said the majority opinion went against the "original understanding" of the Fourth Amendment. Justice Samuel Alito was concerned the Fourth Amendment couldn't have predicted a situation like this. All of the dissenting justices had concerns that the majority suddenly seemed against the "third-party doctrine," which says people who voluntarily give information to third parties, like cell phone companies, banks, and internet providers, have "no expectation of privacy."[323]

Regardless, *Carpenter v. United States* was a big win for privacy and the Fourth Amendment. After the decision, the government had to get a warrant to access records that tracked where citizens moved. With almost everything we do being tracked these days, it's comforting to know these records can't easily be turned over to any government agency.

Still, despite the *Carpenter* decision, Americans today don't have as much privacy. The federal government continues to regularly conduct mass surveillance without warrants.

---

322   www.law.cornell.edu/supremecourt/text/16-402
323   www.nytimes.com/2019/06/18/opinion/facebook-court-privacy.html

After all, this is what led to Edward Snowden speaking out about the National Security Agency in 2013. While most Americans don't seem too bothered by their government or corporations regularly spying on them, it's hard to deny the troublesome implications of such mass surveillance. This is, after all, what George Orwell's *1984* was supposed to warn us about. "Big Brother" *is* always watching, and because of that, the Court will likely have to revisit the issue again soon.

# 95. Bostock v. Clayton County (2020)

This case began in Clayton County, Georgia, in January 2013. That month, Gerald Bostock, a gay man, joined a gay-focused recreational softball league. Bostock had been a child welfare services coordinator for the Juvenile Court of Clayton County for a decade, and he made the fateful choice of promoting the gay softball league at work. After this, Bostock began getting criticized at work for participating in the softball league and for his sexual orientation. In April, Clayton County audited the program funds controlled by Bostock and then promptly fired him for "conduct unbecoming a county employee."

Bostock thought this was an excuse for the country to fire him for being gay. Georgia had no law protecting LGBT+ people from employment discrimination at the time. Still, three years later, Bostock filed a claim for workplace discrimination in the US District Court for the North District of Georgia. Bostock claimed that Clayton County went against Title Seven of the Civil Rights Act of 1964 when it fired him. However, the US District Court for the North District of Georgia dismissed the claim, saying Bostock's claim was based on a loose interpretation that work discrimination shouldn't happen on the basis of sexual orientation. It said Title Seven of the Civil Rights Act didn't include protection against discrimination toward sexual orientation, and it used the US circuit court case *Evans v. Georgia Regional Hospital* (2017) as a precedent to back up its decision.

Bostock then appealed to the same court that made the decision in *Evans v. Georgia Regional Hospital*, the US Court of Appeals for the Eleventh Circuit. As you may have already predicted, it sided with Clayton County and cited the *Evans* decision as precedent. However, two *other* circuit courts, the US Court of Appeals for the Seventh Circuit and the US Court of Appeals for the Second Circuit, found that discrimination in employment based on sexual orientation violated Title Seven of the Civil Rights Act in other cases involving a gay skydiving instructor and a transgender funeral director. In fact, the US Court of Appeals for the Second Circuit said employers couldn't discriminate based on sexual orientation or gender identity. Because of the split circuit courts, the Supreme Court agreed to look at all three cases, combining them and hearing oral arguments on October 8, 2019.

## The Big Question in this case:

- Does Title Seven of the Civil Rights Act of 1964 prohibit employment discrimination based on an individual's sexual orientation?

The Court said yes. On June 15, 2020, it announced it had sided with Bostock and the other employees discriminated against. It was 6–3, with the typically right-leaning Chief Justice John Roberts and Justice Neil Gorsuch siding with the more left-leaning justices. The Court said it was illegal for employers to fire employees for being gay or transgender. Neil Gorsuch wrote the majority opinion, saying, "An employer who fired an individual for being homosexual or transgender fires that person for traits or actions it would not have questioned in members of a different sex." He added, "Those who adopted the Civil Rights Act might not have anticipated their work would lead to this particular result. But the limits of the drafters' imagination supply no reason to ignore the law's demands. Only the written word is the law, and all persons are entitled to its benefit."[324]

*Bostock v. Clayton County* was a huge victory for LGBT+ rights in the United States. More than any other Supreme Court case in history, the *Bostock* decision made it clear that if an employer were to discriminate against an employee based on their sexual orientation or gender identity, they would be breaking the law. The Clayton County Board of Commissioners ultimately paid Gerald Bostock $825,000 in damages for his wrongful termination.

# 96. McGirt v. Oklahoma (2020)

This case began in Oklahoma City, Oklahoma, on June 24, 1997. On that day, the state of Oklahoma convicted Jimcy McGirt, a member of the Seminole Nation, of molesting and raping a four-year-old girl, who also happened to be his wife's granddaughter. For these horrible crimes, the judge sentenced him to a thousand years plus life in prison without the possibility of parole.

On August 28, 1999, Patrick Murphy, a member of the Muscogee Nation, brutally murdered a man named George Jacobs near Henryetta, Oklahoma. How "brutal" was the murder? Murphy had cut off Jacobs' genitals and left him in a ditch to bleed to death. In Oklahoma state court, a jury convicted Murphy and a judge sentenced him to death. Murphy tried to get his conviction overturned, though, arguing that his trial was in the wrong court. Murphy and his lawyers said he should have had a trial in federal court because he was a Native American and the murder occurred on Native American land within Muscogee reservation territory. However, the Oklahoma state trial rejected Murphy's request. He appealed again, this time to the Oklahoma Court of Criminal Appeals, but it also rejected his request.[325] Murphy then appealed the decision to the federal government. He specifically appealed to the US Court of Appeals for the Tenth Circuit, and it *agreed* with Murphy, ordering that he be given a new trial.[326] Keep in mind that, by this point, eighteen years had passed since the murder.

After Jimcy McGirt found out about Murphy's case, he appealed to the District Court of Wagoner County to get a new trial. It denied his request. Next, he appealed to the Oklahoma Court of Criminal Appeals, but it also denied his request. McGirt then appealed to the Supreme Court.

Meanwhile, Tommy Sharp, the Warden of the Oklahoma State Penitentiary, appealed Murphy's case to the Supreme Court, and it heard oral arguments on November 27, 2018. However, the Court had decided to wait to decide on that case until it also heard McGirt's case, mostly since they were deadlocked at 4–4 since Justice Neil Gorsuch had recused himself from it since he had been in the US Court of Appeals for the Tenth Circuit when they heard it. The Court heard oral arguments on May 11, 2020. Due to the COVID-19

325  www.courtlistener.com/docket/5459168/35/murphy-v-trammell/
326  law.justia.com/cases/federal/appellate-courts/ca10/07-7068/07-7068-2017-08-08.html

pandemic, this case was one of twelve in which the Court, for the first time in its history, used teleconferencing for arguments. The Court was fully aware of the optics of this case. It was considering siding with a child rapist and brutal murderer, after all. It also was fully aware of the implications. If they sided with McGirt and Murphy, this might open a huge can of worms in terms of the legal rights of Native Americans.

One law the Court focused on was the Major Crimes Act, a law Congress passed in 1885 that placed certain crimes under federal jurisdiction if they occurred on Native American reservations.

## The Big Question in this case:

- Can a state put a Native American accused of a crime on Native American territory on trial?

The Court said no. On July 9, 2020, it announced it had sided with McGirt, 5–4. Neil Gorsuch again sided with the left-leaning justices to break the deadlock. He also wrote the majority opinion, saying that land reserved for the Seminole and Muskogee nations remains "Indian country" under the Major Crimes Act, and therefore Oklahoma did not have jurisdiction to prosecute McGirt nor Murphy.[327] "States have no authority to reduce federal reservations within their borders," he wrote. "Imagine if they did… It would… leave tribal rights in the hands of the very neighbors who might be least inclined to respect them."[328] Gorsuch added that the federal government has an obligation to fulfill its promises to Native American tribes it had historically made treaties with.

Chief Justice John Roberts wrote the dissenting opinion, arguing that the majority's decision "profoundly destabilized the governance of eastern Oklahoma."[329]

Still, *McGirt v. Oklahoma* was a huge win for Native American rights. Ever since, every Native American tribal citizen who had been convicted under state law for crimes committed on reservation lands could now seek a new trial in federal courts. At the time of the *McGirt* decision, this applied to around 1,900 Oklahoma prisoners alone.[330] More broadly speaking, the *McGirt* decision made it clear that around half of Oklahoma was Native American land, not Oklahoma land. This includes the state's second-largest city, Tulsa. The *McGirt* decision was later somewhat weakened by the Supreme Court case *Castro-Huerta v. Oklahoma* (2022). In that decision, the Court said non-tribal members

327   www.oyez.org/cases/2019/18-9526
328   www.supremecourt.gov/opinions/19pdf/18-9526_9okb.pdf
329   Ibid.
330   www.bbc.com/news/world-us-canada-53358330

could still be prosecuted for crimes in state courts. Regardless *McGirt v. Oklahoma* gave tribal sovereignty a huge boost.

On August 25, 2021, in a new trial in the US District Court for the Eastern District of Oklahoma, Judge John Heil III sentenced Jimcy McGirt to three life sentences.[331] So, the ultimate outcome for him was the same. Patrick Murphy's outcome wasn't the same, though. On May 11, 2022, in a new trial also in the US District Court for the Eastern District of Oklahoma, Judge Ronald White sentenced Murphy to life imprisonment.[332]

331  www.oklahoman.com/story/news/2021/08/25/mcgirt-oklahoma-supreme-court-sentenced-three-life-terms-federal-prison/5590860001/

332  www.justice.gov/usao-edok/pr/patrick-dwayne-murphy-sentenced-life-imprisonment-1999-murder-indian-country

# 97. Mahanoy Area School District v. B.L. (2021)

This case began in Mahanoy City, Pennsylvania, in May 2017. That month, fourteen-year-old Brandi Levy tried out for the cheerleading team at Mahanoy Area High School. To be a cheerleader there, Levy had to agree to a code of conduct that said she would have to show respect to her teammates, coaches, the school, teachers, and other schools' teachers. The code of conduct, which Levy signed, also said Mahanoy Area High School cheerleaders should not use profanity in public. Levy hoped to make the varsity squad, but the two coaches, also teachers in the Mahanoy Area School District, found her only good enough for the JV squad.

Levy was extremely upset by this, thinking she deserved to be on the varsity squad. The next weekend, while hanging out at a convenience store called the Cocoa Hut, she and a friend who also didn't make the varsity squad vented to each other about how unfair they thought it was. Using Levy's smartphone, the two took a selfie with middle fingers raised. They then posted the photo ("Snap") to her Snapchat account with the text "F— school f— softball f— cheer f— everything." After friends responded to the message with concern, they sent a follow-up Snap explaining why they were upset. Levy sent the two Snaps to a group of around 250 friends, many of whom were fellow students. Some were cheerleaders. One cheerleader took a screenshot of the messages. Another cheerleader who got the two Snaps was the daughter of one of the coaches and had been suspended from cheerleading for a short time after talking trash online about another school's cheerleading uniforms. By Monday, the "F— school f— softball f— cheer f— everything" screenshot had been widely shared among students, and it offended some students to the point where they approached the cheerleading coaches about it. At the end of the week one of the coaches took Levy out of class to tell her that she was suspended from cheerleading the next for posting the offensive Snap.

Levy's parents appealed the suspension to the Mahanoy Area School District school board, but it upheld it. Little did the school district know that this little situation was far from over. Levy's parents believed this sort of discipline went against Levy's First Amendment right to free speech. Besides, her parents believed *they* should be the ones disciplining Brandi, not school officials. With the support of the American Civil Liberties Union, or ACLU, her parents sued the school district in the US District Court for the Middle District of Pennsylvania. Levy's lawyers argued that Brandi's Snaps were on her social media account on her time.

In addition, her Snaps consisted of no threats and didn't even mention the specific school. On October 5, 2017, over four months after the cheerleading coaches suspended Levy, Judge Albert Richard Caputo ordered the school district to stop enforcing the suspension. He said, "Simply put, the ability of a school to punish lewd or profane speech disappears once a student exits school grounds."[333] Because the speech was "off campus," Caputo said the precedents set by the Supreme Court decisions in *Bethel School District v. Fraser* (1986) and *Tinker v. Des Moines* (1969) didn't apply in Levy's case.

The school district appealed to the US Court of Appeals for the Third Circuit. There, a three-judge panel admitted that Levy's Snap was "crude, rude, and juvenile, just as we might expect of an adolescent." However, it agreed with the lower court's decision, siding with Levy.

The school district appealed again, this time to the Supreme Court, and it agreed to take on the case on January 8, 2021. By this time, Levy was a senior at Mahanoy Area High School. She ended up on the junior varsity cheerleading squad her sophomore year and had been a varsity cheerleader for the past two years. Despite the national attention and feeling like she never was treated the same way by coaches and teachers again after the Snaps circulated, Levy's life was that of a normal teenager. This case was one of the rare instances when the Alliance Defending Freedom teamed up with the ACLU to support Levy. On the other side, anti-cyberbullying organizations sided with the school district.

The Court heard oral arguments on April 28, 2021. Arguing for Levy, the ACLU's David Cole said if schools could discipline students for off-campus speech, that would dramatically increase their power. He said, "[It] would require students to effectively carry the schoolhouse on their backs in terms of speech rights everywhere they go."[334] While the justices generally seemed sympathetic to Levy, several also expressed there were good reasons for the school to have at least some authority over some types of off-campus speech.[335]

## The Big Question in this case:

- Does the First Amendment prohibit public schools from regulating speech that is off campus?

The Court said mostly yes. On June 23, 2021, it announced it had sided with Brandi Levy (identified as B.L. in this case), 8–1. The Court said the school district's decision to suspend Levy from the cheerleading squad for posting vulgar stuff on Snapchat went against the First Amendment. Justice Stephen Breyer wrote the majority opinion, saying,

333   scholar.google.com/scholar_case?case=5028654821002980824
334   www.npr.org/2021/04/28/991683886/frightened-to-death-cheerleader-speech-case-gives-supreme-court-pause
335   www.oyez.org/cases/2020/20-255

"It might be tempting to dismiss (Levy's) words as unworthy of the robust First Amendment protections discussed herein. But sometimes it is necessary to protect the superfluous in order to preserve the necessary."[336] Breyer added if Levy had been an adult, her Snapchat post most certainly would have been protected by the First Amendment, and since there was no evidence that her Snaps disrupted learning at the high school, they should be protected. It helped Levy's case that her Snaps didn't explicitly name the school or target any individuals. Plus, the Snaps were only sent to her private circle of friends.

That all said, this was a narrow decision. While the Court said the First Amendment heavily limited how public schools could regulate off-campus speech, in certain cases it could, and Breyer established three considerations for courts when dealing with future cases dealing with social media speech:

1. If a social media post was made by a minor off-campus, it generally should be under the responsibility of the parents, not the school.

2. Courts should generally be skeptical of a school's interest in regulating social media speech considering such speech could take place twenty-four hours a day, seven days a week.

3. Schools should generally protect unpopular student speech, since "America's public schools are the nurseries of democracy."[337]

*Mahanoy Area School District v. B.L.* was another victory for the First Amendment. Today, if a student talks trash about their school on social media off-campus, this decision protects them from a school disciplining them for it. Levy, who spent her entire time in high school fighting this case, said after the Court's decision: "I'm really glad that the [Court] ruled in my favor because now it will show to other students, millions of students, that it's OK to express yourself, and you shouldn't be scared to express yourself because of the school."[338] Despite Levy's victory and the Court awarding her one dollar, the Mahanoy Area School District also claimed victory, saying it was happy to see the Court agree that schools could regulate off-campus speech in certain situations.[339]

336   www.law.cornell.edu/wex/mahanoy_area_school_district_v._b.l.
337   Ibid.
338   www.wnep.com/article/news/local/schuylkill-county/a-long-four-years-brandi-levy-reacts-to-
       supreme-court-win/523-0d85f054-64d6-4f81-b4b7-af01fb69fc66
339   finance.yahoo.com/news/mahanoy-area-releases-statement-scotus-103200941.html

# 98. Dobbs v. Jackson Women's Health Organization (2022)

This case began in Jackson, Mississippi, on March 19, 2018. On that day, the Mississippi state legislature passed a controversial law called the Gestational Age Act, banning all abortions after the first fifteen weeks of pregnancy except in cases of rape, incest, or to save the life of the pregnant woman. After Mississippi's governor, Phil Bryant, signed the bill into law, he said, "We'll probably be sued here in about a half hour, and that'll be fine with me. It is worth fighting over."[340] Bryant and others who supported the Gestational Age Act had the true goal of banning abortion and supported *this* law because they knew it would be challenged and hopefully be appealed to the Supreme Court.

Sure enough, within twenty-four hours after the Gestational Age Act passed, Jackson Women's Health Organization sued Mississippi. Specifically, Sacheen Carr-Ellis, a doctor at Jackson Women's Health Organization, sued state officials Thomas Dobbs of the Mississippi State Department of Health and Kenneth Cleveland, the executive director of the Mississippi State Board of Medical Licensure. Jackson Women's Health Organization was Mississippi's only abortion clinic and was already underfunded.[341]

In the US District Court for the Southern District of Mississippi, lawyers representing Jackson Women's Health Organization said that the Supreme Court decisions of *Roe v. Wade* (1973) and *Casey v. Planned Parenthood* (1992) had long established that abortion was a right protected under the Fourteenth Amendment's Due Process Clause. In addition, their lawyers argued that the Gestational Age Act went against a woman's right to privacy as implied through the Ninth Amendment. Finally, they argued that Mississippi attempting to ban abortions before the age of viability, or the age when the fetus could survive outside of the womb on its own, was also unconstitutional as established in the *Casey* decision. Typically, a fetus is not able to survive outside the womb until at least twenty-three weeks.[342] District Judge Carlton Reeves sided with Jackson Women's Health Organization, stating that the Gestational Age Act was unconstitutional and Mississippi had "no legitimate

340   www.npr.org/sections/thetwo-way/2018/03/19/595045249/mississippi-governor-signs-nations-toughest-abortion-ban-into-law
341   www.thisamericanlife.org/774/the-pink-house-at-the-center-of-the-world/act-seven-13
342   pubmed.ncbi.nlm.nih.gov/11753511/

state interest strong enough, prior to viability, to justify a ban on abortions."[343] Reeves ordered Mississippi to not enforce the law.

Mississippi appealed to the US Court of Appeals for the Fifth Circuit, but it agreed with the lower court. In *that* decision, senior Judge Patrick Higginbotham wrote, "In an unbroken line dating to *Roe v. Wade*, the Supreme Court's abortion cases have established (and affirmed, and reaffirmed) a woman's right to choose an abortion before viability. States may regulate abortion procedures prior to viability so long as they do not impose an undue burden on the woman's right, but they may not ban abortions."[344]

Mississippi appealed again, this time to the Supreme Court with the goal of overturning *Roe v. Wade* and *Casey v. Planned Parenthood*. In its request for the Supreme Court, the state said a fetus can detect pain and respond to it at ten to twelve weeks of gestational age and that the viability standard needed to be updated. After the Court agreed to hear the case on May 17, 2021, "pro-choice" advocates, or those who supported abortion rights, got nervous since six seemingly socially conservative justices now sat on the bench. While none of them had explicitly said they would overturn the *Roe* and *Casey* decisions, millions of Americans had voted for socially conservative presidents for decades to get justices in the Supreme Court that would do that.

The Court heard oral arguments on December 1, 2021. Arguing for Mississippi, Scott Steward argued that the Constitution doesn't explicitly guarantee a right to abortion. He added that the *Roe* and *Casey* decisions should be overturned since fetal research has revealed new discoveries. Arguing for Jackson Women's Health Organization, US Solicitor General Elizabeth Carchas Prelogar said the *Roe* and *Casey* decisions should *not* be overturned because the Court "has never revoked a right that is so fundamental to so many Americans and so central to their ability to participate fully and equally in society."[345]

On May 2, 2022, Politico released a draft of a majority opinion by Justice Samuel Alito that revealed the justices had sided with Mississippi. These created media fanfare and protests around the country. This leak of a draft decision was unprecedented, and upset most of the Supreme Court justices, who have traditionally been proud of their ability to keep decisions under wraps until the right moment. As of the time of the writing, we still don't know who leaked the draft.

343   www.cnn.com/2018/11/20/health/mississippi-abortion-ban-15-weeks-ruling/index.html

344   Claeys, Eric (March 2022). "*Dobbs* and the Holdings of *Roe* and *Casey.*" *Georgetown Journal of Law & Public Policy.* 20: 286 (page 5 of the PDF)

345   Shimabukuro 2021, pp. 3–4 and Heritage Reporting Corporation 2021, pages 84–85 (pages 85–86 of the pdf)

**The Big Question in this case:**

- Is Mississippi's Gestational Age
  Act unconstitutional?

The Court said no. On June 24, 2022, it announced it had sided with Dobbs and Mississippi, 6–3. Not only did the Court say that Mississippi's Gestational Age Act was constitutional, but it also said the Constitution does not guarantee a right to abortion. Justice Samuel Alito, who wrote the majority opinion, used the Supreme Court decision *Washington v. Glucksberg* (1997) as a precedent to back up this decision, writing, "The Constitution makes no reference to abortion, and no such right is implicitly protected by any constitutional provision."[346] This was a big deal because by deciding this way, the Court overruled *Planned Parenthood v. Casey* (1992) and *Roe v. Wade* (1973).

This decision caused several state legislatures to immediately pass laws to either severely limit or even outright ban all abortions. In fact, some states had already passed laws that did because they anticipated this decision. At the time of this writing, at least twenty-four states have banned abortion or heavily restricted it.[347]

*Dobbs v. Jackson Women's Health Organization*, as you can imagine, is a controversial decision. According to one poll, 62 percent of Americans disapproved of how the Court decided.[348] The decision has rejuvenated the "pro-choice" movement ever since. In the 2022 midterm elections, millions of Americans showed up to the polls specifically motivated to vote against those who wanted to ban or severely limit abortion.[349] The *Dobbs* decision revealed one thing—the abortion debate isn't going to cool off any time soon.

346   www.supremecourt.gov\opinions\21pdf\19-1392_6j37.pdf
347   www.guttmacher.org/2023/01/six-months-post-roe-24-us-states-have-banned-abortion-or-are-likely-do-so-roundup
348   www.pewresearch.org/politics/2022/07/06/majority-of-public-disapproves-of-supreme-courts-decision-to-overturn-roe-v-wade/
349   www.npr.org/2022/11/25/1139040227/abortion-midterm-elections-2022-republicans-democrats-roe-dobbs

# 99. Kennedy v. Bremerton School District (2022)

This case began in Bremerton, Washington, in August 2008. Inspired by the film *Facing the Giants* and his Christian faith, Joe Kennedy, an assistant football coach at Bremerton High School, began praying after each football game in the center of the field, right at the fifty-yard line. As the season went on, he was joined by his players and even eventually by players and coaches from the opposing team. For the next seven years, Kennedy continued doing this with no issues.

However, in September 2015, the Bremerton School District finally learned what he had been doing. It became concerned that this might be seen as openly going against the separation of church and state, the principle referenced in the Establishment Clause of the First Amendment. Some football players, after all, did not want to join Bremerton on the field for prayer but felt pressured to since they were concerned about getting enough playing time in games. The district's school board negotiated with Kennedy to come up with a plan where he could still pray after games but in a low-key way. It said he could pray off the field or after the spectators left to make everyone know the school district wasn't favoring one religion over another. Bremerton High School's athletic director warned Kennedy that any display of prayer must be student-led, not coach-led.[350]

Well, Kennedy didn't like this so much. He wrote on his Facebook page that he felt like the school district was trying to fire him. A few games later, on October 16, 2015, he returned to praying after the game. By then, the local media was covering the controversy, and because of this Kennedy attracted a big crowd of folks who also joined him on the field. Some of these spectators and reporters knocked down members of the marching band in their efforts to join Kennedy on the field. Others who were angry that Kennedy was doing this shouted profanities at Nate Gillam, the head coach of the football team. He later admitted he was scared he might "be shot from the crowd."[351]

The school district ordered Kennedy to stop, but he continued the practice for two more games. After the season ended, Gillam, who was done with the drama caused by all this, had resigned, and he recommended that Kennedy's contract not be renewed for the following season. However, that didn't matter, as by this time Kennedy had gotten

350   www.cbsnews.com/news/supreme-court-joe-kennedy-high-school-football-coach-prayer-case/
351   www.scotusblog.com/2022/04/in-the-case-of-the-praying-football-coach-both-sides-invoke-religious-freedom/

a lawyer and decided to sue the school district to guarantee that he got his job back. In the US District Court for the Western District of Washington, he argued that the school district had violated his rights of freedom of speech and religion, as protected under the First Amendment. The Bremerton School District said it was trying to comply with the First Amendment, saying allowing the public display of prayer after each game made it look like it favored one religion over all others. By doing this, it was worried it was leading to conflicts and making Bremerton High School less safe. The US District Court for the Western District of Washington sided with the school district.

Kennedy appealed to the US Court of Appeals for the Ninth Circuit, but it agreed with the lower court. Kennedy attempted to appeal the case again to the Supreme Court, but it declined to hear the case. However, Kennedy kept fighting and went through the entire court system again. On January 14, 2022, more than six years after Kennedy had stopped coaching at Bremerton High School, the Supreme Court changed its mind and decided to take on the case. It heard oral arguments on April 25.

## The Big Questions in this case:

- Can a public-school employee pray during school-sponsored sports activities?
- Can a public-school district prevent an employee from praying during school-sponsored sports activities?

The Court said yes and no. On June 27, 2022, it announced it had sided with Kennedy, 6–3. The Court said that the Establishment Clause and Free Speech Clause of the First Amendment protected an individual engaging in a personal religious observance on public grounds or at government-sponsored events. The Court added that, since Kennedy's prayers were not disruptive to the game and he prayed quietly, he ought to be free to do so. This decision effectively overturned *Lemon v. Kurtzman* (1971), the Supreme Court decision that struck down local governments giving special treatment to certain religions. It also overturned the Lemon Test, which, until this point, had been successfully used to evaluate government actions within the scope of the First Amendment's Establishment Clause.[352]

*Kennedy v. Bremerton School District* emboldened Christian religious groups who have been trying to get Christianity back in public schools. More than anything, it signaled that the Court had become much more sympathetic to Christians practicing their religion on public school grounds and during public school activities than it used to be.

352  www.oyez.org/cases/2021/21-418v

While Joe Kennedy has since become a national figure and hero to many Christians in the country, he has also got a lot of hate online from Americans worried about the apparent decline in the separation of church and state. In March 2023, the school district finally rehired him as an assistant football coach.[353]

353  komonews.com/amp/news/local/bremerton-high-school-praying-coach-joe-kennedy-football-
     assistant-us-supreme-court-ruling

# 100. West Virginia v. EPA (2022)

This case began in the District of Columbia on June 2, 2014. On that day, the Environmental Protection Agency, or EPA, led by President Barack Obama, presented new rules to fight climate change. Those rules included requiring that carbon dioxide emissions from electricity generation be reduced by 32 percent by 2030, compared to recorded levels from 2005, at least. States would have to submit plans with how they would move forward to make that happen. They had to submit the plans by 2018 and enforcement would start by 2022. Notice how I keep saying *would*.

Many states weren't so happy about having to do this. Neither were many energy companies. In August 2015, twenty-eight different states, along with hundreds of these energy companies, challenged the EPA's authority to enforce these new rules. They all sued the EPA in the US Court of Appeals for the DC Circuit. In court, these states and companies argued that the Clean Air Act didn't give the federal government the authority to regulate carbon dioxide emissions. The EPA claimed the Clean Air Act *did* give them that authority, and it referenced the Supreme Court case *King v. Burwell* (2015), a decision that gave the federal government broader authority to enforce Obamacare, as a precedent to back that up. The states and energy companies also argued that the EPA was wrongly delegating federal authority to the states. In other words, it was trying to get the states to do the work of the federal government and that went against the Tenth Amendment.

However, things kind of stayed in limbo throughout 2016 as the US Court of Appeals for the DC Circuit never made an official decision. Meanwhile, after Donald Trump won the presidency in November, it became clear he would reverse the EPA rules. In response, the EPA proposed new rules to reduce carbon dioxide emissions that were *much* less strict. The Trump administration was cool with these new rules as it meant the coal and oil industries would make more money, but one EPA analysis found these more lenient rules would lead to thousands of more deaths each year related to respiratory problems.[354] In response to these concerns, the American Lung Association and American Public Health Association sued the EPA on July 8, 2019. Over one hundred other organizations, as well as twenty-three states, joined in to also sue the EPA in the US Court of Appeals for the DC Circuit. They all argued the EPA was epic failing to fulfill its obligations to improve public

354 www.nytimes.com/2018/08/21/climate/epa-coal-pollution-deaths.html

health under the Clean Air Act. They also failed to reduce carbon emissions. On January 19, 2021, the US Court of Appeals for the DC Circuit announced it had sided with the American Lung Association and the others. This was the day before a new president, Joe Biden, would take over, and he had signaled a return to the strict EPA rules first set by Obama.

Before the EPA could make new rules to curb carbon emissions, West Virginia, along with eighteen other states and energy companies, all appealed the DC Circuit's to the Supreme Court. Even though the Biden administration begged the Supreme Court not to get involved, it agreed to take on the case, hearing oral arguments on February 28, 2022.

## The Big Question in this case:

- Does the EPA have the authority to regulate carbon emissions in any industry?

The Court said no. On June 30, 2022, it announced it had sided with West Virginia and the others, 6–3. The Court said when Congress passed the Clean Air Act, it never granted the EPA the authority to regulate carbon emissions. The Court used what's known as the "major questions doctrine" to back up its opinion. The major questions doctrine says when in doubt, courts should assume that Congress doesn't let the executive branch handle policies of "vast economic or political significance."[355] Chief Justice John Roberts wrote the majority opinion, saying that "certain extraordinary cases, both separation of powers principles and a practical understanding of legislative intent make us 'reluctant to read into ambiguous statutory text' the delegation claimed to be lurking there." He added, "To convince us otherwise…the (executive branch) agency must point to 'clear congressional authorization' for the power it claims."[356]

*West Virginia v. EPA* was another controversial decision that further divided those with generally left-leaning political beliefs and those with generally right-leaning political beliefs. Those on the left argued that this stripping of the power of the EPA would be detrimental to the environment. Critics said it would hurt progress trying to fight climate change. Those on the right generally viewed the decision as a win for the coal and oil industries. However folks personally view this decision, it weakened the executive branch and strengthened the legislative branch.

355  opencasebook.org/casebooks/1045-public-institutions-administrative-law-cases-materials/
resources/4.2.4.1-major-questions-doctrine
356  www.law.cornell.edu/supremecourt/text/20-1530

# Why the Supreme Court Matters Today

The Supreme Court of the United States is hot stuff right now.

I started writing this book before June 2022, and before then, it seemed like most Americans didn't care about the Supreme Court. That has changed. It seems like more Americans are paying attention to the Court than at any other point in my life. I have evidence to back up this hypothesis. On February 21, 2023, I reacted to oral arguments in a live stream for the Supreme Court case *Gonzales v. Google*, which could have big implications for how we consume online media. More than a thousand viewers tuned in for the live stream, and hundreds of thousands more have caught the rebroadcast of it since. As I write this, Justice Clarence Thomas has been under increased scrutiny for accepting gifts from a conservative billionaire donor, leading to calls for his impeachment.[357] Perhaps more now than ever before, currently a giant magnifying is on the highest court in the country.

For those who still don't care about why the Court matters today, here's my attempt to change that. *The Court matters today because it has more power than it ever has before.* These nine justices who currently sit on the bench, three of whom were appointed by the unpopular President Donald Trump, have tremendous power expanding or limiting both civil rights and civil liberties. Even though the creators of the United States Constitution, also known as the Founding Dudes, wanted Congress and the president to have more power than the judiciary, today, the opposite is true. You read that correctly. In my opinion, the Supreme Court has more power than the president and Congress.

I'll admit that the ones paying close attention to the Court today tend to lean to the left politically. This is because the Court overwhelmingly leans to the right these days, as seen with the recent trio of decisions in *West Virginia v. EPA* (2022), *Kennedy v. Bremerton School District* (2022), and *Dobbs v. Jackson Women's Health Organization* (2022). However, if you lean to the right politically, I urge you to also closely pay attention to what the Court is doing. Often, progress is only made and our rights and liberties are only protected due to them. The United States currently has a divided Congress unlikely to pass any

357  www.reuters.com/world/us/democratic-lawmaker-ocasio-cortez-wants-us-supreme-court-justice-thomas-2023-04-09/

major legislation until after 2024. Even the president, who has steadily gained more throughout history, is limited as far as what initiatives he can implement. The Supreme Court is often the only part of the federal government truly moving things along. In fact, there's good evidence that recently illustrates this fact. On August 24, 2022, President Joe Biden announced a plan to cancel up to $20,000 of student loan debt for tens of millions of lower-income Americans. However, Nebraska and five other states challenged the constitutionality of the forgiveness program, arguing that the president didn't have the authority to do that under the Administrative Procedure Act. Myra Brown and Alexander Taylor, two citizens with student loan debt who wouldn't benefit from Biden's student loan forgiveness plan, also sued the US Department of Education. In that case, argued in the US District Court for the Northern District of Texas, Judge Mark Pittman sided with Brown and Taylor. The Department of Education appealed to the US Court of Appeals for the Fifth Circuit, but it also sided with Brown and Taylor.[358] The student loan forgiveness program has been put on hold since. However, the Supreme Court has heard oral arguments for both cases, and, by the time this book is published, it likely will have decided on the fate of tens of millions of student loan borrowers. Again, the Court is who all Americans are looking to with bated breath. There is no denying that how they decide will have a tremendous impact.

In Federalist Number 78, Alexander Hamilton predicted the judicial branch would be the "least dangerous branch" since it has "no influence over either the sword or the purse."[359] Well, he was wrong. For better or worse, Americans are currently stuck with a Supreme Court more powerful than ever before. As I mentioned at the beginning of this book, when Americans vote for a president every four years, they are often indirectly "voting" for Supreme Court justices, and hopefully by this point in the book you truly understand why that is. Often, it's these nine people who control our fates, so we might want to start looking at how and why they make these decisions.

358   www.reuters.com/world/us/us-appeals-court-rejects-bidens-bid-revive-student-debt-plan-2022-12-01/

359   guides.loc.gov/federalist-papers/text-71-80

# The Future of the Court

So what will the future of the Supreme Court look like? Well, it's up to you.

Assuming you are an American, you will have to determine the Court's future through the way you vote. You have this power not just in presidential elections but also in Senate and House elections. After all, the Senate has to approve any of the president's Supreme Court nominees. If a Supreme Court justice were to ever misbehave, the House of Representatives would impeach them and the Senate would act as the jury and judges in determining a verdict and punishment. If a president or vice president were to be impeached, the Supreme Court justices would preside over the impeachment trial in the Senate. Most of you also get to vote for judges at the local level. Well, as it turns out, nearly all Supreme Court justices in history were judges in lower courts, and many of them were once elected by voters like yourself.

So what will you decide? How will you vote? As I stated in the last chapter, the current Supreme Court generally leans to the right, and it's been like that for decades. History tells us that the pendulum will likely swing back in the coming years. That said, without term limits, some of the more right-leaning justices on the bench may be around for decades. This will likely only further fuel the movements to call for term limits or the expansion of the Court. While I predict that these movements will continue to grow, ultimately I think it's more likely Americans will attempt to shift more power to Congress. Congress has lost tremendous power in recent decades, mostly due to gerrymandering, which has caused more political polarization, and the filibuster, which has led to much less debate and voting on bills in the Senate. Americans likely will realize that weakening the Supreme Court by empowering Congress might be their best hope for true reforms to be made.

For everyone else reading this who can't vote in American elections, know that your best bet at reforming society is to spread the word about the lessons you learned in this book. Incredibly, I get tens of thousands of viewers who watch my Supreme Court Briefs series on YouTube who are *not* American citizens. Often, however, they watch not because they are concerned about the future of American democracy but because they are amazed at how awesome it is.

Despite the concerns that many have about the future of the Supreme Court, I still have tremendous faith in the institution. It's always been political. It's always angered and frustrated Americans (especially Americans in the federal government). However, it's also often been exceptionally consistent and reliable. That may sound like a bold statement, but the one thing Supreme Court justices have always had in common is their extreme dedication to the Constitution. Sure, they can interpret the Constitution in different ways, but if you read these interpretations, they quickly become redundant. The judicial branch is the least political branch of government, and it's often a breath of fresh air reading their opinions, which are not clouded by partisan attacks. The Court can't get away with being rhetorical like the president or members of Congress often do. They have to back up their decisions with evidence, and that evidence has to be linked directly to the Constitution. Because of that, the Court has continued to provide stability in seemingly chaotic times, and we shouldn't take that for granted.

# About the Author

**Matt Beat** is a teacher, video producer, podcaster, and musician based in Kansas. His YouTube channels, *Mr. Beat* and *The Beat Goes On*, have accumulated more than 850,000 subscribers and 150 million views, helping expand his "classroom" around the world. Mr. Beat's specialty is American history, but he also has a big passion for geography and economics. He has a band called Electric Needle Room, known for original indie pop songs about all of the American presidents. Matt also hosts the podcast *The Beat Pod*; check it out wherever you listen to podcasts. For press and more, visit: www.iammrbeat.com/bio.html.

CPSIA information can be obtained
at www.ICGtesting.com
Printed in the USA
JSHW030819240523
42173JS00004B/4